PUBLICATIONS OF THE
MINNESOTA HISTORICAL SOCIETY

RUSSELL W. FRIDLEY, *DIRECTOR*

JUNE DRENNING HOLMQUIST, *ASSISTANT DIRECTOR
FOR RESEARCH AND PUBLICATIONS*

Capt.ⁿ JONATHAN CARVER.

From the Original Picture in the possession of J. C. Lettsom M.D.

Published as the Act directs, by R. Stewart, N.º 87, near G.º Turnstile, Holborn, Nov. 16, 1780.

THE JOURNALS

OF

JONATHAN CARVER

AND

RELATED DOCUMENTS,

1766-1770

EDITED BY JOHN PARKER

MINNESOTA HISTORICAL SOCIETY PRESS • 1976

Bicentennial Edition

Library of Congress Cataloging in Publication Data:

Main entry under title:
The Journals of Jonathan Carver and related documents, 1766–1770.
   "The manuscript journals are Additional Manuscripts 8949 and 8950 in the British Museum."
   Bibliography: p. 222
   Includes index.
   CONTENTS: Journals of the travels of Jonathan Carver. — Carver, J. Survey journal.— Goddard, J. S. Journal of a voyage, 1766–67. — [etc.]
   1. Mississippi Valley — Description and travel. 2. Northwestern States — Description and travel. 3. Carver, Jonathan, 1710–1780. 4. Goddard, James Stanley, d. 1795. 5. Dakota language — Dictionaries. I. Carver, Jonathan, 1710–1780. II. Parker, John, 1923–   III. Goddard, James Stanley, d. 1795.   F597.J68   917.7'04'10924   76-2643

International Standard Book Number: 0-87351-099-2
MANUFACTURED IN THE UNITED STATES OF AMERICA

❧ *For my Mother* ❧

PREFACE

THIS VOLUME had its origins in the suggestion frequently made by the late historian Theodore C. Blegen that the manuscript journals of Jonathan Carver should be edited and published to stand beside Carver's book, *Travels through the Interior Parts of North America, in the Years 1766, 1767, and 1768*, for which the explorer has been so much praised and criticized. In the pages that follow Carver's journals have been brought together with the journal of James Stanley Goddard, secretary to the Carver expedition, and related letters and documents to provide in one book published versions of the major manuscript sources bearing on Carver's 1766–67 journey to the Midwest.

The manuscript journals are Additional Manuscripts 8949 and 8950 in the British Museum, where I examined and procured microfilm copies of them. They are published here with the permission of the Trustees of the British Museum. Four versions of the journal exist; the development and variations among these copies are discussed in the introduction, pp. 27–30. The first and earliest version is the basis for this edition, but the other three versions have been collated to supplement it in order to create the most complete possible text. Passages here incorporated from Versions II through IV are identified in the margins and by brackets in the text. Version II has been used in the following cases: when a word in Version I was illegible; when a passage in Version I was unintelligible or unclear; when a passage in Version I was similar but less complete than the corresponding passage in Version II; and when Version II contained a passage not present in Version I. The last case was by far the most frequent. In addition, Carver composed a series of numbered inserts to supplement Version II, and these have been placed in the text at

vii

the points where Carver indicated they should be added, except in the case of insert 8, which was moved slightly to improve clarity. Versions III and IV, which are also in Carver's hand and represent clear copies of Versions I and II respectively, have only been used in places where they clarified illegible passages, or where they added information not present in any other versions.

All four versions of Carver's journal contain very little punctuation, and when it is present, it is inconsistent and often unclear. I have therefore incorporated minimal modern punctuation for clarity. In printing all raised letters have been lowered and the periods below them omitted. Carver made little distinction between capital and lower case letters and paragraphed sparingly, so I have used modern capitalization and created paragraphs for greater readability while adhering to his spelling. My objective throughout has been to faithfully reproduce Carver's text to achieve readability in what he intended to be a book, while preserving as much of his own literary technique as possible. The same editorial methods have been used in preparing Goddard's journal and the documents printed in Appendix One, except that Goddard's punctuation has not been altered.

Carver describes his method of determining distances in his journal (see p. 59). The result is a mixture of overestimation, underestimation, and accuracy. Correct distances appear in brackets in the text; since they were measured along water routes, they are in most cases approximate. For such distances as well as latitudes and longitudes I have relied on maps prepared by the United States Geological Survey. Goddard's league averages around three miles, but he consistently exaggerates distances. In Carver's survey journal I have identified points along his route by their modern names, but I have not undertaken to corroborate or correct his estimates of distances or directions, since the former frequently involve very short distances, and the latter are not stated with precision.

The only known copy of the journal of James Stanley Goddard is in the Rare Book Room of McGill University Library, Montreal. It is printed here with permission. The surviving manuscript is an 18th-century copy, and its date and purpose are unknown; some speculations on its origin can be found on p. 180. The copy is in a clean, clerical hand, and seems to have few glaring errors of transcription, with several exceptions which are noted. The documents in Appendix One are printed with the permission of the Université de Montréal and the Public Record Office, London.

In undertaking this work I have received the generous assistance of many institutions and individuals. The following libraries have provided substantial help: the Library of the Society of Friends, Euston House, London; the Friends' Reference Library, Devonshire House, Bishopsgate, London; the Peabody Museum and the Essex Institute, Salem, Massachusetts; the Newberry Library; the Henry E. Huntington Library; the American Antiquarian Society; the American Philosophical Society; the Library of Congress; the John Carter Brown Library; the William L. Clements Library; the New York Public Library; the Michigan Historical Collections; the State Historical Societies of Vermont, Massachusetts, Michigan, Wisconsin, and Minnesota; and the libraries of Amherst College, Yale University, Tulane University, the University of Pennsylvania, the University of Cincinnati, and the University of California, Los Angeles. To all of them I express my gratitude for their good service. To my colleagues in the University of Minnesota Library, I have a very special sense of obligation.

Jonathan Carver's comments on the Indians of the region through which he passed have sent me among anthropologists and others for assistance. I am especially indebted to Raymond J. DeMallie for his work on Carver's Dakota vocabulary which appears in Appendix Two, and I am grateful also to Cecil D. Lewis, E. Adamson Hoebel, Nancy Oestreich Lurie, Ruth Landes, and Timothy Dunnigan. Donald L. Farren provided a description of the Dutch edition of Carver's *Travels*, and Dmitri Tselos and Robert Olson helped me identify the Greek edition. Charles J. Tannenbaum and Mary Turnbull supplied useful biographical information on Carver and his family. To Merrily Smith I am very grateful for numerous typings and retypings of the manuscript as it emerged from Carver's journals, to Carol Urness for many suggestions in the area of natural history, and to Bernadette Pyter Muck for her work in preparing the index. The Publications Department of the Minnesota Historical Society has been most helpful in all aspects of preparing this work for publication, and special recognition is due Carolyn Gilman for her editorial assistance and for editing James Stanley Goddard's journal for inclusion in this volume. I am grateful to my family for a decade of patience during which Jonathan Carver became a household word.

Two grants were of great assistance in partially defraying the costs of publication. Both the Minnesota Historical Society and the editor wish to thank the Elmer L. and Eleanor J. Andersen Foundation and General Mills, Incorporated, for making it possible for this book to appear in the nation's Bicentennial year. Since Jonathan Carver was the only British-American explorer to visit the Minnesota region during the period immediately preceding independence, his journals are an appropriate contribution to the literature of the period.

JOHN PARKER

CONTENTS

28

The Dialect of the Winebagoes is the most difficult to be pronounced of all Nation they pronounce very hard from their throats, when they say when I Drink to thee, in their tongue is Chouerarro. Ukh charrigaugh, I found the utmost Difficulty in pronouncing the Last of these words

Septem. 20 left this town the principal part of the Winebagoes went with us in order to seek their place for a winter hunt determining to Travel with us to the Carrying place into the Ouisconsin

Sep. 29 Intered a small Lake calld the Foxes Lake, at this place upward of 40 year ago the Saugies and the Olligomis had a Castle on the west side of this Lake, the French & Menomonies who were at the time at war with these two Nations Came with an Army upon them at unawares in the winter Cut them to piece in a most Cruel maner which nearly destroyed them both these two Nations

October 4th this day passd the upper Town of the Winebagoes where more of this Nation Joynd who were bound for the Ouisconsin. This Village is but very small Containing eight or ten Hutts on the South Ed of a small Lake this with all other Indian Towns is Laid Down in the Map

Oct. 11 arived at the Great Carrying place between the Saxs River and the Ouisconsin. this portage wants a little of being two Miles from one of the Rivers to the Other, one half of the way is a Marsh which makes the Carriage much more Difficult, the other part is very good going being a Sort of an Oak Plain. The Country on the Saxs River is very good Land and apears to me the best for Grass I saw

A page of Carver's journal, Version I.

INTRODUCTION

Jonathan Carver's Journey, 1766-68

JONATHAN CARVER'S *Travels through the Interior Parts of North America in the Years 1766, 1767, and 1768* was published in London in 1778. The book was widely read in Great Britain, in America, and in Europe, achieving for its author recognition as an important traveler to the hinterland of North America. Shortly after Carver's death in 1780, however, questions were raised about the authorship and authenticity of his observations, and by the beginning of the 20th century, he was being set down as a plagiarist and an ignorant shoemaker incapable of writing such a book on his own. His name was further tarnished by his descendants' questionable claims to a vast tract of land in the upper Mississippi Valley. But Carver could not be totally dismissed or disgraced for long. Too much of his story was obviously authentic, and it was useful to early 19th-century travelers and explorers who followed him into what is now Wisconsin and Minnesota.[1]

[1] Carver's main detractor was Edward Gaylord Bourne, "The Travels of Jonathan Carver," in *American Historical Review*, 11:287–302 (January, 1906); on Bourne's criticisms and the questionable land grant, see pp. 47–51, 54, below. General sources on Carver's life and work include William Browning, "The Early History of Jonathan Carver," and Louise Phelps Kellogg, "The Mission of Jonathan Carver," both in *Wisconsin Magazine of History*, 3:291–305, 12:127–145 (March, 1920, December, 1928); and Milo M. Quaife, "Jonathan Carver and the Carver Grant," in *Mississippi Valley Historical Review*, 7:3–25 (June, 1920). An account of Carver's travels based on the journals appeared in Kellogg, *The British Régime in Wisconsin and the Northwest*, 49–75 (Madison, 1935). Documents relating to Carver are printed by John Thomas Lee, "A Bibliography of Carver's Travels," in State Historical Society of Wisconsin, *Proceedings*, 1909, pp. 143–183 (Madison, 1910); Lee, "Captain Jonathan Carver: Additional Data," in *Proceedings*, 1912, pp. 87–123 (1913); T. C. Elliott, "The Origin of the Name Oregon,"

Continued research has gradually yielded information about Carver's life that justifies conclusions which are no longer easily assailed. The authenticity of his book is firmly established by his manuscript journals, unquestionably the record of his journey from Boston to the Minnesota River and back between 1766 and 1768. Heretofore unpublished, these journals in the collections of the British Museum in London offer insights into Carver's character, interests, and literary style which are to a considerable degree obscured in the heavily edited *Travels* based on them. They also invite an explanation of the differences between their texts and that of the published *Travels,* as well as a discussion of the controversy over Carver's accuracy, literacy, and honesty. It is the purpose of this introduction to assess these topics.

He was known in his later years as Captain Jonathan Carver, that being his rank when he was mustered out of a Massachusetts regiment at the conclusion of the French and Indian War. But his early years are almost entirely lost to us. Born in Weymouth, Massachusetts, on April 13, 1710, Carver migrated with his parents, Ensign David and Hannah Dyer Carver, to Canterbury, Connecticut, about 1718. In both Canterbury and Weymouth, David Carver held positions in town government. Hannah Dyer's family included two brothers, John and Thomas, both of whom held the rank of colonel. Eliphalet, son of Thomas Dyer, was destined to be a member of the Continental Congress and chief justice of Connecticut. The Dyers had settled in Connecticut ahead of the Carvers and probably were an inducement to the latter's emigration from Massachusetts. Young Jonathan Carver may have acquired a knowledge of shoemaking from his uncle Thomas, who practiced that trade in Windham County, Connecticut.[2]

It is apparent that Jonathan Carver came from a family that was stable, thrifty, respectable, and ambitious, with a regard for religion, education, and civic responsibility — a "good" family. Jonathan was likely kept aware of an ancestry on his father's side that may have gone back to a Robert Carver (1594–1680) who

and "Jonathan Carver's Source for the Name Oregon," in *Quarterly of the Oregon Historical Society*, 22:91–115, 23:53-69 (June, 1921, March, 1922); Kenneth Roberts, ed., *Northwest Passage Appendix* (Garden City, N.Y., 1937).

[2] Browning, in *Wisconsin Magazine of History*, 3:291–305; Connecticut Historical Society, *Records of the Congregational Church in Canterbury, Connecticut, 1711–1844* (Hartford, 1932).

settled at Marshfield, Massachusetts, about 1638. Some position of importance may have been expected of Jonathan, but there is no evidence that he satisfied any such expectation in his early years. He obviously acquired sufficient education to enable him to write with clarity and tolerable orthography. He may have studied medicine briefly as his first biographer, John Coakley Lettsom, suggested, but considering Lettsom's other known errors concerning Carver's early life, this suggestion is not dependable. Carver's own writing indicates a knowledge of religious subjects, and we may assume he had discussed such topics with his sister Sarah's husband, Solomon Pain, a leader in the Separatist Church movement in Connecticut.[3]

When Jonathan was nearly 18 years old, his father died, leaving an estate of 2,036 pounds, 15 shillings, 10 pence, of which Jonathan's share was £193, 19s., 6d. His guardian was Colonel John Dyer. From the probate of his father's estate on February 13, 1728, until Jonathan's marriage to Abigail Robbins on October 20, 1746, nothing is known of him. Apparently he did not own land or practice any profession for which records have been kept. His marriage to Abigail is recorded in Canterbury, indicating that he must have remained in that vicinity. By this time Jonathan was 36 years old. His bride was perhaps 20. After two daughters were born to them in Canterbury (Mary on April 8, 1747, and Abigail on May 29, 1748), the family moved to Montague, a frontier town in the Connecticut River Valley of northwestern Massachusetts. There is no record that Carver ever returned to Canterbury. A third daughter, Sarah, was born in Montague in 1750, and the first son, Rufus, in 1754. Again we have no consistent record of what trade Carver followed there, but in nearby Northfield he is supposed to have delivered 20 pairs of shoes to Moses Field. This, and the fact that his eldest son, Rufus, became a shoemaker, may indicate his possible occupation in Montague. Apparently he also lived for a time in Deerfield, another town on the Massachusetts frontier.[4]

[3] Browning, in *Wisconsin Magazine of History*, 3:300, 303. John Coakley Lettsom, "Some Account of Captain J. Carver," in Carver, *Travels through the Interior Parts of North America in the Years 1766, 1767, and 1768*, 1–22 (Reprint Ed., Minneapolis, 1956); on Lettsom's errors, see p. 54, below.

[4] Browning, in *Wisconsin Magazine of History*, 3:294, 297; *Congregational Church Records*, 60, 168; George Sheldon, *History of Deerfield, Massachusetts*, 2:102, 104 (Deerfield, 1896); J. H. Temple and George Sheldon, *A History of the*

In the mid-18th century western Massachusetts was steadily exposed to the threat of Indian and French dominance westward beyond the ribbon of English influence along the eastern coast. Boston was English. Montague, some 80 miles to the northwest, was almost no man's land. It was this frontier environment that determined the course of Carver's life, for the skills of survival even in times of peace were those of the woodsman and the soldier.

Carver's career in the colonial militia spanned eight years, involving several enlistments for short periods of time when troops were needed for particular campaigns of the French and Indian War. He reputedly purchased an ensigncy to begin his military career in what was probably a regiment raised in the Connecticut River Valley of Massachusetts. His name is on the roll of Captain Elijah Williams of Deerfield for 1755. A petition Carver filed with the Massachusetts Bay House of Representatives in May, 1756, refers to his participation in the expedition against Crown Point in the upper Hudson Valley and claims that he was taken ill at Lake George, near the New York-Vermont boundary, presumably after the battle there on September 8, 1755, in which colonial troops under William Johnson were badly mauled by a French force commanded by the Baron Ludwig August von Dieskau.[5]

Carver enlisted again in 1757, when the threat of Indian attacks called the Connecticut Valley's farmers and townsmen to arms once more. He served that year in a ranger company under Captain John Burk, whose troops were posted in groups numbering from 7 to 26 men at various frontier stations. It was during this enlistment that Carver was captured at Fort William Henry on the southern end of Lake George. The battle there resulted in the slaying of a number of British prisoners by Indians fighting for the French. Carver's blood-chilling account of the incident in *Travels* tells how he escaped with no more than a leg wound.[6]

Town of Northfield, Massachusetts, for 150 Years, 418 (Albany, N.Y., 1875). There is conflicting evidence and a 3-year discrepancy concerning Abigail Carver's age. Lee, in *Proceedings,* 1912, p. 106n, quotes her tombstone inscription, indicating she died in 1802 at the age of 73. However, *Congregational Church Records,* 60, list her baptismal entry on April 17, 1726.

[5] Lee, in *Proceedings,* 1912, pp. 90, 107; Sheldon, *Deerfield,* 2: 102.

[6] Lee, in *Proceedings,* 1912, pp. 91–93; Temple and Sheldon, *Northfield,* 300–302; Carver, *Travels,* 313–329.

Carver's military service did not take him beyond the Connecticut and Hudson valleys. In 1758 he served as a second lieutenant under Captain John Hawks in the campaign at Lake George.
In 1759 he was a lieutenant under Captain Salah Barnard at Fort
Edward, New York, and he still held that rank at Charlestown,
New Hampshire, the following year. He was at Crown Point
with Colonel Richard Saltonstall's unit in 1762, and he was a
captain when peace was concluded in 1763.[7]

The frontier troops from western Massachusetts, New Hampshire, and New York were the guardians of the northern flank of
the British colonies, the road from Montreal to New York. They
were also the most capable soldiers in His Majesty's service,
ingenious, wise to the ways of Indian warfare, and at home in the
woods. From this sector emerged one of the war's greatest
heroes, Robert Rogers. A New Hampshire native born in 1731,
Rogers was the commander of the redoubtable Rogers' Rangers,
whose daring feats and bloody engagements made them the
most romantic figures of the French and Indian War. Rogers'
debts, excessive drinking, and reputation for independent action
made him a controversial figure both in England and America
long after the war's end. His grandiose peacetime plans would
involve Jonathan Carver. It is possible that the two men met
during one of the northern campaigns (they both served at
Crown Point in 1755), but this is not certain.[8]

While the war years were disruptive, they did not entirely
remove Carver from life at Montague. Enlistments were for
specific periods or campaigns, between which Carver was back
at Montague or possibly at Deerfield, a garrison town offering
more security against Indian attack. In 1759 he served as a

---

[7] Sheldon, *Deerfield*, 2: 102; Lee, in *Proceedings*, 1912, pp. 91n, 93n; Charles H.
Lincoln, ed., "The Orderly Book of Lieut. William Henshaw," in American
Antiquarian Society, *Transactions and Collections*, 11: 225 (Worcester, Mass.,
1909). In September, 1759, a periodical named the *Royal Magazine* published a
letter from "J. C–r" describing Fort Niagara. "C–r" stated that he was taken
prisoner near Oswego on May 16, 1758, and held at Fort Niagara until August 24,
when he escaped. The piece has been attributed to Carver, but his authorship is
improbable in view of the records cited above, which list his name in the billeting
roll of John Hawks's company until June 3, 1758. On the other hand, the opinions expressed in the letter strongly resemble Carver's statements in his journals.
See Paul L. Ford, ed., *A Short History and Description of Fort Niagara, with an
Account of Its Importance to Great Britain (Winnowings in American History: New
York Colonial Series,* no. 1 — Brooklyn, 1890).

[8] On Rogers and the rangers, see John R. Cuneo, *Robert Rogers of the Rangers*
(New York, 1959).

selectman of Montague. A fourth daughter, Olive, was born in 1757; a second son, Jonathan, in 1759; and a fifth daughter, Mindwell, in 1762.[9]

This father of seven, now 53 years of age, was mustered out of the army in 1763 without rights to the half pay which was received by the regular officers, called the Establishment. Nor was Carver entitled to any grant of land. As a volunteer with several enlistments for limited periods, he had no claim to compensation at the conclusion of the war. His petition to the House of Representatives of the province of Massachusetts Bay in 1764 for command of a fort "at the Eastward" in what is now Maine was discussed and dismissed. The only capital that Carver claimed in his journals was frontier experience and knowledge that gave him an insight into the western country. To build upon that capital, he tells us that he bought books which would help him learn the arts of surveying and map making, with the intention of using them in the vast western territories which the Treaty of Paris in 1763 decreed should belong to Great Britain rather than France.[10]

When Carver looked west, it was to a region which the development of the fur trade by the French had revealed to be a vast land dominated by three waterways: the Mississippi and its branches flowing south, the St. Lawrence-Great Lakes system to the east, and the rivers flowing into Hudson Bay on the north. Since 1670 the northern watershed had been exploited for furs by the British Hudson's Bay Company, but the St. Lawrence and upper Mississippi waterways had been avenues of French commerce with the Indian tribes.

The French monopoly of trade in the Great Lakes area had created a French monopoly on firsthand knowledge of the region. But, like the French, the British hoped to find a great waterway that flowed westward into the Pacific from a point near the meeting of the other three watersheds. Since the 16th century, men like John and Sebastian Cabot, Jacques Cartier, Martin Frobisher, and Henry Hudson had sought a western outlet to serve as a trade route to China. Such a passage would be

[9] Edward P. Pressey, *History of Montague, A Typical Puritan Town*, 242 (Montague, 1910); Sheldon, *Deerfield*, 2: 104.

[10] Massachusetts Bay Province, *Journal Of the Honourable House of Representatives*, 65 (Boston, 1764). See also p. 58, below.

shorter, safer, and more profitable than the long journeys around the southern tips of Africa or South America, which remained the only sea routes from Europe to the East. French searches for a northwest passage had focused first on the Great Lakes chain and later on river routes west and north of Lake Superior. The last concerted French effort to find a route to "La Mer de l'Ouest" had been led by Pierre Gaultier de Varennes, Sieur de la Vérendrye, in the 1730s and 1740s. His explorations had been based in the Lake Winnipeg area, from which he probed west along the Missouri and Saskatchewan rivers in the very region where Carver later imagined he would find the mythical "River of the West."[11]

British searches had worked out from Hudson Bay. Seventeenth-century expeditions launched from England under such men as Thomas Button, Luke Foxe, and Thomas James had met with no success in finding a passage in the Hudson's Bay Company's territories. Renewed northern efforts in the 1740s, inspired by Arthur Dobbs, the archpublicist of the northwest passage in England, had likewise failed. Upon Britain's acquisition of Canada at the end of the French and Indian War in 1763, attention naturally turned farther south. Carver's optimism about the ease of discovering the western link shows the British ignorance of the extent to which the French search had already been carried out down the western waterways of this hinterland empire.[12]

The very organization of the French fur trade had encouraged exploration. By the middle of the 17th century Frenchmen and Canadians were going west to meet the fur trade of the interior. From Montreal, where at first the Indians came to exchange furs for European goods, the white men's trade articles passed westward from one tribe to another, preceding the Canadians along the rivers and lakes. Eventually, French traders filtered as far as the Saskatchewan River and the western branches of the

[11] Carver, *Travels*, xi, 76. For a summary of searches for a northwest passage, see Lawrence J. Burpee, *The Search for the Western Sea: The Story of the Exploration of North-Western America*, 1: xviii–xx (Toronto, 1935). On La Vérendrye, see Nellis M. Crouse, *In Quest of the Western Ocean*, 379–404 (New York, 1928).

[12] Glyndwr Williams, *The British Search for the Northwest Passage in the Eighteenth Century*, xv, xvi, 31 (London, 1962). On the expeditions mentioned, see Crouse, *Western Ocean*, 174–178, 187–196, 421–444. See also Ernest S. Dodge, *Northwest by Sea* (New York, 1961).

Mississippi, replacing Indian middlemen in what is now the Midwest.[13]

In an attempt to provide some control over this far-flung commerce, the French colonial government established western posts with military garrisons, and licenses were granted to traders working out from these posts. But outside of this western establishment, free-lancers, or *coureurs des bois,* operated as private, unregulated merchants. Living among the Indians, they became little different from them, and much the same could be said of the authorized *hivernants,* who lived in the Indian villages to be present with European goods when a quantity of furs became available. Not infrequently these "winterers" became blood relatives of the bands with which they lived.

The fur trade as the Indian knew it in 1763 came to him in his village. Though there were changes in French administrative policy with respect to the West, and corruption within the system, there was no change in the basic French technique of going to the woods with the Indians. Nor did it lose its centralized character in which churchmen, merchants, and government officials were agents in the implementation of a national policy. A consistent ingredient of this system was the practice of giving presents to the Indians, a feature of diplomacy which was also a part of Indian intertribal relations.[14]

British policy at first dictated a direct reversal of that formerly implemented by the French. Even before the end of the French and Indian War, Sir Jeffrey Amherst, commander of the British colonial forces, announced his intention to decrease the amount of goods to be distributed among the Indians as gifts. He was against letting them have gunpowder — even for a price — which the French had supplied as a gift. While he was hoping to encourage self-sufficiency and self-reliance among the western tribes, his policies lent credibility to the French-inspired belief among the Indians that the English intended their destruction. Amherst was not opposed to trading with the Indians. He wished to establish a new colony in the Great Lakes area, and he

[13] On the French fur trade here and in the following paragraphs, see Louise Phelps Kellogg, *The French Régime in Wisconsin and the Northwest,* 364–385 (Madison, 1925); Rhoda R. Gilman, "The Fur Trade in the Upper Mississippi Valley, 1630–1850," in *Wisconsin Magazine of History,* 58: 3–8 (Autumn, 1974).

[14] Wilbur R. Jacobs, *Diplomacy and Indian Gifts: Anglo-French Rivalry Along the Ohio and Northwest Frontiers, 1748–1763,* 5–45 (Stanford, Calif., 1950).

opened the Michilimackinac post at the junction of Lakes Michigan and Huron to British trade in 1760 after it and Detroit had been secured by British arms. Traders quickly moved up the lakes, and by 1761 they were in the Rainy River country northwest of Lake Superior, a part of Michilimackinac's natural hinterland. But they brought new methods and manners, and often reaped little more for their long journeys than the hostility of the Indians, who preferred the French way of doing business.[15]

The Indians soon had numerous reasons to wish for the return of the old French regime. In addition to the lack of gifts and powder, the Indians found the prices of English goods going up and the supply of liquor on the decline, although those near the frontier had been abundantly supplied by the British when they had hoped thereby to cause trouble for the French. Sir William Johnson, British superintendent of Indian affairs in the north, issued a set of regulations designed to control the western trade more effectively. In Johnson's system, the fur trade was to be restricted to certain garrisoned forts, and the giving of credit to the Indians was forbidden. As a result, the western Indians had to make long journeys to reach a fort instead of having traders come to them. Moreover, when the Indians reached such a post, accustomed to the French system of easy credit, the British often refused them hunting supplies. To make matters worse, the eastern lands of the Delaware and the Iroquois were being invaded by illegal settlers.[16]

Pontiac, the great Ottawa leader, began to advocate rebellion against the British in order to reinstate the French. In May, 1763,

[15] Marjorie G. Reid, "The Quebec Fur-Traders and Western Policy, 1763–1774," in *Canadian Historical Review*, new series, 6: 15–32 (March, 1925); Howard H. Peckham, *Pontiac and the Indian Uprising*, 72, 92, 93 (Princeton, N.J., 1947); Marjorie Gordon Jackson, "The Beginning of British Trade at Michilimackinac," in *Minnesota History*, 11:239 (September, 1930). Michilimackinac, always a strategic fur post, was in the 1760s the most western fort authorized for Indian trade. For Carver's account of it, see *Travels*, 18. A description based on a visit there in 1761 is in James Bain, ed., *Travels & Adventures In Canada and the Indian Territories Between the Years 1760 and 1776 by Alexander Henry*, 40 (Boston, 1901). At the time of Carver's visit, the fort was located on the mainland at the south point of the straits. On its several early locations, see Calvin Goodrich, *The First Michigan Frontier*, 255–283 (Ann Arbor, 1940). Now a part of the Michigan State Park system, the fort's painstaking excavation is described in Moreau S. Maxwell and Lewis H. Binford, *Excavation at Fort Michilimackinac, Mackinac City, Michigan, 1959 Season* (East Lansing, Mich., 1961).

[16] Peckham, *Pontiac*, 73, 87, 101–103; Jackson, in *Minnesota History*, 11:235, 244.

under Pontiac's initiative, the storm of resentment broke into war. Within a month posts were taken at Sandusky, now in Ohio, St. Joseph and Michilimackinac in present Michigan, Miami in present Indiana, and Presque Isle and Venango in Pennsylvania. The brunt of the attack fell on Detroit, where Pontiac and his allies, the Potawatomi and Huron, besieged the fort from May to October, 1763. Major Henry Gladwin, commander at Detroit, was able to hold the post despite Pontiac's effective blockade of the Detroit River, its only supply route. In Pontiac's War, Robert Rogers again distinguished himself, leading a company of rangers who went along with Captain James Dalyell's reinforcements to Detroit and took part in the battle of Bloody Bridge.[17]

News of Pontiac's attack on Detroit reached the Board of Trade in London early in August, 1763; it was immediately proposed that an announcement be issued to satisfy the Indians. A policy statement was hurriedly composed, and the Proclamation of 1763 was published on October 7. One part of it was designed to restrict westward settlement until land could be purchased from the Indians. For this reason, it forbade settlement anywhere west of the Appalachian Mountains. Ignoring the French settlements in the Illinois country, it unrealistically advised persons already settled in the West "forthwith to remove themselves." The proclamation also decreed that the Indian trade was to be "free and open to all our Subjects whatever," but strictly licensed and closely governed.[18]

The proclamation did not provide a permanent solution. Between 1763 and 1769 the British continued to search for a western policy that would at once keep the Indians at peace, prevent French and Spanish influence from reaching up the eastern tributaries of the Mississippi, and make the newly acquired land an economic asset to the empire. Perhaps the most elementary fact that the new rulers needed to know was that this western land had grown dependent upon European goods. The Native Americans required arms, gunpowder, steel traps, hatchets, and other European tools to ply their trade as hunters. Another fact deserving consideration was that many Indians and French

[17] For a full account of Pontiac's War, see Peckham, *Pontiac,* 130–242.

[18] For the information here and below, see Clarence W. Alvord, "The Genesis of the Proclamation of 1763," in *Michigan Pioneer and Historical Collections,* 36: 18, 22 (1908); R. A. Humphreys, "Lord Shelburne and the Proclamation of 1763," in *English Historical Review,* 49: 241–264 (April, 1934).

Canadians associated with the fur trade already lived in the West. These people could look to two outlets for their furs: Montreal, which was now a gateway to the English markets, or New Orleans, which was still a funnel to France in spite of the fact that the city as well as French lands west of the Mississippi had been turned over to Spain in 1762 to keep them out of English hands.

All of these facts were cited at the time by proponents of an expansionist policy for Britain in America. Jonathan Carver reflected this expansionist point of view. He expressed concern at the number of Frenchmen he found trading in the interior and at the amounts of furs from the headwaters of the Mississippi which were being shipped to New Orleans. His recommendations for a vigorous trade and settlement policy were those of a man in the field who foresaw the impending loss of the western trade unless British policy makers realized that the stability of the fur trade depended upon highly mobile merchants living close to the Indians.[19]

In Carver's time, an expansionist western policy presented difficulties for Britain. Before the mid-18th century her American interests were largely commercial rather than territorial. The mercantilist tradition of holding and defending what was of immediate commercial value and doing so as cheaply as possible called for defense of the sea and its harbors. Land must yield a high profit in proportion to the cost of its defense. What, then, had a vast continental heartland to offer in return for the expense of defending it? Only furs. And they were being supplied by the Hudson's Bay Company and the western outposts of New York. In the view of General Thomas Gage, who in 1763 succeeded Amherst as commander of British forces in America, expansion in the West would prove a sure liability to Britain, since trade required policing and settlers required protection — and both were expensive. He condemned opportunistic traders who "shew little Regard to the Regulations that have been made, to oblige them to traffick only at the Forts; which they avoid, and rove at pleasure." Though Gage knew that French merchants in New Orleans profited by the Indians' displeasure with the British system, he maintained "to take Post in any Place, where our small Garrisons are at their Mercy . . . seems a Measure not to be pursued without some very cogent Reasons." But

[19] See pp. 122–125, below.

if Gage and other British policy makers were seaboard-minded, the seaboard looked to the West. Americans felt a need to tame this empire, where English was still the minority language and where the continued presence of the French presented a threat sufficient to call for some modification in the traditional British colonial policy.[20]

After Pontiac's War the trade was not reopened until January, 1765, when Governor James Murray of Quebec began issuing trading licenses. Sir William Johnson's regulations were still in force, and both Indians and traders were discontented with them. Montreal merchants were acutely aware that restriction of the trade to garrisoned forts such as Oswego, Niagara, and Detroit not only favored New York fur merchants, but encouraged French competition in the West — and the West was the area Montreal depended upon for furs. The merchants therefore sent agents to London to lobby for a relaxing of the restrictions against wintering out from Michilimackinac.[21]

Trouble had already begun at Michilimackinac as a result of Johnson's order that trade be restricted to the fort. William Howard, the commandant, realized soon after the reopening of trade in the spring of 1765 that if no traders went among the Indians, the furs of the West would go to New Orleans. To compromise with the protesting merchants and Indians, he allowed a few traders to go out from the fort. Those who were held back complained and Howard was recalled. In the meantime, Robert Rogers was in London seeking an appointment. On October 12, 1765, he was granted the command of Fort Michilimackinac, and he was later given permission to relax restrictions on wintering out, making the British system more nearly comparable to the old French practice.[22]

While in London, Rogers had presented a plan to the Board of Trade proposing a three-year expedition to discover a northwest passage. The scheme was partly an effort to recoup his fortunes, for Rogers' skills as a frontiersman were matched by his inability

[20] Stanley M. Pargellis, *Lord Loudon in North America*, 1–5, 17–21 (New Haven, Conn., 1933); Gage to Lord Shelburne, November 11, 1766, and to Lord Halifax, March 10, 1764, in Clarence E. Carter, ed., *The Correspondence of General Thomas Gage with the Secretaries of State 1763–1775*, 1: 19, 113 (New Haven, 1931).

[21] Jackson, in *Minnesota History*, 11:242n, 244, 249–256; Paul C. Phillips, *The Fur Trade*, 1: 574–582 (Norman, Okla., 1961).

[22] Reid, in *Canadian Historical Review*, 6:22–24; Cuneo, *Rogers*, 179.

to keep within a budget, and since 1744, the British government had offered a £20,000 reward to the discoverer of a northwest passage. The stated objective of his plan, however, was to find a route of communication from North America to China "for the benefit and Advantage of the British Interests in that Wide-Spread Empire." Rogers claimed he had "a Moral certainty" that the northwest passage existed, and that to find it, one had only to travel up the Mississippi to its source "and from thence to the River called by the Indians Ouragon, which flows into a Bay that projects North-Eastwardly into the [country] from the Pacific Ocean." Although he did not receive official permission for a western expedition, Rogers interpreted his receipt of the command of Michilimackinac as the first stage in approval of his plans. Charles Townshend, one of London's prominent political figures, encouraged him in this assumption.[23]

Rogers returned to America in 1766, arriving at New York. In March he was in New England, where he apparently made arrangements with Captain James Tute to participate in a western expedition. Tute was a native of Hardwick, located near Deerfield, Massachusetts. It seems probable that he and Carver were acquainted, for Carver served with Amos Tute, James's brother, in the French and Indian War. James Tute had a turbulent career as a captain in Rogers' Rangers and was captured twice during the course of the war. He remained in close touch with Rogers after the coming of peace, joining with him in petitions for land grants in New Hampshire. When Rogers met him again in 1765, he was living on half pay as a British officer. It may have been Tute who introduced Carver to Rogers. At any rate, the two men met in Boston, and Carver's newly acquired map-making abilities seem to have recommended him to Rogers. He was hired as the expedition's draftsman. When Rogers set out in the

---

[23] Cuneo, *Rogers*, 177–180; Crouse, *Western Ocean*, 434. The name Oregon first appeared in print in *Travels*, ix, 76. On its origin and use by Carver and Rogers, and for Rogers' petition, see T. C. Elliott, "The Strange Case of Jonathan Carver and the Name Oregon," in *Oregon Historical Quarterly*, 21: 341–368 (December, 1920), 22: 91–105. Townshend was also involved with Rogers in land speculation along the south shore of Lake Superior. Rogers claimed to have been granted a large tract near the Ontonagon River by the Indians at Detroit in 1760. Townshend purchased part of this land from Rogers for £200 on October 10, 1765. A photocopy of the deed, December 23, 1760, is in Rogers Papers, Minnesota Historical Society; the original is in the National Archives, Washington, D.C.

spring of 1766 to assume command of Michilimackinac, Carver followed closely behind him.[24]

This association between Carver and Rogers was not explained in the introduction to the *Travels*. There Carver indicated only that upon leaving military service, "I began to consider . . . how I might continue still serviceable, and contribute, as much as lay in my power, to make that vast acquisition of territory, gained by Great Britain, in North America advantageous to it. . . . To this purpose, I determined, as the next proof of my zeal, to explore the most unknown parts . . . and to spare no trouble or expence in acquiring a knowledge that promised to be so useful to my countrymen." This is not entirely false, but it omits the paramount place of Rogers as the master planner and strategist behind Carver's western journey, an omission that is readily understandable, for during the time Carver's *Travels* were being readied for publication, Rogers was in disgrace, frequently in debtor's prison in London. The journals, however, clearly indicate that Carver had no thought of slighting Rogers' role in the expedition.[25]

Carver left Boston on May 20, and nine days later was at Albany. Possibly he traveled with Rogers, for the major and his wife, the former Elizabeth Browne of Portsmouth, New Hampshire, were at Johnson Hall about 40 miles northwest of Albany on June 3. They followed the usual route west from Albany to Oswego, and Carver arrived there on June 13 in the company of a group of merchants bound for Detroit. Rogers' party at this point must have been near but not with Carver's, for on June 28 Rogers was at Fort Erie, where he wrote of meeting the famous Chief Pontiac. While Carver's journals supply neither chronology nor comment on this part of his trip, it is difficult to believe that he would not have recorded meeting an Indian chief so widely known in America. Carver and Rogers were undoubt-

[24] Cuneo, *Rogers*, 185. On Tute's family, see Sheldon, *Deerfield*, 348; Temple and Sheldon, *Northfield*, 300. On his association with Rogers, see Franklin B. Hough, ed., *Journals of Major Robert Rogers*, 150, 151 (Albany, N.Y., 1883); Burt G. Loescher, *The History of Rogers Rangers: Officers and Non-Commissioned Officers*, 3:32–37 (Burlingame, Calif., 1957). After the exploration scheme failed, Tute continued in the western trade; in 1774 he was west of Lake Winnipeg near Fort Dauphin. He died in the smallpox epidemic which swept the western plains in 1781–82. See W. Stewart Wallace, *The Pedlars from Quebec and Other Papers on the Nor'Westers*, 14 (Toronto, 1954).

[25] Carver, *Travels*, i; Cuneo, *Rogers*, 246, 250, 252; and pp. 58, 59, 121, below.

edly together in Detroit, but they took separate passage from there to Michilimackinac. Sailing aboard the schooner "Gladwin," commanded by Captain Patrick Sinclair, Major and Mrs. Rogers reached Michilimackinac on August 10. Carver left Detroit on August 5 and arrived at the fort, presumably by canoe, on August 28.[26]

While waiting for Carver to arrive, Rogers prepared a commission for him. Dated August 12, 1766, it sets Carver's pay at 8 shillings per day and outlines his duties. He was to proceed west to the Falls of St. Anthony (within present Minneapolis), making maps and plans along the way, noting the Indian towns with the numbers of inhabitants, and other pertinent facts. He was to report back in the spring unless he should receive orders to proceed northwestward in search of a waterway to the Pacific Ocean, in which case he was to send back his journal by some "safe hand." Apparently Rogers was awaiting approval of his northwest passage expedition before sending Carver beyond the Falls of St. Anthony. If not ordered to go farther west, he was to return via the Illinois River farther down the Mississippi. On September 3, 1766, Carver set out in company with William Bruce, a Montreal man who had been one of the first British traders to enter the Northwest in 1762 and who had wintered in Wisconsin in 1763–64.[27]

On September 17, two weeks after Carver left Michilimackinac, Rogers despatched Captain James Tute and James Stanley Goddard on a related mission. Goddard, a Montreal merchant who knew the West, had been at Green Bay in present Wisconsin as early as 1761. In 1768 it was said that he had more influence among the Indians than any other single man trading around Lake Michigan. Rogers appointed him secretary of the expedi-

[26] Cuneo, *Rogers*, 189, 190; on Carver's route, see pp. 60, 69–71, below. On Sinclair, see Reuben G. Thwaites, "Papers from the Canadian Archives — 1778–1783," in *Wisconsin Historical Collections*, 11:141n (1888).

[27] For Carver's commission, see p. 192, below; Kellogg, *British Régime*, 17, 33n. After 1767 Bruce traded along the Mississippi until an altercation with the Indians forced him to move north. He became a partner of James Tute, wintering near Pasquia and the Red Deer River, west of Lake Winnipeg. In 1781 he and Charles Boyer fought off an Indian attack at Fort des Trembles near present Portage la Prairie, Man. He died of smallpox in 1781 or 1782. Wallace, *Pedlars*, 11, 13, 14; Arthur S. Morton, "Forrest Oakes, Charles Boyer, Joseph Fulton, and Peter Pangman in the North-West, 1765–1793," in Royal Society of Canada, *Proceedings and Transactions*, 3rd series, vol. 31, sec. 2, p. 95 (Ottawa, 1937).

tion and instructed him to keep a record of the journey. His journal, of which one known copy survives, supplements and corroborates Carver's account. It is printed in Chapter 3, below.[28]

The instructions which Rogers gave Tute directed him to go via Green Bay to the Falls of St. Anthony, where he was to meet Carver (who was supposed to be wintering with William Bruce) and proceed up the Mississippi to winter. The next spring the party was to travel on up the Mississippi and then overland to Fort des Prairies, the westernmost post the French had held, at the confluence of the north and south branches of the Saskatchewan River near present Prince Albert, Saskatchewan. Here Rogers would send sufficient supplies for them to press on northwest to "the great River Ourgan which rises in several diff[e]rent branches between the latitudes of fifty six and forty eight." The men were to follow this river 700 leagues until it reached the Pacific.[29]

Tute and Goddard did not make contact with Carver in the winter of 1766–67. Instead they wintered near Prairie du Chien on the Mississippi in what is now western Wisconsin — Goddard on the "Dard" (Dinde or Turkey) and Tute on the "Jone" (Jaune or Yellow) rivers, both on the west side of the Mississippi in present Iowa. Carver wintered with the Sioux or Dakota Indians farther north on the Minnesota River. The exact location of his wintering place has been questioned ever since fur trader Peter Pond in 1773 visited a hut which he supposed to be Carver's only 14 miles up the Minnesota River. Carver's vagueness about this part of his tour and his doubtful claim to having traveled 220 miles up the Minnesota do nothing to clarify the point. The only clue he offers is the mention in his survey journal of the Green River, which was the name sometimes given to the Blue Earth River after 1700 when Pierre Charles Le Sueur built a post there. This would suggest that Carver reached a spot beyond the site of present Mankato, Minnesota, where the Blue

[28] For Goddard's "Journal," see pp. 180–191, below. On Goddard, see Reuben G. Thwaites, ed., "The British Regime in Wisconsin," in *Wisconsin Historical Collections,* 18: 285n (1908); Daniel Claus to Sir William Johnson, August 10, 1768, in Alexander C. Flick, ed., *Papers of Sir William Johnson,* 6: 319 (Albany, 1928).

[29] For the instructions, see p. 193, below. On Fort des Prairies, see Bain, ed., Henry, *Travels & Adventures,* 275n; Charles M. Gates, ed., *Five Fur Traders of the Northwest,* 98n (Reprint Ed., St. Paul, 1965).

Earth River joins the Minnesota. Possibly Carver wintered at nearby Swan Lake in present Nicollet County, Minnesota, an ancient village site of the Dakota.[30]

At the end of April, 1767, Carver invited a group of Dakota from both the plains and the river bands to visit Major Rogers, hopeful of opening trade between Michilimackinac and the upper Mississippi. He then proceeded to Prairie du Chien, where he met Tute and Goddard. Here the party apparently gave away as gifts the greater part of the trade goods with which Rogers had supplied them — goods amounting to the sizable value of £500. This generosity was to bring down on them accusations of stirring up the Indians and creating unfair competition for the traders.[31]

With their supply of gifts depleted, they then started up the Mississippi under Tute's command, but instead of continuing to the river's source, as Rogers had ordered, they detoured via Wisconsin's Chippewa, Namekagon, and Brule rivers to Lake Superior, where they hoped to receive more goods from Rogers at Grand Portage. Thus equipped, they planned to follow the waterways northwest to Fort des Prairies. When they reached Grand Portage, however, no supplies were forthcoming. Instead Tute received a letter from Rogers complaining that he was "astonished at your heavy drafts on me but that convince me on the other hand that you must have now goods enough with you to compleat your expedition." Rogers declared that otherwise he would be "ruined by your extra[va]gance." He ordered the men to continue to the northwest "and be more prudent than you have hitherto been."[32]

[30] See pp. 160, 186, below; Gates, ed., *Five Fur Traders*, 45; Warren Upham, *Minnesota Geographic Names, Their Origin and Historic Significance*, 57 (Reprint Ed., St. Paul, 1969); Willoughby M. Babcock, "Sioux Villages in Minnesota Prior to 1837," in *Minnesota Archaeologist*, 11:142 (October, 1945); N. H. Winchell, *Aborigines of Minnesota*, 199 (St. Paul, 1911). Royal B. Hassrick makes an interesting case for the advance of the Dakota in this period to the Big Stone-Lake Traverse region on the present Minnesota-South Dakota border, suggesting that Carver may in fact have traveled the full length of the Minnesota River. See Hassrick, *The Sioux: Life and Customs of a Warrior Society*, 61 (Norman, Okla., 1964).

[31] See p. 204, below; Thwaites, in *Wisconsin Historical Collections*, 18:278n.

[32] Grand Portage, now a national monument on the north shore of Lake Superior in northeastern Minnesota, was the logical place to receive supplies from the east as well as the departure point on the best route to the northwest. British traders had been operating there since 1761. See Eric W. Morse, *Fur Trade*

The fact was that Rogers had never received authorization for his costly western expedition, and the economy-minded government was displeased with his expenses. Sir William Johnson was complaining to London that Rogers "has employed so many persons under extravagant promises and given them Rank and powers to go with large cargoes of goods amongst all the Nations, the Traders began to take the alarm & . . . are now in the utmost consternation." Lacking supplies, the explorers could not continue, and the scheme collapsed. In August the disappointed party set out from Grand Portage on the return trip to Michilimackinac.

The purpose of this undertaking was clearly not confined to the discovery of a northwest passage, its avowed goal. A major portion of the party's energies and expenses went into alerting the Indians of the West, from the Illinois country well into the trading territory of the Hudson's Bay Company, that Michilimackinac was favorably disposed to them and to their trade.

At Michilimackinac less innocent intentions were quickly attributed to Tute and his party. Rogers' free interpretation of his orders concerning the fur trade and his inability to get along with Benjamin Roberts, Sir William Johnson's agent at Michilimackinac, resulted in considerable tension at the fort. In the summer of 1767 Nathaniel Potter, Rogers' secretary, went to Roberts with a tale that Rogers planned to desert to France if he was not given a free hand at Michilimackinac. Roberts immediately suspected Tute's party of negotiating with the western Indians in order to secure their support in the event of Rogers' defection. While Tute's party was making its way toward Grand Portage, Roberts and Rogers were quarreling over a man named Phinehas Atherton, a former member of Rogers' Rangers, who had escaped from prison at Albany and fled to Michilimackinac. There Rogers apparently employed him and protected him from Roberts' efforts to arrest him on behalf of the sheriff of Albany.

Canoe Routes of Canada/Then and Now, 75 (Ottawa, 1968); Solon J. Buck, *The Story of the Grand Portage* (Minneapolis, 1931); Nancy L. Woolworth, "Grand Portage in the Revolutionary War," in *Minnesota History*, 44: 199–201 (Summer, 1975).

See also Kellogg, *British Régime*, 76. For material quoted here and in the paragraph below, see p. 198; Sir William Johnson to the Earl of Shelburne, October 26, 1767, in E. B. O'Callaghan, ed., *Documents Relative to the Colonial History of the State of New-York*, 7: 989 (Albany, 1856).

When Rogers sent the questionable Atherton off to meet Tute's party at Grand Portage, Benjamin Roberts saw another link in the treason plot. On August 20 Roberts wrote in dismay to Sir William Johnson's secretary that the Cree at Grand Portage were "very much dissatisfied," and he was afraid that Rogers' men were distributing unauthorized trade belts among them. On August 29, the very day Tute's party returned, Nathaniel Potter left for Montreal to make his deposition accusing Rogers of treason. Tute and Atherton, Potter declared, "design to go off with him [*Rogers*]." Goddard was accused of embezzlement. Surprisingly, Carver's name was never seriously dragged into the affair.[33]

He spent the winter of 1767–68 at Michilimackinac. From there on September 24 Carver wrote his wife that a part of his reports on the interior had been "sent back with some Indians, which plans and letters Governour Rogers has sent sometime ago by Mr. Baxter, a gentleman belonging to London, to be laid before the Lords of Trade." He added that he was preparing an account of his travels subsequent to that first dispatch, "which is the reason of my not coming home this fall." The first installment of Carver's observations may have been brought before the Board of Trade in London by Alexander Baxter or Henry Bostwick, a Michilimackinac trader who sailed with Baxter to England late in 1767. If the second installment of Carver's report was ever written, it is unlikely that it ever reached London.[34]

[33] Cuneo, *Rogers*, 216; Benjamin Roberts to Guy Johnson, August 20, 1767, and Nathaniel Potter deposition, both in Frederick Haldimand Papers, in *Michigan Pioneer and Historical Collections*, 10: 225, 228, 229 (1888); Allan Nevins, ed., *Ponteach or, The Savages of America, A Tragedy by Robert Rogers*, 143 (Chicago, 1914). Atherton went to London about the same time as Carver, and there began legal proceedings in 1771 to recover £ 4,000 in alleged losses from Roberts. In 1772 he joined Carver in a petition for employment in Rogers' new exploration plan discussed on p. 24, below. On Atherton, see Loescher, *Rogers Rangers*, 3: 54–56; Roberts to William Johnson, June 7, 1771, in Flick, ed., *Johnson Papers*, 8: 134 (Albany, 1933); Hough, ed., *Rogers' Journal*, 240; Kellogg, *British Régime*, 90; Goddard, p. 191, below.

[34] Carver's letter to his wife Abigail is printed in *Boston Chronicle*, February 15–22, 1768, and reprinted in Appendix 1, below. Alexander Baxter, son of the Russian consul at London, had gone to Michilimackinac to investigate mineral deposits in the Great Lakes area in response to a mining scheme Rogers had publicized in London; see p. 142n, below. Bostwick sailed to London with Baxter in connection with the same scheme. Kellogg, *British Régime*, 107, 108. Board of Trade records contain no mention of Carver's report, but petitions by Bostwick and others for mining rights in the Great Lakes area were numerous. Great Britain, Public Record Office, Colonial Office, Class 391, vol. 75: 51, 80, 88, 154; 76: 129, 136, 144, 146; 78: 146, 152, 166, 172, 178. Hereafter cited as G.B., P.R.O.

On December 6, 1767, a dispatch from General Gage arrived at Michilimackinac, ordering the arrest of Rogers on a charge of treasonable negotiations with France. Subsequent suspicion that Rogers would attempt to escape resulted in his being placed in solitary confinement, his legs shackled in irons. His arrest certainly dimmed the hopes Carver had expressed to his wife that Rogers would "take special care to acquaint the Government at home of my services" and that he would receive £200 in payment from the Crown in the spring. In December Carver appealed to General Gage for payment for his services, but Gage turned him down, saying that his employment by Rogers had not been authorized. These setbacks must have added to the discomforts of the winter at Michilimackinac, of which Carver complains briefly in the journals. Yet it was probably during these dreary months that he wrote his western journals with a view toward publishing them.[35]

In May, 1768, Major Rogers was taken east to Montreal, where his trial for treason was to be held. Carver traveled east through Ohio and Pennsylvania carrying with him a manuscript prepared by Rogers which set forth the costs and opportunities for exploiting the fur trade at Michilimackinac. It was September 1, 1768, when Carver reached Boston, and on September 12 he advertised in the *Boston Chronicle* for subscriptions to "An Exact Journal of his TRAVELS" which would be published "as soon as a sufficient number have subscribed, to indemnify the expence of the printing and engraving." Clearly he had no capital to invest in a book, and the subscription price of "TWO SPANISH DOLLARS for every copy" comprised his only immediate prospect of remuneration for his previous two years' work. Public response apparently was not sufficient to encourage publication.[36]

[35] Cuneo, *Rogers,* 225, 227; pp. 134, 202, below; Thomas Gage to James Tute, and Gage to Carver, May 2, 1768, Gage Papers, in William L. Clements Library, University of Michigan, Ann Arbor.

[36] A transcript of Rogers' trial is published in David A. Armour, ed., *Treason? at Michilimackinac* (Mackinac Island, Mich., 1967). The manuscript Carver carried was Rogers, "An Estimate of the Fur and Peltry Trade in the District of Michilimackinac," in American Philosophical Society Library, Philadelphia, copy in Minnesota Historical Society. Most of the latter document was published in William L. Clements, ed., "Rogers's Michillimackinac Journal," in American Antiquarian Society, *Proceedings,* new series, 28:258–273 (Worcester, Mass., 1919). The manuscript was addressed to Thomas Barton of Lancaster, Penna., and contained some notes by Carver. For Carver's Boston activities, see p. 203, below.

Carver's only hope lay in taking his case to England. The acquittal of Rogers on October 31, 1768, may have given him encouragement, for the removal of suspicions of treasonable intent on the part of his superior made Carver's journey more nearly a legitimate government service. He sailed for London late in February, 1769, to carry his case for reimbursement through the maze of the English bureaucracy.[37]

Carver in London, 1769-80

ALTHOUGH JONATHAN CARVER was unknown in London when he arrived there early in the spring of 1769, he was destined to become acquainted with some of the city's foremost scientists, politicians, and publishers. He carried with him a letter from Samuel Cooper, Calvinist preacher and pamphleteer of Boston's Brattle Square Church, to Benjamin Franklin, colonial agent for Pennsylvania, who thanked Cooper "for giving me an opportunity of being acquainted with so great a traveller." Franklin added that he would be glad to help Carver if he could.[1]

Carver's best potential claim to fame — his association with Rogers — could not have done him much good in London. Although Rogers had been acquitted of treason, both he and Carver in the eyes of British officials represented an unpopular expansionist western policy that called for vigorous trade and settlement. The personalities of the two men may also have conjured up visions of the opportunistic frontier traders regarded by General Gage as "generally of no Character, and of desperate fortunes, and for the consideration of a present profit have never thought of consequences." Moreover, Carver's travels had taken him to a part of North America which was of little interest to the Board of Trade in London, since the upper Mississippi Valley was seemingly of small commercial importance compared to Hudson Bay and the Detroit and Illinois areas.[2]

[37] Cuneo, *Rogers*, 242; Lee, in *Proceedings*, 1909, p. 144.

[1] Jared Sparks, ed., *The Works of Benjamin Franklin*, 7: 438 (Boston, 1838); on Cooper, see *Dictionary of American Biography*, 4: 410 (New York, 1930).

[2] Gage to Sir Henry Conway, June 24, 1766, in Carter, ed., *Gage Correspondence*, 1: 97.

With hindsight, one can see that there was little reason for Carver to be optimistic when he presented his petition for reimbursement to the Crown. On May 3, 1769, it was forwarded to the lords' committee of the Council for Plantation Affairs. On June 21 they in turn passed it on to the Board of Trade. Carver was called before the board on July 4. He showed the members his commission from Major Rogers allowing him 8 shillings per day. To this amount Carver added other incidental expenses, making the total due him £ 735, 11s., 3d. He supplied documents from General Gage setting forth the reasons why payment had not been made. The members of the board also examined the journals and maps Carver submitted, and concluded that "no discoveries of general and national importance appear to have been made in the course of his Travells." The board agreed with General Gage that Carver's commission from Rogers was irregular. But in view of his efforts, sufferings, and apparent good character, the board passed the petition back to the Council for Plantation Affairs in July as "a case of compassion but not as including any just demand upon the Crown." On November 20 the council recommended to the Crown that Carver's petition be acted upon favorably if he would agree to deposit all his "Maps Charts plans Discoveries and observations" with the Board of Trade. On November 29 the Crown agreed to this proposal.[3]

By January 20, 1770, however, the treasury was still asking the board what amount Carver should be paid, and the board had made no specific recommendation. Possibly it was still awaiting Carver's delivery of his papers. Later, Carver claimed that during his interview the board had given him permission to publish them, and consequently he "disposed of them to a bookseller," meaning that he had sold them for publication. After the order to deliver them to the board for deposit, he had to buy them back. This he was in no financial condition to do at once, although he did eventually turn them over to the board.[4]

Six months later the hardy colonial was still trying to get his money. On June 7, 1770, he addressed a memorial to the Earl of Gower, lord president of the Privy Council, in which he recited

[3] See pp. 205–209, below; G.B., P.R.O., Colonial Office, Class 391, vol. 76: 130, 136. A different version of the latter document was printed by Lee, in *Proceedings*, 1912, pp. 110–112. Carver's first petition is published by Elliott, in *Oregon Historical Quarterly*, 22: 111–113.

[4] G.B., P.R.O., Colonial Office, Class 391, vol. 77: 19; Carver, *Travels*, xiii.

the history of his efforts, noting that he had now been four years in traveling and petitioning and that the latter had cost him dearly. His total expenditure was now given as £1,129, 15s., 3d., and he said that he was "reduced to great Want and distress." He pleaded for speedy action on this or whatever sum he was to be allowed. Apparently he was planning to return to America soon, for he attached a schedule of expenses which included "time and Expence . . . to the first of July 1770 the Time the pet[itione]r expects to Arrive in America." He also added an alternative schedule of expenses which totaled only £600, 4s. In it he substituted an allowance of 4 shillings daily for provisions for himself and two men while on the expedition instead of the 8 shillings per day promised by Rogers.[5]

It has been stated that Carver received £1,373, 6s., 8d., from the treasury at last. Although no official document has yet been found to confirm this figure, it is consistent with Carver's statement that he was given "a little more than Equivolent to the Expenses he was at." He must have received the money before November 19, 1770, for on that date James Rivington, an American bookseller, wrote to Sir William Johnson: "they have paid the accounts of the Expedition . . . to make discoveries in the back countries, to one Carver."[6]

It would seem that the Crown's reimbursement kept Carver alive "For near three Years . . . without pay or Employment," or so he implied in another appearance as a petitioner on February 10, 1773. On that date he asked the Earl of Dartmouth, secretary of state for America, to "put him into Some Employment, Civil or Military whereby Your memorialist may git a Support." He continued his residence in England, probably because he still hoped to gain some income from the publication of his journals

[5] Lee, in *Proceedings*, 1912, pp. 114–117.

[6] The sum Carver received was stated by Samuel Peters in the course of his testimony concerning the Carver grant. For this and Carver's own statement, see Lee, in *Proceedings*, 1912, pp. 97, 118. Stephen Cottrell to the treasury, June 7, 1770, in G.B., P.R.O., Treasury, Class 1, vol. 475: 240, copy in Rogers Papers, recommended that Carver be paid £1,129, 15s., 3d. For Rivington's letter, see Milton W. Hamilton, ed., *The Papers of Sir William Johnson*, 12: 877 (Albany, 1957). Rivington was a Londoner who emigrated to America and had bookstores in Philadelphia, Boston, and New York. The source of his information is unknown, but he would have been in touch with gossip in the London bookselling and publishing trade. G.B., P.R.O., Treasury, Class 1, vol. 478: 321–330, and Colonial Office, Class 323, vol. 28: 303–306, contain references to Carver, but no statement of payment made to him.

or anticipated the possibility of obtaining an appointment. His intention to return to America was underlined in a second memorial to Dartmouth 15 days later when he requested an appointment as superintendent of Indian affairs for the lands west of Lake Huron between the Illinois River and the Hudson's Bay Company territories.[7]

Nothing came of this memorial, and Carver remained in London. Rogers was there too, having arrived in September, 1769, also to seek financial assistance. Although Rogers spent much of the following four years in debtor's prison, he and Carver were again associated in proposing an expedition to find a western passage to the Pacific. On February 11, 1772, Rogers submitted to the king a plan which closely resembled his proposal of 1765: the explorers would follow the Minnesota River westward to a branch of the Missouri, portage to the "River Ourigan" leading to the Pacific, where a post was to be founded to support a search of the northwest coast of North America. Carver petitioned in May, 1772, for employment in the expedition. Two years later the plan was being forwarded under the patronage of Richard Whitworth, member of Parliament for Stafford. But the uneasy relations between England and the American colonies in 1774 prevented Whitworth's scheme from materializing.[8]

Rogers went back to America in 1775 to serve the loyalist cause as the leader of the Queen's American Rangers. Carver stayed on in London, apparently reconciled to remaining there, for in 1774 he took a second wife, a Mrs. Mary Harris, widow of a captain in the royal navy. (This despite the fact that he had a wife still living in America.) Possibly this union brought him some financial support, for no further petitions from him appear after 1773. His connection with Richard Whitworth yielded some employment in 1775, for Whitworth set him and an obscure map maker named Isaac De Costa (who had joined in Carver's petition for employment in Rogers' 1772 northwest passage scheme) to making "A Plan of the Town and Harbour of

---

[7] Carver's petition is printed by Lee, in *Proceedings*, 1912, p. 117. For a similar petition dated November 4, 1773, see Elliott, in *Oregon Historical Quarterly*, 22:113–115.

[8] Cuneo, *Rogers*, 246; for Rogers' petition, see Elliott, in *Oregon Historical Quarterly*, 22:106–110; for Carver's, see Roberts, ed., *Northwest Passage Appendix*, 63–65; Carver, *Travels*, 541–543.

Boston," which was published in London on July 29 of that
year.[9]

By 1776 Carver was apparently finding employment among
the major map publishers of London. In that year R. Sayer and J.
Bennett, map sellers, offered "A New Map of the Province of
Quebec . . . from the French Surveys Connected with those
made after the War. By Captain Carver, and Other Officers in
His Majesty's Service." Its southern border is the very northern
part of New York, an area Carver makes no claim to having
visited after his self-preparation as a draftsman; it is therefore
unlikely that he could have had any part in surveying for it. It is
possible that he put it together, however, from French and
British sources. In this period he may also have become acquainted with Samuel Dunn, a mathematician, teacher, author,
and cartographer, who in 1776 published "A Map of the British
Empire in America . . . improved from the Surveys of Capt.
Carver."[10]

How and when did Carver get his journals and maps from the
Board of Trade in order to prepare them for publication? In his
memorial to Dartmouth on February 10, 1773, Carver said that
the money he had received from the treasury in exchange for
giving up his papers was inadequate, and his "Draughts and
Plans wou'd then by a publication produce Your Memorialist a
Considerable Relief." His request for the return of his papers
produced the reply that the Board of Trade had lost his journals;
luckily, he had kept copies. Whether his "Draughts and Plans"
were also misplaced is not known, but he did eventually receive
the loan of some documents deposited with the board, for a note
on Rogers' 1772 proposal for an exploring expedition reads,
"lent the two Plans to Capt. Carver 15 Feb. 1775." It is likely
that the board found and returned his maps at least before 1776,
since Dunn's map of that year "improved" by Carver appears to

[9] Cuneo, Rogers, 257, 266; Samuel Peters to Samuel Harrison, February 4,
1805, Samuel Harrison Papers, in Minnesota Historical Society; Lee, in Proceedings, 1912, p. 101; Roberts, ed., Northwest Passage Appendix, 65. De Costa was
probably the nephew of Emanuel Mendes da Costa, a Jewish naturalist and friend
of Dr. John Fothergill. Dictionary of National Biography, 12:271 (New York,
1887); Emanuel Mendes da Costa, "Familiae Mendesianae & Da Costianae," in
Gentleman's Magazine And Historical Chronicle, 82:24 (January, 1812).

[10] Thomas Jefferys, The American Atlas, plates 8, 19 (London, 1776); on Dunn,
see Dictionary of National Biography, 16:210–212 (1888).

agree with the revisions Carver made of his map before publishing it in the *Travels*. [11]

In his negotiations with the board, it seems probable that Carver received some support from Joseph Banks. That illustrious gentleman, to whom Carver dedicated his *Travels,* was in 1778 named president of the Royal Society of London for the Improvement of Natural Knowledge, the dominant scientific organization in Britain. The explorer's journals were in Banks's library before being entrusted to the British Museum, and the sparse remaining record suggests that Banks rendered Carver some important favors relative to the journals. [12]

In claiming the attention of Joseph Banks, Carver had truly arrived in London scientific circles, and he made other important connections as well. In addition to Whitworth and Dunn (who was also a member of the Royal Society), Carver became known to an unnamed "private society of gentlemen" for whom he offered to undertake a journey to North America by way of northern Asia to study the ethnic origins of the American Indians. The Society for the Encouragement of Arts, Manufactures and Commerce would patronize his pamphlet entitled *A Treatise on the Culture of the Tobacco Plant* when it was published in London in 1779. Also among his acquaintances in his last years was Dr. John Fothergill, one of London's most prominent physicians and Joseph Banks's collaborator in collecting botanical specimens. [13]

Connections of this kind were essential to an aspiring explorer or author in London. By 1775 Carver was 66 years old, hardly an age to command exploring parties. He had but one exploration story to tell, and London was by no means lacking in travel narratives. Captain James Cook had won the praise of all England with two voyages around the world between 1768 and 1775, and travel tales flowed in steadily from all parts of the empire. How then did Carver go about getting his travels to the little-known upper Mississippi published? [14]

[11] Lee, in *Proceedings,* 1912, p. 118; Carver, *Travels,* xiv; Elliott, in *Oregon Historical Quarterly,* 22:110.

[12] See p. 33, below. On Banks's career, see Hector C. Cameron, *Sir Joseph Banks* (London, 1966).

[13] On Carver's proposed Asian expedition, see *Travels,* 216. On Fothergill, see *Dictionary of National Biography,* 20:66 (1889).

[14] Joseph Banks accompanied Cook on his first voyage. In 1776 Cook set out again to seek a northwest passage from the west coast of North America, prov-

The four versions of Carver's journals preserved in the British Museum offer some clues as to how their author went about preparing his account for publication. Although none of the versions is dated, the order in which they were written can be inferred from internal evidence and from the order of binding. Version I, the basis for the present edition, is the shortest and probably the earliest of the four. It is a day-by-day account (in part) of Carver's journey, essentially beginning and ending at Michilimackinac, with one long digression in the middle on the customs of the Sioux. In it Carver concentrated on topics which Rogers had directed him to document: geographical information, locations and numbers of Indians, and descriptions of trading posts. He also made observations on resources of the regions through which he passed (on food, soil, and transportation routes, for example), and commented on French and Spanish activity in the area. This version was largely geared to the interests of the government and the military who were its intended audience. To illustrate it Carver included a page of drawings depicting a Sioux tent, a calumet, a buffalo snake, and two Indian weapons, and a large, roughly drawn manuscript map, probably made at Michilimackinac during the same months in which the journal was composed.[15]

In Version II Carver enlarged his story by more than a third, adding 14 sometimes substantial numbered inserts and indicating in the manuscript where they were to be placed. He also made other additions in the form of both small details and larger sections in an attempt to improve the readability and organization of the manuscript. The 14 numbered inserts supply considerable background on Carver himself, Rogers, the fur trade, and the French and Indian War. They also offer more specific obser-

ing that no usable sea route existed through the ice-free portion of the continent. See J. C. Beaglehole, *The Exploration of the Pacific*, 278, 348 (London, 1934). Cook's accounts of his first two expeditions were originally published as "An Account of a Voyage round the World," in John Hawkesworth, *An Account of the Voyages Undertaken by the Order of His Present Majesty*, vols. 2 and 3 (London, 1773); James Cook, *A Voyage towards the South Pole and Round the World* (London, 1777).

[15] Versions I and II are bound together as British Museum Additional Manuscripts 8949. The illustrations were later misbound with Version II, but page numbers referring to the text of Version I show that they belong to the earlier draft. The engravings in Carver's *Travels*, Plate 4, were closely modeled on these drawings, which presumably were made by the explorer. The map is bound at the end of Version I.

vations on various places — Detroit, Grand Portage, and Michilimackinac, for example — as well as the dubious story of the tame rattlesnake and a description of what is now known as Carver's Cave. Other additions which do not appear in the numbered insertions provide comments on Indian foods and customs, Pontiac's War, place names, the weather, and his return trip from Michilimackinac to the East in 1768.

It would appear that the enlargements served at least two purposes: they supported Carver's view of the importance of the fur trade in the Michilimackinac hinterland, and they incorporated specific data on the people, the flora, and the fauna of North America which might be of interest to English readers.

The additions also contain several puzzles. In one of them near the end of the manuscript, Carver refers to Thomas Hutchins in a way indicating that he was aware of his book, *A Topographical Description of Virginia, Pennsylvania, Maryland and North Carolina.* This volume was published in London in 1778 during the same month that Carver's *Travels* apparently appeared. This would seem to indicate either that Carver knew about Hutchins' book before it was published, or that at least some of the enlargements were added to his own manuscript very late in 1778.[16]

Carver's journal enlargements also show his awareness of the earlier works of Father Louis Hennepin, Pierre François Xavier de Charlevoix, and Baron Lahontan, all of whom he mentions by name. But a comparison of his additions with the volumes of these three authors does not indicate any wholesale plagiarism from their works. Unlike the published *Travels,* Carver's journals appear largely to report his own observations. Such overlapping details as do appear are either attributed, or they are consistent with facts Carver could have known from his own experience.[17]

[16] See p. 140, below; on Hutchins' book, see Frederick C. Hicks, ed., *A Topographical Description of Virginia, Pennsylvania, Maryland, and North Carolina,* 55 (Reprint Ed., Cleveland, 1904). Hutchins is also mentioned in *Travels,* 531.

[17] Some works of all of these authors would have been available to Carver in English. The book of Louis-Armand de Lom d'Arce, Baron de Lahontan, was translated as *New Voyages to North-America* (London, 1703). Louis Hennepin's books, *Nouvelle Decouverte d'un Tres Grand Pays Situé dans l'Amerique* (Utrecht, 1697) and *Nouveau Voyage d'un Pais plus grand que l'Europe* (Utrecht, 1698), would have been available to Carver in a combined translation, *A New Discovery of a Vast Country in America, Extending above Four Thousand Miles* (London, 1698). Hennepin's *Description de la Louisiane* was not translated until 1880. Pierre François Xavier de Charlevoix's *Journal d'un Voyage Fait Par Ordre du Roi dans*

Between the text and the numbered inserts in Version II is a page headed "To the Reviser" in which Carver defined certain American terms which might need to be explained to a British audience and offered the reviser considerable latitude in making changes in the text. Carver wrote that anything which would "embellish or give better sence to the journal will I dare say be very agreable to the publishers and to the author." This license to "embellish" was to become a major cause for criticism of the book that emerged from these journals.[18]

Versions III and IV of the journal, also in Carver's hand, seem to show the author moving closer to the publication of his book. The former bears a title page: "A Journal of the Travels of Captain Jonathan Carver from Michilimackinac to the Country of the Nadouwesie or Sioux from August, the 12th, 1766, to August, ye 30, 1767." This version, which begins with the survey journal recording the distance and direction traveled each day, was copied in a large, clear hand on one side of the page only. Version III is in part an early copy of the original manuscript, for it contains no indication of where inserts are to be made, nor does it add the description of lands and tribes included in Version II. The 14 inserts from Version II were copied and placed at the end of the text, although the first six were later misbound and numbers 12 and 13 appear to have been lost. Greatly improved drawings of the tent, calumet, and Indian weapons are present, but the sketch of the buffalo snake is omitted.[19]

Version IV may have been the one intended as the manuscript for the publisher. At least it is so labeled by some near-contemporary of Carver's who wrote: "The following is the same Journal put by the Author into a form which he intended for Publication with Several Additions, Seem to have been made from Memory." In copying Version IV, Carver made many simple transcription errors, although the text closely follows that of Version II with indications for the insertions. The latter are not, however, incorporated into the body of the text nor is the

---

l'Amerique Septentrionnale (Paris, 1744) was translated as *Journal of a Voyage to North-America* (London, 1761). The more exhaustive work of Charlevoix, *Histoire et Description Generale de la Nouvelle France* (Paris, 1744) was not translated in Carver's time.

[18] For Carver's note, see p. 142, below.

[19] Versions III and IV are bound together as British Museum Additional Manuscripts 8950.

survey journal included. In addition, insert 11 giving an account of Carver's visit to the "great cave" on May 1, 1767, is omitted. The incident is reported, however, through the inclusion of "Speeches interchanged between Capt. Carver and the cheifs [sic] of . . . the Naudouwessee," which appear as an appendix to the manuscript proper. Carver's additions concerning the lands and tribes in Version II are included, and the buffalo snake is restored to the illustrations. Three new illustrations are added: two drawings of an Indian man, woman, and child (subsequently printed in the Travels as Sioux and Fox), and a "safe conduct" given Carver by a Sioux chief with the explorer's explanation of it.[20]

Versions II, III, and IV, therefore show the development of Carver's manuscript toward book form, with Version II being the critical one from the standpoint of additions to the original text. These various stages reflect Carver's adjustment to the realities of the publishing business — the need to make his book impressive, more than a thin piece contending for attention among folios. Perhaps the cost of production when weighed against its possible interest for readers determined him to omit the survey journal from Version IV.

But Carver's experiences, his knowledge, and his own journals were not enough. Before the book we know as the Travels was published, further additions from the writings of other authors were incorporated, in some cases with only casual acknowledgment. The alterations consisted of rearranging and distributing Carver's text around these additions. For example, much of Carver's material on the Indians (pp. 100–113, below) was placed in a section entitled "Of the Origin, Manners, Customs, Religion, and Language of the Indians." His description of rattlesnakes in the early part of the journals (pp. 62–65) was placed in a section near the end of the Travels entitled "Of Serpents." Within the published account of his journey, there are some differences in the dates of arrival and departure from various points. Notably, the Travels report a trip of 60 miles northward from the Falls of St. Anthony, while the journals take him immediately from the falls southward to the Minnesota River (p. 94).[21]

[20] For the speeches and "safe conduct," see pp. 118–120, 143, below. The handwriting on the near-contemporary label is not that of Joseph Banks.

[21] For the section on Indians, see Travels, 181–419; on serpents, 478–488; on the trip above the Falls of St. Anthony, 71–73.

More important is the attempt in the published book to enhance Carver's position and give his journey loftier purposes
than the journals indicate. The *Travels* make the search for a
western passage the dominant objective of the expedition,
whereas the journals emphasize the fur trade. The *Travels* ap-
pend as a secondary motive "the introduction of more polished
manners, and more humane sentiments" among the Indians. No
such motive is expressed in the manuscript journals. Throughout the published version, it is Carver who seems to be in charge
of the expedition, but the journals state frankly that from Prairie
du Chien northward in 1767 Captain Tute was "commander of
the party" (p. 125). The importance of Rogers as the mastermind
of the undertaking and the prominence of Goddard and Tute are
downgraded in the *Travels,* where Carver's companions at any
stage of the journey are seldom mentioned. On the other hand,
the *Travels* introduce much more historical background, although some of it is not entirely pertinent. Another significant
difference lies in the language and general tone of the two accounts. The manuscript journals in Carver's own hand are forth-
right and matter-of-fact, while the arrangement of the *Travels* is
more sophisticated and the language is ornate, involved, and
often flowery.[22]

According to Elkanah Watson, who was in London on government and personal business in 1782 and made many acquaintances there, "Carver had very little agency in bringing forward
the superadded matter" in the *Travels*. Who then made these
additions and alterations in the hope of creating greater public
appeal for what had been a simple explorer's journal? Only one
person ever claimed the honor. He was Alexander Bicknell, a
fairly productive but insignificant English author. Just after
Carver's death in 1780, Bicknell was apparently advertising himself in London literary circles as the explorer's editor, for the
Gentleman's Magazine of August, 1780, contains a corre-
spondent's wish "to know more of Mr. Bicknell, who calls himself editor of the former edition of his [*Carver's*] Travels." A
decade later on the title page of his book *Doncaster Races,*
Bicknell listed some of his earlier works and identified himself as
"Editor of . . . Captain Carver's Travels." No one has ever

[22] On the expedition's purposes, see *Travels,* vi, 178, 539–541; on Carver's
role, ix–xi.

challenged his claim. Indeed, during the years of greatest controversy over Carver's book, Bicknell's role was either unknown or ignored, although there was nothing unusual about a publisher employing someone to improve a manuscript, and Dr. Johnson's London was well supplied with literary hacks who made their spare livings filling this need.[23]

An additional piece of evidence lends credence to Bicknell's claim. In November, 1783, the *European Magazine* carried an "Anecdote of the late Captain Carver" signed "A. B." It concerned a dream Carver had before he left America in 1769, a dream which, after the fact at least, appeared to foretell the independence of the American colonies. Bicknell was interested in the subject of dreams and apparitions and their relationship to the location and function of the soul, a topic upon which he had published in 1777 a treatise entitled *Philosophical Disquisitions on the Christian Religion*. In relating Carver's dream, "A. B." stated: "In the year 1778 he [*Carver*] more than once repeated the circumstances of the foregoing dream to the writer of this." Since "A. B." indicates no previous acquaintance with Carver and since the publication of the *Travels* was the dominant event in Carver's life in 1778, it is likely that the book brought them together. The initials "A. B." seem to point once more to Alexander Bicknell.[24]

While Bicknell copied copiously from the pages of Hennepin, Lahontan, and Charlevoix, weaving them into material from Carver's own experience, Carver worried about the increased costs of printing and sought subscribers to cover expenses. He could see that publishing costs were outrunning the probable income from the first edition. By August 13, 1778, his concern

[23] On Watson, see *Dictionary of American Biography*, 19: 541 (1936); his information on Carver is recounted by Henry R. Schoolcraft, in *Historical and Statistical Information Respecting the History, Condition and Prospects of the Indian Tribes of the United States*, 1: 138 (Philadelphia, 1851). On Bicknell, see *Dictionary of National Biography*, 5: 9 (1886); anonymous letter, in *Gentleman's Magazine*, 50: 374 (August, 1780); Alexander Bicknell, *Doncaster Races; or the History of Miss Maitland; a Tale of Truth*, title page (London, [1790]). Bourne, in *American Historical Review*, 11: 302, considered John Coakley Lettsom the most likely author and editor of *Travels*. Lee, in *Proceedings*, 1909, 1912, was of the opinion that Carver wrote his own book.

[24] A.B., "Anecdote of the late Captain Carver," in *European Magazine and London Review*, November, 1783, p. 346; on Bicknell's mystical interests, see anonymous reviews of his books in *Monthly Review; or, Literary Journal*, 57: 331 (October, 1777), 63: 467 (December, 1780).

found expression in a letter to Joseph Banks, who must have been somewhat aware of the book's progress toward publication. Carver wrote:

SIR

The present season proves unfavourable for publishing my travels, and is a misfortune I did not expect, owing to the delay of the Printers, and the increase of the subject beyond my first thought; tho' I have been favoured with a number of subscribers, they are not more than sufficient to pay one third of the expences of printing: to settle only a part of the rest, I have been obliged to make over part of the Copies; and I fear all must go, and not enough, and into hands possessed of little Mercy or Justice.

And tho' all greatly approve of my choice in the Dedication, yet many have censured me for not making a property of it: in either I have the greatest satisfaction, and am happy in the opportunity I have, of making some acknowledgment, for the favours and kindness I have heretofore had the Honour of receiving from you. Pardon me if I again presume to ask for some further assistance: I am impelled by the most urgent necessity: a small favour may do great service, nay, save me from ruin — I think I shall be able to repay it soon — Such an additional favour, if possible, will increase my gratitude, which (tho' I should be denyed) will not diminish, but Bless ever the name of Banks while I live.

I am Sir, with the greatest respect Your much obliged and most obedt Humble servt.

J. CARVER

It seems probable that Banks made a further contribution, for Carver's book with its dedication to Banks was published not more than three months after this letter was written.[25]

Another problem that must have added to Carver's expenses was the re-engraving of the map he had probably drawn at Michilimackinac in the winter of 1767–68. Some time in 1769 he had his first rough draft copied in preparation for engraving. The

[25] A copy of the original letter is in the British Museum, Natural History, Dawson Turner Collection, 1: 197. It is calendared in Warren R. Dawson, ed., *The Banks Letters,* 204 (London, 1958). It is printed by permission of the Trustees of the British Museum (Natural History).

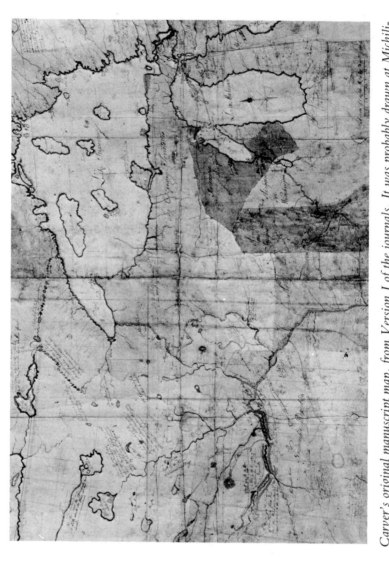

Carver's original manuscript map, from Version I of the journals. It was probably drawn at Michili-mackinac in the winter of 1767–68. The original in the British Museum measures 730 by 535 mm.

copying was for the most part accurate, but in the process the size was reduced from 730 by 535 mm. to 340 by 270 mm. Space was left on the copy version for a dedication. An engraving was executed by Thomas Kitchin, a prominent engraver of the period. Perhaps in the hope of obtaining reimbursement, Carver had Kitchin add a dedication to "the Earl of Hillsborough & the rest of the Lords, Commissioners for Trade & Plantations." Kitchin again altered the map's size, enlarging it slightly to 362 by 280 mm.[26]

These first three versions of the Carver map are alike in all major features, but as publication approached it became obvious that the rendering was inaccurate. Carver had given his map too great an extension westward, placing the western end of Lake Superior 100 degrees west of London. So the version Kitchin engraved did not conform to either English or French contemporary maps of the Great Lakes area. A new engraving had to be executed. Some stylistic changes within it indicate that a different — and inferior — engraver was retained, but the resulting map was much improved in accuracy. Where the earlier three versions had depicted Michilimackinac at 88 degrees west of London and Carver's wintering place at 105 degrees, the final version published in *Travels* located these points at 85 and 97 degrees respectively. The north-south limits of Carver's journey were also altered from 50 degrees, 20 minutes, and 40 degrees, 20 minutes, to 49 degrees and 41 degrees, 40 minutes. The general shorelines of the Great Lakes and the courses of rivers were not significantly changed, although in the final version, Carver inserted "heads of Origan" in the northwest portion of the map, perhaps to give credibility to his hope for another westward expedition.

The first edition of Carver's *Travels* was published in the fall of 1778, just ten years after the journals on which it was based had been written. Only a little more than a year before his death, Jonathan Carver's narrative became a part of American travel literature, and his name became known to the English reading public. A second edition appeared in 1779 and his *Treatise on the*

---

[26] John Parker, "Jonathan Carver's Map of his Travels," in Hellmut Lehmann-Haupt, ed., *Homage to a Bookman,* 197–208 (Berlin, 1967). All the maps are bound between Versions I and II except for the manuscript copy, which follows the inserts in Version III.

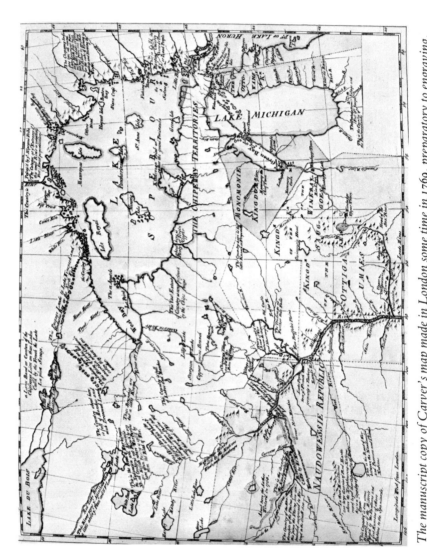

The manuscript copy of Carver's map made in London some time in 1769, preparatory to engraving.
The original, which measures 340 by 270 mm., is bound with Version III of the journals.

The version of Carver's map as published in Travels with corrected latitude and longitude lines, and the "heads of Origan" added on the far left. From the 1779 edition.

Culture of the Tobacco Plant was published in the same year. His name also appeared as the author of *The New Universal Traveller*, a catchall volume of travel literature issued in 1779. Whether he was paid for the use of his name or whether it was stolen to give this compendium some acceptability, is not clear, but in 1781 his London widow stated "to prevent imposition on the public" that Carver was not the author of it. Indeed, the work was put together in much the same way as Bicknell's additions to Carver's *Travels*. Soon after it came out, a writer noted its numerous borrowings from other travelers in comments that appeared in the *Critical Review*.[27]

The income from these books did not sustain Carver, however, and he attempted to support himself in his last year as a lottery clerk. He died on January 31, 1780, in extreme poverty, leaving widows and children on both sides of the Atlantic. His London widow had the philanthropic aid of Dr. John Coakley Lettsom, her husband's last attending physician, and she also received an annuity from the Crown. Abigail Carver, his American widow, received nothing, but Carver's American heirs were to seek their reward in land claims in the upper Mississippi Valley. Jonathan Carver's reward was the fame which was to live after him in the attention that his book has received for nearly two centuries.[28]

Carver's *Travels*
The History of a Book

JONATHAN CARVER'S BOOK was a success. Its numerous editions in English and in translations made Carver a familiar name to explorers, geographers, literary figures, speculators, teachers, students, and others who became interested in the American West in the century following its publication. Yet despite its

---

[27] Anonymous note, in *Gentleman's Magazine*, 51:80 (February, 1781); anonymous review, in *Critical Review*, 50:429–434 (December, 1780).

[28] Lettsom, in *Travels*, 18, 22; Quaife, in *Mississippi Valley Historical Review*, 7:11.

appeal, the prospect of disrepute dogged the *Travels* through the 19th and into the 20th century.

The *Travels* was probably published in October or November, 1778. The first note on it, which appeared in the *Critical Review* of December, 1778, was generous, praising Carver's motives and describing him as "a judicious and faithful observer" whose objective was "Contributing to the Commercial advantage of his country." According to the anonymous reviewer, the claim in the *Travels'* introduction that the French had falsified their descriptions of North America was confirmed; the northwest passage objective was noted. Much of the 10-page review was devoted to quotations from the book, including the descriptions of the Indians, the accounts of Lake Pepin, Carver's Cave, and the "shining mountains." [1]

Similarly, the *Monthly Review* found it an entirely praiseworthy book. To those mourning the "presumed loss" of the American colonies, Carver's volume was offered as a consolation, demonstrating that there was still an abundance of "fine country, yet unsubjected to European colonization, — and to the property of which, *we* have, at least, as good pretensions as we had to most of the provinces which have lately bidden *good bye* to us." Extending through two issues, the review included extensive quotations, chiefly from the unusual material in Carver's narrative: the rattlesnake story, the Lake Pepin "fortifications," the rumored smaller and whiter Indians farther west, the Cree priest and his magic, and other accounts of the Indians. Nowhere in the review is there anything derogatory or in the least critical of the book, which, incidentally, sold for 7s., 6d. [2]

With such favorable reception in review journals that were not at all loath to destroy a book and its author, it is not surprising that a second London edition should have appeared in 1779. Offered by a new group of booksellers, this edition bore the marks of some incidental revision by the author, who by this

[1] *Critical Review*, 46:441–450 (December, 1778); for the passages mentioned, see *Travels*, ii–iv, 54–56, 63, 121. A search for the records of Carver's various publishers in the British Museum and the files of the Company of Stationers, London, proved fruitless.

[2] Anonymous review, in *Monthly Review*, 60:90–95, 281–289 (February, April, 1779); for the passages mentioned, see *Travels*, 43–45, 56, 118–120, 123–129.

time was near, if not in, his final illness. Errata noted in the first edition were corrected, but only minor changes were made in the text, largely in material relating to natural history. The section on Indians was not changed significantly; a footnote was added calling attention to Carver's recently published pamphlet on tobacco, and an illustration of the tobacco plant, "Drawn and Engrav'd for Carvers Travels . . . by F. Sansom," was included.[3]

The apology in the 1778 edition for the unscientific arrangement of the natural history material was omitted in the 1779 printing, but an interesting "Address to the Public" was added, which stated that the first edition was enjoying a brisk demand and that in this new edition errors were being corrected. The author of the "Address," ostensibly Carver, admitted to some questioning of the stories about the prognostications of an Indian priest at Lake Superior and of the rattlesnake that returned to its master's box after an absence of some seven months. Of the first of these he said he was an eyewitness, and the second story he insisted was related to him by a Frenchman of "undoubted veracity."[4]

The popularity of the *Travels* in London induced a group of Dublin booksellers to bring out in 1779 another printing obviously pirated from the 1778 version. These three editions satisfied current demand, but the publishers were seemingly unwilling to admit it. The 1779 London sheets were reissued in

---

[3] The errata in the 1778 edition are on the verso of p. 543. The dedication was changed from "To Joseph Banks, Esq. F.R.S." to "Joseph Banks, Esq., President of the Royal Society." The former dedication was dated June 20, 1778; the latter is undated. The "Contents" reflect additions to the text and contain the following changes: p. 151 (1778) was changed to 153 (1779); "Dress of the Chipéways" on p. 229 was changed to "Dress of the Ottagaumies"; p. 489 was changed to 488, 489. Minor alterations were made within the text: on p. 66 (both editions) the 1779 edition altered the distance at which the Falls of St. Anthony could be heard from 50 to 15 miles. At p. 347 "unwanted" (1778) became "unwonted" (1779). At p. 446 "exceedingly" (1778) became "extremely" (1779). At p. 467 the descriptions of the "whipperwill" and the fish hawk were interchanged. The following brief descriptions were added: wood pigeon (p. 471); silkworm (p. 490); tobacco worm, bees (p. 491); vines, mulberry tree (p. 503); and sweet gum (p. 505). The description of the skunk (p. 450) was altered somewhat, and the footnote and drawing of the tobacco plant appeared on pp. 521, 522.

[4] The apology was on p. 526 of the 1778 edition; the "Address" was inserted after the dedication; the questionable passages can be found on pp. 43–45, 123–129. For a list of the various editions discussed here and below, see Appendix 3.

November, 1780, with a title page labeling them as the third edition, though only a line was changed in the "Address to the Public," from "A large edition . . ." to "Two large editions." Included was an engraving of Carver from a portrait in John Coakley Lettsom's possession.

Nine months before this printing appeared, subscribers to the *Gentleman's Magazine* of March, 1780, read: "We are sorry to inform our readers that we are well assured Capt. Carver . . . died absolutely and strictly starved, leaving a wife and two small children, for whom Dr. Letsome [*sic*], with his wonted humanity, interests himself, and has disposed of many copies of his Travels, which, notwithstanding their great merit, could not procure him a competent provision." Lettsom subsequently used Carver's death and previous financial difficulties as an example in advocating a "Society for Promoting Useful Literature." Both authors and public, he felt, would benefit from such patronage of writers. The part of the proposal which related to Carver found a response in London, and one who signed himself "A Friend to Humanity" wrote to the *Gentleman's Magazine* in May, 1780, proposing some assistance to Carver's family by way of a subscription edition under Lettsom's sponsorship. Lettsom replied in June that he approved of the plan and had already taken it in hand. All of this was testimony to a continuing regard for both Carver and his book. The only — and probably the first — reservation concerning the *Travels* in this period was the previously quoted anonymous query in the *Gentleman's Magazine* of August, 1780, regarding Alexander Bicknell, who was claiming to be the editor of the book.[5]

When the new issue sponsored by Dr. Lettsom appeared in 1781, it was prefaced by a biography of Carver written by the doctor. It also included an index and a reproduction of a deed granting land to the explorer by two Sioux chieftains in the upper Mississippi country. In July, 1781, the book was reviewed for the first time in the *Gentleman's Magazine*. The reviewer quoted at length from Lettsom's biography. Carver's failure to reach the northwest passage was noted, but "is now less to be

[5] Lettsom, "Hints for establishing A Society for Promoting Useful Literature"; "A Friend to Humanity," May 13; Lettsom letter of June 10; all in *Gentleman's Magazine,* 50: 153, 183, 219, 264, 374 (March, April, May, June, August, 1780).

regretted, as Captain Cook has since shewn the impracticability of a N.W. passage in those parts." The major emphasis of the review was on Carver's account of his travels; the much larger portion of the book devoted to the origins, manners, and customs of the Indians was passed over with little comment. While this may constitute a value judgment by the reviewer on the relative merits of these two parts of the book, no question was raised about the quality, authorship, or originality of the latter section. Nor did anyone observe that this issue was in fact made up of the unsold sheets of the 1779 London edition, buttressed by the new introductory material and an index. Questions about the authorship and quality of the *Travels* were to be raised in America, and for the most part the conflict over Carver's book was to be an American affair.[6]

The first transatlantic edition appeared in Philadelphia in 1784. Three years later the *American Museum*, a miscellaneous news, comment, and culture journal patterned after those of London, published an unsigned essay entitled, "Indians indifferent about dying." This was an extended, but unattributed, excerpt from Carver's *Travels*. Two more years passed before an unnamed reader wrote the editor in July, 1789, that he had "several times heard and read of doubts being suggested, whether Carver made the extensive tour he had described; or whether his book be not compiled from those of Charlevoix, Hennepin, &c." Subsequent issues of the *American Museum* show no reply to this letter, but doubts were clearly going around.[7]

Jedidiah Morse, publishing his *American Geography* in 1789, apparently was not aware of them, for he stated: "Mr. Carver has travelled higher up this river [*Mississippi*], and appears to be better acquainted with its northern parts and source, than any European or American, who has published his observations. He is my authority for what follows." Morse then gave Carver's interpretation of the interior, including his observations on the four rivers that found their sources in this region, among them the Oregon. For this faith in Carver's narrative, Morse was chided privately by Oliver Wolcott, secretary of the treasury under Presidents Washington and Adams. His letter to Morse, dated May 6, 1792, indicated a view of the *Travels* that was not yet

[6] Anonymous review, in *Gentleman's Magazine*, 51:324 (July, 1781).
[7] *American Museum*, 1:216, 6:23 (March, 1787, July, 1789).

widespread, but was apparently present in some minds that had reason to be concerned with the interior territories of the United States. Wolcott wrote: "I know not whom you can take for a guide, more consistently with the present state of public opinion, and yet I suspect but little credit is due to the book published in his [Carver's] name. By information which I have obtained respecting Carver, I am satisfied that his book was compiled under very inauspicious circumstances. He doubtless resided a number of years in the western country, but was an ignorant man, utterly incapable of writing such a book. . . . There is reason to suspect, that the book styled Carver's Travels, is a mere compilation from other books and common reports, supported by some new remarks which Carver may possibly have made."[8]

Perhaps Morse was similarly advised by other friends. At any rate, when in 1793 he signed the preface to a "new edition, revised, corrected and greatly enlarged," which was published in London the next year, he described the Mississippi River, the Falls of St. Anthony, and "the four most Capitol rivers on the Continent of North America" without reference to Carver. Although the information was little changed, it was based, Morse said, on "the best accounts that can be obtained from the Indians." He also omitted Carver's estimate of the length of Lake Superior's shoreline. In his *Geography Made Easy,* the first six editions of which were published between 1784 and 1798, Morse altered measurements of Lake Superior and Lake of the Woods from his first edition, bringing them into conformity with Carver's figures, but he made no mention of his source. In his *American Gazetteer,* he referred to "Carver's River" as a branch of the Minnesota River, but he gave no indication of the origin of its name. Again, Morse relied upon Carver's *Travels* in describing the Falls of St. Anthony and the "St. Pierre" (Minnesota) River, but without acknowledgment.[9]

While Carver was receiving this silent treatment in North America's most popular geographies, he was not otherwise for-

---

[8] Morse, *The American Geography: or, A View of the Present Situation of the United States of America,* 42 (Elizabethtown, N.J., 1789); George Gibbs, ed., *Memoirs of the Administrations of Washington and John Adams,* 1: 76 (New York, 1846).

[9] Morse, *American Geography,* title page, 126, 131–133 (London, 1794); *Geography Made Easy,* 112 (New Haven, Conn., 1784), 67 (Boston, 1798); and *American Gazetteer,* n.p. (Boston, 1797).

gotten. The 1784 Philadelphia edition of the *Travels* was followed by others in 1789, 1792, 1794, and 1796, with Boston supplying one in 1797, and Charlestown, Massachusetts, in 1802. Meanwhile, Carver's *Travels* found a wide readership in Europe. Translations were made into German, French, and Dutch during the last two decades of the 18th century, and the book was published in Edinburgh as well. The narrative must have reached thousands of young readers through its abridgment for children by Joachim Heinrich Campe, a German educator, author, and translator of numerous juvenile titles, many of them dealing with geography and exploration. Carver's account was first included in Campe's series of travel narratives for young people in 1796. It went through many editions in German, was translated into French, Swedish, Dutch, and eventually into Greek.[10]

It was not long before Carver's observations could be put to the test by travelers in a position to make observations of their own. While disagreement with him was frequent, there is no doubt that many later explorers read his book before embarking on their own journeys. John Long, a fur trader who in the late 1770s covered some of the same ground, found no cause to question Carver's narrative or his map, both of which Long had studied well. He did have some reservations about Carver's remarks on the Chippewa language. Carver's authority was at this point sufficient to call forth no challenges in print, although there was undoubtedly considerable private sniping in the form of observations like those written down about 1800 by Peter Pond, an old fur trader who knew the West well. His account of his travels in the Northwest was not published until 1906, but he clearly thought Carver gullible and of no great consequence, stating "his Hole toure I with One Canew Well mand Could make in Six weekes."[11]

In the early 19th century the Louisiana Purchase inspired new American interest in exploration of the West. Zebulon M. Pike commanded an expedition to the headwaters of the Mississippi in 1805. In his journal of this trip, Pike made only one reference to Carver, an uncritical, casual one that merely indicated a familiarity with the *Travels*. When Meriwether Lewis and William Clark's narrative of their journey was first published in London

[10] See Appendix 3, below.

[11] Long, *Voyages and Travels of an Indian Interpreter and Trader,* ix, 62, 83, 84, 130 (London, 1791); Pond, in Gates, ed., *Five Fur Traders,* 17, 45.

in 1815, it was obvious to a writer in the *Quarterly Review* that they had "made free use of Carver's Travels without referring to them." The anonymous reviewer thought "it would not have misbecome the American journalists [*Lewis and Clark*], if they had bestowed upon their able and enterprizing forerunner, the commendation which he anticipated and desired." Although Carver had not visited the region traversed by Lewis and Clark, he had written of the nations near the source of the Missouri, and, according to the reviewer, Carver's veracity "could not be called in question." [12]

Less than a decade later it was called in question, however, by William H. Keating, who in 1823 accompanied Major Stephen H. Long's expedition to the Northwest, the first formal excursion up the Minnesota River since Carver's. In his *Narrative of an Expedition to the Source of the St. Peter's River,* Keating often referred to Carver's book, noting "many circumstances which might induce us to question the accuracy of his report." Although Keating expressed no doubt that Carver made such a journey and used the *Travels* as a point of reference in his own observations, he spoke of the unwillingness of Long's men "to ascribe to Carver a scrupulous adherence to truth." He added, "we feel strongly inclined to say of him, as he said of his predecessor [*Hennepin*], 'the good father, I fear, too often had no other foundation for his accounts than report, or at least a slight inspection.'" Keating doubted that Carver had gone any considerable distance up the Minnesota River or that he had learned the Dakota language. Visiting the region 55 years after Carver, Keating analyzed the second part of the *Travels,* which concerned the Indians, and found that Dakota marriage customs and others described there did not conform to those in use by that tribe at the time of Long's visit. Rather, Keating said, the customs Carver described were those of other Indian nations. Carver's Indian vocabulary, he said, may have been obtained from the Dakota along the banks of the Mississippi, "but was more probably copied from some former traveller, for a reference to old works

---

[12] Elliott Coues, ed., *The Expeditions of Zebulon Montgomery Pike,* 1: 50 (Reprint Ed., Minneapolis, 1965); [Meriwether] Lewis and [William] Clarke [*sic*], *Travels to the Source of the Missouri River, and Across the American Continent to the Pacific Ocean* (London, 1815); *Quarterly Review,* 12: 318–320 (January, 1815). The reviewer alluded to the request to later discoverers, "And whilst their spirits are elated by their success, perhaps they may bestow some commendations and blessings on the person that first pointed out to them the way." *Travels,* vii.

will prove that Carver derived much of his information from them, though no credit is given to their authors for it."[13]

George W. Featherstonhaugh, an English geologist who visited the Minnesota River in 1835, and whose own observations were subject to question, published a report containing testimony on Carver's behalf in 1836. He wrote: "Having a copy of Carver's Travels with me, and having always found his descriptions deserving of very great confidence, I had been anxious to discover a remarkable locality he speaks of, and which, from the doubts expressed by other travellers, they evidently had never seen." This referred to Carver's account of a fortlike formation just below Lake Pepin which was questioned by Keating and others, since Carver said it was man-made. Featherstonhaugh, after examining it, concluded that it was a natural phenomenon, yet "sufficiently remarkable to justify the description" Carver had given of it. Featherstonhaugh followed the Mississippi to its junction with the Minnesota and then traveled up the latter, confident that he had found Carver's Cave and the branch of the Minnesota which Carver had named for himself. In his *Canoe Voyage up the Minnay Sotor,* a later book based on the same trip, Featherstonhaugh was less willing to concede that the "fortifications" at Lake Pepin were works of nature, although he thought that the *Travels* was extravagant in comparing them to the work of Marquis de Vauban, the great French military engineer.[14]

Joseph N. Nicollet, the French scientist who headed expeditions to the Minnesota River sponsored by the United States government in 1838–39, paid little attention to Carver's book, although he indicated familiarity with it. His major references were to its deficiencies: Carver's failure to properly identify the Missouri River and to comment on the Coteau des Prairies, both of which were beyond Carver's own experience. Nicollet gave

[13] Keating, *Narrative of an Expedition to the Source of St. Peter's River,* 1: 10, 277, 297, 324, 325 (Philadelphia, 1824). See also note 96, below.

[14] Featherstonhaugh, *Report of a Geological Reconnoissance Made in 1835,* in 24 Congress, 1 session, *Senate Documents,* no. 333, pp. 129–131, 135, 138 (serial 282); Featherstonhaugh, *A Canoe Voyage up the Minnay Sotor,* 1: 241–245 (Reprint Ed., St. Paul, 1970). See also G. Hubert Smith, "Carver's Old Fortifications," in *Minnesota History,* 16: 152–165 (June, 1935), which noted that the manuscript journals do not mention these "fortifications." Smith credited Carver's description of them in *Travels,* 56–59, as giving "an initial impetus to American archaeology."

more credence to Lahontan, who was at that time generally discredited.[15]

By the mid-19th century Carver's *Travels* was no longer considered a useful book. The exploration and settlement he had predicted were sufficiently advanced to justify Henry R. Schoolcraft's remark in 1851 that Carver "is not an author to glean much from." At that point the explorer might have been retired to honored obscurity, if another controversy had not brewed up about him. While western travelers had been doubting or defending his book, a scandal was tarnishing Carver's name far more than his lack of accuracy could ever have done.[16]

The unsavory story of the fraudulent "Carver grant" began in London in 1781 after the charitable Dr. Lettsom reissued the 1779 edition of the *Travels* for the benefit of Carver's widow and children. We have noted that Lettsom added the text of a curious land grant, purportedly given to Carver on May 1, 1767, by two Sioux chiefs at a council held in the great cave described in the *Travels*. It conveyed to Carver, "in return for the many presents, and other good services," a tract of land that stretched from the Falls of St. Anthony along the east side of the Mississippi River south to the mouth of the Chippewa River, then due east for 100 miles, due north for 120 miles, and back in a straight line to the Falls of St. Anthony. It included what is now the west-central portion of Wisconsin and the southeastern corner of Minnesota, encompassing the site of present St. Paul. The deed was signed by Hawnopawjatin and Otohtongoomlisheaw, names mentioned in the *Travels* as belonging to two Sioux chiefs whom Carver had known. After publishing it, Lettsom apparently gave the deed to Carver's London widow. At her death he sought to locate it, but without success, and in 1804 he concluded that it no longer existed.[17]

[15] Nicollet, *Report Intended to Illustrate a Map of the Hydrographical Basin of the Upper Mississippi River,* in 28 Congress, 2 session, *House Executive Documents,* no. 52, pp. 20, 28 (serial 464). On Lahontan, see A. H. Greenly, "Lahontan: An Essay and Bibliography," in Bibliographical Society of America, *Papers,* 48: 334–340 (4th quarter, 1954).

[16] Schoolcraft, *Personal Memoirs of a Residence of Thirty Years with the Indian Tribes on the American Frontiers,* 168 (Philadelphia, 1851).

[17] Lettsom, in *Travels,* 12–14. Slightly different spellings of the chiefs' names appear on p. 380 of *Travels.* The boundaries of the grant were roughly the same as those of tract "No. II" mapped in blue in *Travels* and described on pp. 533, 534, as a "heavenly spot" which "exceeds the highest encomiums I can give it." See also Quaife, in *Mississippi Valley Historical Review,* 7: 13.

The matter was not to rest there. In the same year Samuel Harrison of Chittenden, Vermont, who was related by marriage to one of Jonathan Carver's American granddaughters, took it upon himself to establish the rights of Carver's heirs to the land grant. He wrote to the Reverend Samuel Peters, a fellow New Englander living in London, asking him to take up the search for the original deed. Peters, a 70-year-old former Episcopal minister, was a fervent loyalist who had been forced to leave his native Connecticut in 1774 as a result of his political opinions. In 1804, when he received Harrison's letter, he was living without income, and the Carver grant probably looked like a potential pot of gold. He promptly embarked on a 20-year-long quest for the validation of the grant.[18]

Peters did not find the original deed in London. Instead he found that a complex of fraud and deception already existed around the grant. "I find Captn. Carver Sold a Quarter of the whole to R. Smith — and two thirds of the whole to A. B. C and D and gave Deeds accordingly," Peters wrote Harrison. In all, he said, only one-twelfth of the land could legitimately be claimed by Carver's heirs, "and People here from N. York tell me Rufus & Jonathan Carver & their Sisters Sold the greater Part on Speculation Since 1792." This was true; the interest of Carver's children in the grant had been sold at least once, to Edward Houghton of Vermont. But as the purchase price had never been paid, Carver's American heirs continued to deed away land. At the same time, other speculators were investing in the grant on behalf of Carver's daughter Martha in London.[19]

The land grant was worthless if it was not certified by the government in whose territory it lay, and Peters was aware of this. Returning to America in 1805, he took on the task of getting the deed ratified on two fronts: in the United States Congress and by the Dakota at the Falls of St. Anthony. For the former purpose, Peters' partner, Samuel Harrison, petitioned Congress to confirm the grant on behalf of 98 heirs of Carver. For the latter purpose, Peters petitioned for an appointment as superintendent of Indians in the Falls of St. Anthony region. The petitions were referred to a committee, and Peters besieged the

[18] Quaife, in *Mississippi Valley Historical Review*, 7: 13, 14.

[19] Peters to Harrison, April 22, March 5, 1805, Harrison Papers; Quaife, in *Mississippi Valley Historical Review*, 7: 15.

congressmen until a decision was reached. The result was uninspiring; the committee declared that "a Confirmation of Carvers Deed by the present Sachems, or Chiefs of the Noudowissie . . . would not induce the Committee to report in favour of the Claim of Carver; for they Consider the Claim, in toto, bad." Still Peters was not discouraged. Blaming his failure on corruption in Congress, he urged Harrison to obtain a passport into Indian territory to negotiate with the Sioux for their approval of the grant. Peters would wait patiently "until Jefferson is out of office & an honest man is placed in his Room." But the Carver heirs concluded that they could not raise enough funds to send a representative to the Sioux, and so they allegedly sold their interest to Peters in return for a promise that the latter would reimburse them once he had obtained congressional confirmation of the deed.[20]

Between 1807 and 1812 Peters said he sent four representatives to the Falls of St. Anthony to obtain Indian approval of the deed. The first two got no farther than Michilimackinac, the third arrived at the Falls of St. Anthony and failed to return, and the fourth was stopped by the outbreak of the War of 1812. These failures did not prevent Peters from selling shares of land as if the deed were already ratified and he were sole owner of it. His procedure was to deed his customers large tracts of land for an advance amount of $1,000 or more. This money purportedly went to finance a mission to obtain confirmation of the deed from the Sioux. During the subsequent four years, the purchaser of the land would sell as many tracts as possible, splitting the income with Peters. At the end of this time all the unsold land would be returned to Peters, except for one township; the advance money was then to be repaid. Since the proceeds from sales were likely to exceed the expense of an expedition to the Sioux, Peters would profit handily. The arrangement was clever, and a number of sales were made.[21]

The scheme of the Reverend Samuel Peters was defeated by the fact that no one had a clear claim to the Carver grant and a multitude of opportunists began to pretend that they did. The

[20] Quaife, in *Mississippi Valley Historical Review*, 7: 15–17; Peters to Harrison, March 9, 1807, Harrison Papers.
[21] Peters to Joshua Goss, August 22, 1812, Harrison Papers; Quaife, in *Mississippi Valley Historical Review*, 7: 17–19.

Carver heirs, apparently feeling that Peters had forfeited his claim by his failure to reimburse them, began to dispose of the land to others. In 1812 Jonathan P. King, Carver's grandson, was selling land allegedly inherited through his mother. In 1815 Benjamin Munn acquired a title through Rufus, Carver's oldest son, and with this proof in hand exposed Peters' fraudulent dealings. Peters' dismayed customers appealed to him to produce his deed to the land, but Peters had never possessed one. Harrison, apparently not having trusted Peters, had kept Peters' deed in his own possession after Peters purportedly had assumed ownership of the land. Harrison was now dead, and Munn had bought his papers, including Peters' deed. But turnabout was the only fair play which emerged from the fraud, for before long several of the Carver heirs came forward to refute Munn's claim as well as that of Peters.[22]

In 1817 the King and Peters factions both sent missions to the Sioux. The representatives of the former group were two cousins, Jonathan P. King and a man named Gunn, grandsons of Carver through his daughters Mary and Olive. They traveled north from Prairie du Chien with an expedition led by Major Stephen H. Long, which was exploring and mapping the course of the upper Mississippi. At the Falls of St. Anthony the Sioux who met King and Gunn denied that the grant was authentic, or that any chiefs named Hawnopawjatin or Otohtongoomlisheaw had existed among them. The Peters expedition to the falls was no more successful. Although he was 83 in 1817, Peters finally decided to go in person to meet the Sioux at Carver's Cave. He never reached his goal. Lacking official permission to travel into Indian territory, Peters was ordered by the commander of Fort Crawford at Prairie du Chien to wait there until he should receive a passport to allow him to proceed up the Mississippi. This permission never came. After spending a winter at the isolated outpost, Peters had to turn back to New York to face a new round of scandals. He made two more appeals to Congress for

[22] Peters to Goss, August 22, 1812, and Harrison to Peters, September 7, 1812, Harrison Papers; Quaife, in *Mississippi Valley Historical Review,* 7: 19, 20; Rufus Carver to Robert McClenachan, May 4, 1816, Carver Land Grant Papers, in the James Ford Bell Library, University of Minnesota, Minneapolis. On King's relationship to Carver, see indenture between William B. Peabody and Leonard Vanalstine, October 4, 1839, Carver Deeds, in Minnesota Historical Society.

ratification of the grant in 1823 and 1825, but was not successful. He died impoverished and disappointed in 1826.[23]

Although the refusal of the House of Representatives committee on private land claims to recognize the grant in 1825 imposed a legal barrier to titles based on the Carver grant, this did not prevent Carver's heirs from continuing to traffic in lands within it. In 1827 Martha Pope, Carver's daughter by his London wife, arrived in New York, full of hopes that she might secure her land. In the 1830s great-grandsons and great-granddaughters of Carver were still profiting by sales of land. In 1897 a flurry of speculation was produced when the original deed was allegedly found in Chillicothe, Ohio, and as late as 1921 it was noted that "If the present governor of Minnesota has not been addressed by some person believing himself a rightful beneficiary of the claim, his experience is exceptional."[24]

No document of Carver's survives to link him with the grant. The principal evidence that he knew about it rests on Peters' statement that Carver used it during his last impecunious years to raise money by sales of land to R. Smith and others. Though Peters was an eminently untrustworthy witness when any twisting of the truth could serve his purpose, there is no proof that he fabricated this statement. All the later chicanery associated with the Carver grant could not be laid at Carver's door, but it is likely that the grant itself — as published by Dr. Lettsom — could be, and in popular opinion it certainly was.[25]

[23] For the descent of the Gunn family, see *Vital Records of Montague, Massachusetts, to the End of the Year 1849*, 24, 25, 63 (Salem, Mass., 1934). On King and Gunn's expedition, see Long, "Voyage in a Six-Oared Skiff to the Falls of Saint Anthony in 1817," in *Minnesota Historical Collections*, 2: 8, 10 (1889); Keating, *Narrative*, 1: 325. On Peters' efforts, see Quaife, in *Mississippi Valley Historical Review*, 7: 22–24; Willard Keyes, "A Journal of Life in Wisconsin One Hundred Years Ago," in *Wisconsin Magazine of History*, 3: 339–363 (March, 1920); D[aniel] S. Durrie, "Captain Jonathan Carver, and 'Carver's Grant,'" in *Wisconsin Historical Collections*, 6: 247, 250 (1872).

[24] Quaife, in *Mississippi Valley Historical Review*, 7: 24; Martha Pope Sexton to Martha Mary Pope, November 2, 1827, in the possession of Alan D. Ridge, Edmonton, Alba., photocopy in Minnesota Historical Society; indenture of Peabody and Vanalstine, October 4, 1839, and deed from Martin King to Ichabod A. Holden, June 13, 1838, Carver Deeds; S. R. Holt to Henry C. Harrison, February 2, 1897, Harrison Papers; William W. Folwell, *A History of Minnesota*, 1: 64 (Revised Ed., St. Paul, 1956).

[25] Carver could have gotten the idea from Rogers, who was using an Indian land grant to raise cash in London as early as 1765; see p. 13n, above.

With Carver's accuracy and honesty thus impeached, only the literary merit of the *Travels* survived to prop up his reputation. But it was not long before scholars began to have doubts about this as well. In 1844 historian Robert Greenhow revived the old accusation of plagiarism. He stated that the *Travels* "was written, or rather made up, at London, at the suggestion of Dr. Lettsom and other gentlemen." He added that Carver's description of the Indians, making up about two-thirds of the book, "is extracted almost entirely, and, in many parts, *verbatim,* from the French journals and histories." He goes on: "read his [*Carver's*] magisterial and contemptuous remarks on the works of Hennepin, Lahontan, and Charlevoix, in the first chapter . . . and then compare his chapters describing, as from personal observation, the ceremonies . . . of the natives of the Upper Mississippi countries, with those of Lahontan, showing the conduct of the Iroquois, of Canada . . . by which it will be seen that *Carver has simply translated from Lahontan the whole of the accounts, even to the speeches of the chiefs.*"[26]

In 1851 Henry R. Schoolcraft, one of the most widely read authorities on the peoples of the inner continent, defended Carver against the discredit which had been thrown on the *Travels*. As early as 1821 Schoolcraft had praised Carver's "great personal courage" and his "persevering and observing mind." Having been appointed mineralogist to the 1820 expedition organized by Governor Lewis Cass of Michigan to explore the sources of the Mississippi, Schoolcraft was early in a position to criticize Carver's book from firsthand observation, but he found nothing to cause him doubt then or in 1834 when he cited Carver for his ascent of the Chippewa River. By the middle of the 19th century, however, Schoolcraft acknowledged the charges of plagiarism which had been leveled against Carver, but advanced a theory that "the booksellers, owning his [*Carver's*] personal narrative, found it necessary to . . . swell the size of his volume, and arrest the public eye." He argued that "some literary hack" had been employed to pad the book from French sources — someone whose efforts were so faulty as to leave French orthog-

[26] Greenhow, *The History of Oregon and California, and the Other Territories on the North-West Coast of North America,* 142n, 144n (Boston, 1844).

raphy in the Chippewa vocabulary. His conclusion was that Carver himself had been "underrated."[27]

The latter part of the 19th century saw a resurgence of confidence in Carver and his story, though no new editions of the *Travels* appeared in the United States between 1838 and the end of the century. Citizens of Minnesota trooped to Carver's Cave in 1867 to observe the centenary of his travels, and works were published praising him as "an acute and close observer, an industrious student of ethnology, and a careful, discriminating journalist." These sentiments were echoed by Daniel S. Durrie when, in 1872, continued flurries over land grants called for a defense of Carver. John Heckewelder, a historian of the frontier, wrote in 1876 that Carver had been imposed upon in some instances by Indian magicians but was "deserving of credit for the greatest part of what he has written on the character of the Indians." In 1891 James C. Pilling honored the *Travels* by describing 16 editions of it in his *Bibliography of the Algonquian Languages*. Two years later, A. W. Greely wrote in his brief and sometimes erroneous biography of Carver, "it seems difficult to determine on what grounds his truthfulness has been questioned by a few hostile critics."[28]

Further scholarly approval was given to the explorer by Elliott Coues, the editor of Zebulon Pike's journals, who in 1895 summed up his several defenses of Carver with, "I think that he . . . had no occasion to deceive anyone but himself, and always intended to tell the truth as it seemed to him — in short . . . I accept Carver's statements, as I do those of Pike, Long, and other honest persons, for what they may prove to be worth." Carver was praised alike by the Parkman Club and by Moses Coit Tyler, who apparently had not read Carver's critics, for he lauded most

[27] Schoolcraft, *Narrative Journal of Travels through the Northwestern Regions of the United States*, xi, xii, xiii (Albany, 1821); Schoolcraft, *Narrative of an Expedition through the Upper Mississippi to Itasca Lake*, 121 (New York, 1834); Schoolcraft, *Indian Tribes*, 1: 138; Schoolcraft, *Personal Memoirs*, 169.

[28] "The Carver Centenary," and John Mattocks, "The Life and Explorations of Jonathan Carver," in *Minnesota Historical Collections*, 2: 257, 267; Durrie, in *Wisconsin Historical Collections*, 6: 220–270; Heckewelder, *History, Manners, and Customs of The Indian Nations Who Once Inhabited Pennsylvania and the Neighbouring States*, 322 (Pennsylvania Historical Society, *Memoirs*, vol. 12 — Philadelphia, 1876); Pilling, *Bibliography of the Algonquian Languages*, 68–71 (Bureau of American Ethnology, *Bulletins*, no. 13 — Washington, D.C., 1891); Greely, *Explorers and Travellers*, 84 (*Men of Achievement Series* — New York, 1904).

highly the questionable cribbed section on Indians, rejoicing that
"we have no other 'Indian book' more captivating than this." A
leading ethnologist, W. J. McGee, in his essay on the Siouan
Indians, written for the Bureau of American Ethnology in 1897,
placed Carver side by side with George Catlin, Lewis and Clark,
and Stephen Long as authorities on the Sioux.[29]

It appeared that Carver was going to be accepted as an accurate though sometimes gullible observer and a partner to borrowings from French sources without credit. But controversy
again flared around the explorer in 1906, with the publication of
a devastating critique of Carver's life and book by Edward
Gaylord Bourne, a prominent historian and disciple of the "new
history," which advocated careful examination of texts and
sources. Bourne first exposed the multitude of falsehoods concerning Carver's life that had been perpetrated by the explorer's
two earlier biographers, Dr. Lettsom and Samuel Peters, the land
speculator. Lettsom had written that Carver was born in
Stillwater, Connecticut, and studied medicine at Elizabeth
Town. Bourne pointed out there was no town of either name in
Connecticut. As for Peters' account, Bourne quoted his statement that Carver was descended from John Carver, the first
governor of the Massachusetts Bay Colony, and noted that John
Carver had no male issue. Bourne pointed to Carver's biga-
mous marriage to further damage the credibility of the two biographers, who had praised the explorer's fine moral character.[30]

Having thus raised doubts about the earlier accounts of
Carver's life, Bourne turned to the plagiarized parts of the
Travels. He lined up in incriminating parallel columns the passages from the Travels and their nearly identical counterparts in
Lahontan and Charlevoix. After speculating on why such
plagiarism would be necessary, Bourne concluded that Carver
must have been too ignorant to write a book such as the Travels;
he was "the source rather than the author of the narrative." In
conclusion Bourne stated that "the Travels of Jonathan Carver

[29] Coues, ed., Pike, Expeditions, 1:60n; John G. Gregory, "Jonathan Carver:
His Travels in the Northwest in 1766–8," in Parkman Club Publications, no. 5, pp.
73–101 (Milwaukee, 1896); Tyler, The Literary History of the American Revolution,
1763–1783, 1:150 (New York, 1897); McGee, "The Siouan Indians: A Prelimi-
nary Sketch," in Bureau of American Ethnology, Fifteenth Annual Report, 170,
173, 175 (Washington, D.C., 1897).
[30] Bourne, in American Historical Review, 11:289, 290.

can no longer be ranked as an authentic record of the observations of the supposed author." He compared Carver to Sir John Mandeville, the notorious borrower of other travelers' tales.[31]

None of these facts were new; the incorrectness of Lettsom's biography had been pointed out by Lyman C. Draper in 1872, and charges of plagiarism went as far back as the query in the *American Museum* of 1789. Nevertheless, Bourne's accusations were to stick. Reuben Gold Thwaites, one of the great authorities on the exploration of the Great Lakes region, took Bourne's word in dismissing Carver as "an ignorant shoemaker" who "has long enjoyed unearned literary and historical fame." Thwaites went even further than Bourne in his skepticism, questioning both Carver's presence at the siege of Fort William Henry and his receipt of a gratuity from the British government; the historian added, "there is no evidence that he ever held any military office."[32]

The counterattack came quickly. In 1909 John Thomas Lee took on Carver's detractors with two reprints from the *Boston Chronicle,* which documented Carver's travels through a letter written to his wife from Michilimackinac, and his attempts to get his book published in America. Lee's conclusion was that the explorer was "a man of intelligence and fair education." Commenting on the "ignorant shoemaker" remark by Thwaites, Lee wrote, "Carver may at one time have been a shoemaker; but the only point worthy of consideration is whether or not he was an *ignorant* shoemaker." Having disposed of doubts concerning Carver's literacy and travels, Lee later went on to produce documents from the Massachusetts archives certifying Carver's enrollment in one military unit or another from March 21, 1758, to March 2, 1763, his rank progressing from sergeant to captain. Evidence from the British Board of Trade clarified Carver's London activities. Finally, the British Museum produced Carver's journals in his own hand, together with the revisions written by the author in preparation for its publication. They had come from the library of Sir Joseph Banks, to whom Carver had dedicated his book. The author, his journey, his manu-

---

[31] Bourne, in *American Historical Review,* 11: 300–302.

[32] Draper, in *Wisconsin Historical Collections,* 6: 221n; Thwaites, *Wisconsin: The Americanization of a French Settlement,* 125 (Boston, 1908); Thwaites, in *Wisconsin Historical Collections,* 18: 281.

scripts, his patron, and his book were clearly and logically linked together.[33]

Subsequent studies concerning Carver have sought to fill in biographical background and to establish the motivation for his travels. What now seems most needful is a printing of the text of Carver's own journals, as he wrote them.

[33] Lee, in *Proceedings,* 1909, pp. 143, 148–151; 1912, pp. 91, 107–121.

❧ Chapter One ❧

Journals of the Travels
of Jonathan Carver

⟨As I had served several years in the provincial troops of the Massachusetts Bay in New England, who were mostly employd on the frontiers between the English provinces and the French settlements during the late [*French and Indian*] war, I thereby became prety well acquainted with the French settlements in Canada and on some of the small lakes. My curiosity became thereby more excited by imagining that the intire conquest of Canada and its dependencies actually opened a door for many valuable and interesting discoveries (which before was intirely impossable as the French had a string of settlements from the Gulf of Mexico to the Gulf of St. Lawrence about 3000 miles in length through the interiour part of the continent which servd them as a sort of line of circumvallation round the back of the whole English-American provinces) on that vast continent between the New England provinces and the South Sea.

⟨*Version II*
Insert 1

After the late treaty of peace [*1763*] I shared the fate with the rest of my fellow officers of the same province of being dischargd without any advantages of half pay nor of any share of land in the conquered country which was granted to the officers on the Establishment with whom we did equal duty through the whole of the several campaigns in the late war.[1]

In this situation I yet wishd for an oppertunity of serving my king & country, being for some time out of employ was very disirous for an oppertunity of being employd in some business

---

[1] On Carver's military status, see pp. 4–6, above.

whereby I might be useful in making some further discoveries in these new acquisitions. I having by several circumstances strengthened my hopes of traveling, that as I had acquired but a very slender knowledge in geography, I privatly procured some books on subjects of that nature and studiously endeavoured to inform my self in every science necessary for a compleet draghts man.

Some time in the year 1765 I being in company with a gentleman[2] of my acquaintance, with whom I had had the pleasure of serving in the army and was then an half pay officer on the Establishment, one I knew to be well approvd of as a very ingenious man in surveying and drawing, to him I communicatd my desires of aplication to government for liberty to go on some discoveries toward the South Sea. He seemd to like the proposal and signified his desires of undertaking, but before we had entered upon any perticular plan of proceeding, I heard that Major Rogers, who was then in England, had laid a plan before the Board of Trade by which he proposd to find a passage through the continent to the South Sea, which by the accounts at that time I thought it likely he would succeed in this undertaking, by which means I changed my purposes of application and contented my selfe to wait for Majr Rogers' return to America with a determination of taking the first opertunity of offering my service to joyn in the opperation of the plans, which by accounts I thought he had adopted, in consequence of which I waited in Boston untill his arrival which was some time in March 1766. Upon my mentioning the affair and my designs to him he replyd he had proper athority to employ persons for that purpose.[3]

Accordingly I entered into an agreement not suspecting any defect on account of his orders which then appeared probable as he was at that time invested with the command of the important post of Michilimackinac and its dependencies, tho it afterwards appeared that he had only some small encouragement from some of the Lords of Trade but nothing certainly concluded on when he left England. Yet I will so far apologize for Major Rogers'

[2] Carver supplied the name "Francis Miller esqr." in a note at the bottom of the page. Miller is known to have been involved in settling the Massachusetts-New York boundary line in 1773; Massachusetts Historical Society to the editor, March 11, 1969.

[3] On Rogers' plans and movements at this time, see p. 13, above.

conduct on that account that by what I have understood since he
somwhat expected that orders in consequence of the plan of the
undertaking would have been completed and sent after him,
which when I was in England took care to enquire into and by
credible information that it was thought by some who might be
depended upon that his measures would have been perfectd had
it not been for the change of the ministry happening at that time.
And though it appears that some at the head of affairs at that
time might in some degree favour the measures that he had
adopted for this undertaking yet the public can easily judge how
far Major Rogers may be excusd for his undertaking this service
with no better authority. I look upon my self obliged to make
mention of this circumstance only to do my self that justice that I
am confident that I have a just right to, and am very sorry to give
any hints to the public that may in the least hurt or injure the
character of one who has been any ways servicable to his country
as I am sure Major Rogers has, and more especially at a time
when some have endeavourd to ruin and destroy not only his
character but his person also. No one that ever knew the perticu-
lars of his sufferings on this account but must have a feeling for
anyone who has done any service to his country. I hope the
reader will pardon this digression.[4]

As 'tis likely some may have the curiossity to enquire how I
could measure distances in such a vast extent of travels, I answer that as I had determined to calculate all my distances by
miles and half miles before I undertook in this voyage, in order to
enable me the better to ascertain the distances by my judgment
only, I practiced several times the pacing out the lengths of a
mile by land and then would go the same distance in a battou or
canoe by water, which by frequent practicing I could by that
means judge prety exact as to the distance of a mile.)[5]

Version II
Insert 1⟩

[4] On the post at Michilimackinac, see p. 9n, above. The change of ministry to
which Carver refers involved the fall in 1766 of the government headed by Lord
Rockingham, and the subsequent reorganization of the Board of Trade under
William Pitt's ministry. Sir Henry Conway, who had seemed favorable to Rog-
ers' exploration plan when the latter presented it in London, was replaced as
secretary of state by Lord Shelburne. See Clarence W. Alvord, *The Mississippi
Valley in British Politics,* 1: 251–253, 269, 276 (Cleveland, 1917). At the time
Carver's rather well-hedged apology was written, Rogers was recruiting men for
the Queen's American Rangers, a loyalist military unit. See pp. 14, 24, above;
Cuneo, *Rogers,* 179, 230, 274–276.

[5] See pp. 62, 70, 89, 140, for instances of Carver's inconsistent inaccuracies in
measuring distances.

MAY 20, 1766. Took my departure from Boston in New Eng-
land, on the 29th of May, arrivd at Albany; June 13th arrivd at
Oswego, and from thence in company of some traders bound to
Detroit.[6]

⟨Version II
Insert 2⟩ ⟨As I aim at giving a general account of every thing any ways
remarkable that came to my knowledge during the course of my
travels, yet I hope the reader will excuse my not entering into
any particulars of the countries between New England and Detroit as several accounts have been published heretofor of those
parts.[7] For that reason my journal will be confind more perticular to those countries that have been hitherto least known.

I shall in my way make mention of the falls of Niagara perhaps
considering the vast quantity of water that here has a perpendicular fall is one of the greatest cataracts in the known world and
may be with propriety reconed among the greatest rarities and
curiosities in nature. The French writers differ with regard to the
height of this fall and tho several have undertaken to give an
account of this fall of water yet I don't remember of two that
agree in their discriptions. Father Henepin and Baron LaHonton
have been so extravagant in their accounts that I think one might
well suspect their ever having seen them at all. Charlevoix comes
nearer to the truth in this perticular then any French writer I have
ever seen. The land about the falls is somthing mountainous as is
generally the case near large cascades. The English have taken
great pains since their being acquainted in these parts to ascertain
the height and its form, and it appears by the best and latest
intelligence I was able to obtain that the perpendicular fall is
about 160 feet and about three leagues of prity rapid swift water
below. The form is somthing like a half moon. It has an island

---

[6] The editor's efforts to identify the traders with whom Carver traveled from
New York to Detroit have been unsuccessful; Carver himself states, however,
that he traveled from Detroit with William Bruce. See pp. 70, 73, 77, below.

[7] At the time Carver wrote, the most recently published among such works
was Thomas Hutchins, *A Topographical Description of Virginia, Pennsylvania,
Maryland, and North Carolina* (London, 1778). Other works in English to which
he may be referring were: Thomas Pownall, *A Topographical Description of Such
Parts of North America as are Contained in the (Annexed) Map* (London, 1776);
Robert Rogers, *A Concise Account of North America* (London, 1765); John Mitch-
ell, *The Contest in America Between Great Britain and France* (London, 1757); Lewis
Evans, *Geographical, Historical, Political, Philosophical and Mechanical Essays*
(Philadelphia, 1755); Thomas Jeffreys, *The Natural and Civil History of the French
Dominions in North and South America* (London, 1760); and translations of the
authors cited in note 8, below.

[*Goat*] in the middle bearing to a point where the water takes its fall and is about half a mile long. The two parts of the water divided by this island connects again before it reaches the bottom. The fall occasions for upwards of a league above a considerable suction or draught so that it is dangerous for any vessels within that distance, and several Indians by accounts have been drawn down these falls by their not taking sufficient precaution. Fish are frequently found on the shores below dashd to pieces by attempting to get over. Some French travellers have reported that birds have when attempted to fly over been drawn into the vortex formed in the air by the violence of the torrent, which account I beleave is premature as I could not learn that any of late years had seen anything like it. The noise of these falls as the thunder is commonly heard at several miles distance but much farther below then above. The violent dashing of the waters here occasion a mist which rises at a distance like smoke or fogg in which when the sun shines is to be seen the parts of a rain bow.⟩[8]   *Version II*
                                                                                Insert 2⟩

JUNE 23, 1766. Arrivd at Niagara. ⟨About twenty miles from   ⟨*Version II*
the falls of Niagara up the river of that name I came to the east   *Insert 3*
end of Lake Erie. On the enterence of this lake is a bar of rocks extending from the north side almost across the river. Only a small chanel [exists] where vessels of sixty or eighty tuns is taken up with the advantage of a strong wind and without being loaded. Fort Erie stands on the north side at the east end and is now commanded by Lieutenant Cardin [*John Carden*] with about 40 soldiers who assist in loading the vessel and forwarding provisions for the troops at Detroit and Michilimackinac.[9]

From Fort Slosser [*Schlosser*], a small garrison a little above the

---

[8] In the editions of their works which Carver may have seen, Hennepin gave the height of Niagara Falls as 600 feet, Lahontan as 700 or 800 feet, and Charlevoix as not less than 140 or 150 feet. The highest point is actually 167 feet. See Hennepin, *New Discovery,* 29 (1698); Lahontan, *Voyages,* 1:82 (1703); Charlevoix, *Journal,* 1:352–355 (1761). The latter, who visited the falls in 1721, mentioned the dead fish and, like Carver, deplored the story of the birds. More accessible and more useful to modern readers are the later editions of these authors edited by Reuben G. Thwaites (Hennepin and Lahontan) and Louise P. Kellogg (Charlevoix), which will be cited hereafter in these notes. The Kellogg edition of Charlevoix (1923) includes page references to the earlier version which Carver might have consulted. For other early accounts of this landmark, see Charles M. Dow, *Anthology and Bibliography of Niagara Falls,* vol. 1 (Albany, N.Y., 1921).

[9] Harlan Hatcher, *Lake Erie,* 18 (Indianapolis, 1945), pointed out that a strong easterly wind rolls back the water from the east end of the lake and exposes its

falls of Niagara now without any men except one or two to take care of the king's stores that yet remain here, to Lake Erie there is a prety good depth of water sufficient for to take up the vessels built at some of the islands near Fort Slosser in to Lake Erie. The land about here is tolerable good and well timbered.[10]

Lake Erie is about 300 [245] miles long lying nearly east and west and is about 50 miles in bredth. 'Tis remarkd for having a very long and narrow point [*Long Point*] begining near the middle on the north side extending its course east southeast about 40 [20] miles or better. The canoes which generally coast these lakes are carried over a carying place about 50 rods across within a little ways of the northern shore. This point is very sandy and produces aboundance of scrubby small trees and vines. This lake has in many places for several miles together very high banks which makes it somwhat dangerous passing with canoes or battoes, as 'tis common for suden squalls to rise especially in spring and fall whereby many battoes & canoes loaded with goods, and lives are lost. In this lake is a great plenty of fish and at some seasons of the year there is a great resort of fowl. The land about here is very good, sutably timbered, a vast plenty of chesnut trees, oak, hickery, maple, ceeder, and fir. In the woods is abundance of game such as bear, deer, and turkies, partridges, and pidgeons.

The land about Lake Erie is very good for settlement and a very pleasant country and nothing can make it so disagreable as the multiplicity of snakes of several sorts. The most numerous is the water snake which tho pretty common through all the setled provinces yet are found no where in such numbers as at this place. They are frequently seen in the middle of the day lying coild up on the leaves of water lillies, which are near a foot broad and rest on the surface of the water and are so close to each other that in many places they cover the water for several acres together; and on these I have seen such multitudes of these snakes

rocky bottom. Carver may have seen the east end of the lake under these conditions.

Fort Erie, a rectangular enclosure with four bastions, was built in 1764 as a supply base for Detroit on the west bank of the Niagara River just above the present town of Fort Erie, Ontario. See Ronald L. Way, *Ontario's Niagara Parks: A History*, 256–258 (Hamilton, Ont., 1946). Lieutenant Cardin is identified as John Carden by Peckham, *Pontiac*, 289.

[10] Fort Schlosser was built by the British in 1760 as one of a string of posts to protect the Niagara portage. Way, *Ontario's Niagara Parks*, 222.

that the whole surface of the water for some distance appeard quite black. These water snakes when grown are about as large in the middle as a man's ankle and are about two feet and half in length, of a brown colour interspersd with rows of spots of a yellowish shade about the bigness of an English shilling in the middle lessoning toward each end in proportion with the different sizes of the snake. I never heard that this snake was ever esteemed poisonous and whenever people approach them they appear shy and run into the water.[11]

The rattle snakes here which are very numerous are not at all different from those in the provinces or other parts of America. However, as not all my readers may have seen a particular discription of this reptile I shall give a particular discription of them. This snake when grown to its common size is about four feet in length and about eight inches in circumference in the middle, tapering to the neck which is no larger then a man's middle finger. The head is wider on each side but not thicker then the neck perpendicular wise. In his upper and under jaws are small teeth somthing resembling those in a small fish, but in the forepart of its upper jaw are two teeth much longer then the rest very much like the claws of a cat, and like those will either project in an erect posture when he is about to bite which he does by letting fall his under jaw, or contract them under a thin sort of a flimsey skin which nature seems to have provided. For they bite not their food with these teeth; if they did it would prove as fatal to them as to any other animal. They have a small bag full of mortal venom which they emit at the same time that their teeth touches or enters what they bite. This I have frequently seen when I have vexd them and made them bite at a rag fastened to the end of a stick. They emit their poison through a hollow place in their teeth. This is only seen when the tooth has been dryd for some months for I have lookd on purpose when they were first killed but could not see any such thing. This poison is of a dirtyish green colour. From their middle to their tails it tapers to the bigness of a man's little finger where begins their rattles by pairs of a dry callous substance increasing one every year, the first partly covering the second which seems loosly

---

[11] On the watersnake, *natrix sipedon insularum,* see Albert H. and Anna A. Wright, *Handbook of Snakes of the United States and Canada,* 1: 529–535 (Ithaca, N.Y., 1957).

riveted in to the first; tho one of these is added every year, yet the
number they are found with gives no certainty of their age for
they frequently lose some of them. I have found them with
fourteen which takes up about four inches in length. There appear to be two sorts of these snakes, the one commonly are called
the black the other the yellow sort. The poison of the yellow sort
is esteemd the most mortal, but whether really so or not I cannot
say. Those of the black sort have from one end to the other rows
of yallish spots about ye bigness of a shilling with a shade of a
purplish colour beautifully mixed. The yellow sort have spots in
the same manner of a dark purple on one side of the spots which
decreases to a yellow except the edges of the spots are intirely of
a darkish cast. Each colour by changing its position to the light
shades different. These are very beautiful.[12]

The rattle snake when he is disturbd imediatly coils himself
into a round heap with his head prominent in the middle with a
few inches of his tail and rattles perpendicular, which with a sort
of a quick trembling motion he makes a noise which may with
attention be heard more than a score rods. This is frequently a
sufficient warning to the unwary traveller and he either kills or
shuns the venomous reptile. The different seasons of the weather
very much effect this snake, & his bite is very venomous in the
dog days, but when the weather is but moderatly warm he rather
appears harmless and will endeavour to get out of the way.

The poison of this snake is more or less venomous not only to
all human beings but to every sort of beast, the hog only ex-
cepted. This annimal that live where rattle snakes are frequently
found eat them of choice and when bit will not regard it more
then the bite of one of their own kind, nay they will rather hunt
after them for their food. I flung a large old one for curiosity's

---

[12] Carver's description here and below is reasonably accurate. Wright and
Wright, *Handbook of Snakes*, 2: 957, note two color phases, yellow and black, for
the rattlesnake *crotalus horridus horridus*, but indicate no difference in the poisonous quality of their venom. On its use for a great variety of medicinal purposes in
the 19th century, hogs, and the gravity of the snake's bite mentioned below, see
Laurence M. Klauber, *Rattlesnakes, Their Habits, Life Histories, and Influence on
Mankind*, 2: 790–796, 822–825, 1038–1040 (Berkeley and Los Angeles, 1956). This
author concluded that the venom now "has no recognized place in regular medi-
cal practice," that hogs are not immune but are protected by their tough hides
and layers of fat which prevent the venom from entering their circulatory sys-
tems, and that the variation in the gravity of the bite is not affected by climate,
although the snake is generally more active in warm weather.

sake among a drove of hogs. Each one strove for a bit as if it had been their natural food. I observed one who eat the head eagerly without being in the least effectd. If the head of the rattle snake be cut off in the forenoon 'tis common for life to remain in him til sun sett. Their galls taken out and mixd with powdered chalk and made up into balls are sold to the apothecaries and are esteemd very good and cooling in fevers, especially with children. 'Tis observed that the rattle snake is the most docile of all serpents. In winter they den in holes in the rocks and remain thro that season in a state of inactivity and stupifaction. As to their food or whether they eat anything during this time is a matter of uncertainty as yet.

There is another snake about Lake Erie which I have never seen anywhere else. These are calld the hissing snake, are about twenty inches in length, speckled with small yellow and purple spots with some faint appearance of stripes of a yellow and purplish colours. These snakes are about three inches in circumference round the middle. Their way of emiting their poison is in this manner: when they are vexd they will flat their heads and necks for several inches long and near two inches in bredth, & at the same time make a sort of hissing, belching out a most unsavory smell, which if a person at the leeward takes full in his breath is immediately taken into a decline which carries him off in a few months.[13]

There is another snake about this lake that I have never yet seen anywhere else. This appears to be somthing of the species of the black snake and differs from them only by being somwhat larger and its belly of a scarlet or red colour. I killd several which I measured about seven feet or upwards in length and about six inches in circumference in the middle. I never heard that these were any way poisonous.⟩ *Version II Insert 3*⟩

JUNE 26, 1766. At Fort Erie on the east end of Lake Erie, the 27th entered the lake in company with several traders, and arrivd at Detroit.

⟨Detroit which in English signifies the straits. The fort the ⟨*Version II Insert 4*

[13] Wright and Wright, *Handbook of Snakes,* 1: 306–310, identified the hissing snake or spreading adder as *heterodon platyrhinos platyrhinos,* but did not mention poisonous breath, which was perhaps a frontier legend. The snake described in the paragraph below is the red-bellied or copper-bellied watersnake, *natrix erythrogaster erythrogaster;* Wright and Wright, *Handbook of Snakes,* 1: 477.

French had here was called Ponchartrain and is only a stockaid garrison in which is contained near an hundred houses chiefly belonging to the traders, the principal of which are English. Here is at present about 300 troops of the 17th regiment commanded by Col. [John] Campbell whose mild administration has gained him the esteem of the traders and others in these parts. The French have several plantations scattered along on the shore of the straits for about ten miles below the fort and about twelve miles above as far as Lake St. Clare [Clair]. The French have been settled in these parts upwards of forty years.[14]

The land is very good, producing all the necessaries of life in aboundance, but by reason of the inactivity and idleness of the French inhabitants provisions are very dear, they themselves living but a little better then the Indians and even here seem fully to possess that spirit of gaity so natural to that nation, for it is not uncommon to see a Frenchman with Indian shoes and stockings, without breeches, wearing a strip of woolen cloth to cover what decency requires him to conceal. Yet at the same time he wears a fine ruffled shirt, a laced waistcoat with a fine handkerchief on his head. But since the English have frequented these parts the French have laid by many of their savage customs.

At Detroit in [blank in mss.] the day became as dark as night; at the same time it raind water as black as ordinary ink which continued for some hours.[15]

About this time Pontiac, an interprizing chief of the Miamies, a nation of the west side of Lake Erie, by his influence over several nations it seems had determined to extirpate the English in all these new acquisitions and in particular had laid a plan to cut off the garrison of Detroit with all the English traders without hurting the French. But this was timely discovered by the ex-

[14] On the fort, founded in 1701 by Antoine de Lamothe Cadillac, and the French settlement there, see C. M. Burton, "Fort Pontchartrain du Detroit — 1701 to 1710 — under Cadillac," in Michigan Pioneer and Historical Collections, 29: 240–317 (1899–1900); Almon E. Parkins, The Historical Geography of Detroit, 46–84 (Lansing, Mich., 1918). During the British occupancy from 1760 to 1796, Col. John Campbell succeeded Col. John Bradstreet as commander in 1765, according to Nelson V. Russell, The British Régime in Michigan and the Old Northwest, 1760–1796, 292 (Northfield, 1939). See also F. Clever Bald, Michigan in Four Centuries, 50, 55, 62, 77 (New York, 1954).

[15] Travels, 153, stated that this abnormal darkness occurred in July, 1762. On Carver's belief in portents, see p. 32, above.

traordinary viligence and prudent conduct of Colonel [*Henry*] Gladwin, who then commanded a battallion of Royal Americans at that post, a discovery that was of the greatest advantage to the English who resided there and especially to those whose fortunes lay in goods for trade which they had just brought. In 1763 the confederates under Pontiac laid seige to this place and continued before it near a year, but most of the time was rather a blockaid than a regular seige. At length provisions became scarce & the garrison and the people within the fort were reduced to great extremities.[16]

Meanwhile the Indians made some very strenuous efforts to destroy all communication between the provinces and this place and in this war several good officers lost their lives. Captain [*Donald*] Campbell who was a prisoner among the Indians in Pontiac's camp was inhumanly murdered in cold blood to revenge the death of one of their chiefs whom the English had a little before killd in battle. Captain Delzel [*James Dalyell*], a very brave officer at the head of a party of English, sallyed out of the fort and made an attack on Pontiac's camp in which he lost his life as did several others, & the whole party would probably have suffered much more had it not been for Lieutenant Braham [*Dietrich Brehm*], who sailed up the river from the fort in a boat armed with some swivels & with these he kept up a heavy fire on the front of the enemy who by this means was kept from annoying the rear of our party while they retreated to the fort.[17]

However notwithstanding the violent efforts the Indians made to stop the communication a vessel [*"Huron"*] by the good behaviour of Mr. Jacobson the mate in a smart engagement in the river a little below the fort (the captain being killd in the begin-

[16] On Pontiac's War, see p. 9, above. Peckham, *Pontiac*, 15, considered Pontiac a member of the Ottawa nation, but of mixed parentage, one parent being either Chippewa or Miami. A more extended account of these events appeared in *Travels*, 153–166.

[17] Campbell went to Detroit in 1760 during the English occupation, and commanded the post until relieved by Gladwin in 1761. He was killed in revenge for the death of the nephew of Wasson, the Chippewa chief from Saginaw. See Peckham, *Pontiac*, 67, 194; M. Agnes Burton, ed., *Journal of Pontiac's Conspiracy, 1763*, 208 (Detroit, [1913?]). On Dalyell and Brehm, see Peckham, *Pontiac*, 202–208. For biographical sketches of all three soldiers, see Thwaites, in *Wisconsin Historical Collections*, 18: 225n, 252n.

ning) he fought his way through and arrived at the fort with a sutable supply of provisions and stores which with Col. Gladwin's resolution of maintaining the post so discouraged the Indians that soon after they made a peace.[18]

The land about Detroit is very good for agriculture, tho some lyes a little too low. Yet this will serve for very good grass & pasture land and nothing seems to be wanting but good farmers to possess itt. Indeed every thing I have heard said or mentioned in history concerning this tract of country is far from being extravagant.

After having tarried at Detroit a few days to refresh myself and to prepare such emplements as was requisite for the ascer-

Version II
Insert 4 ⟩

taining the lattitude of places and to enable me to keep a journal.⟩[19]

JULY 13, 1766. The country I have passd through to this and about here is so well known and layd down by draughtsmen of more abilities than I can pretend to that I shall not undertake to give any discription of it.[20] What ever account I have yet met with treating of the excellency of Detroit its situation, soil, produce &c is far from being extravagant. The manners, customs and commerce of the Windotts [*Huron*], Chippeways, Ot-

[18] The engagement here referred to probably took place on September 3, 1763. The mate's name was given as Jacobs in *Travels*, 164, where the name of the boat is erroneously said to be the "Gladwin" rather than the "Huron." Henry R. Howland, "Navy Island and the First Successors to the Griffon," in Buffalo Historical Society, *Publications*, 6: 36 (1903), gave the captain's name as Horst; Russell, *British Régime*, 167, identified him as Sergeant Miller of the Royal Americans.

[19] The instrument probably used to determine latitude was a reflecting quadrant designed by John Hadley, a London instrument maker; it is mentioned two paragraphs below, and in Carver's schedule of expenses, p. 207, below.

[20] Carver, *Travels*, ii, was critical of French maps of the West, and most English maps preceding his were based largely on French sources. Those he may have used include Guillaume de l'Isle, *Carte de la Louisiane et du Cours du Mississipi* (Paris, 1718), reprinted in his *Atlas Nouveau, Contenant Toutes les Parties du Monde,* map 48 (Amsterdam, 1730), and in his *Atlas Universel, Contenant les Cartes Generales et Particulieres* (Paris, [1769]); maps of Jacques Nicolas Bellin in Charlevoix's *Histoire et Description Generale* (1744), and Bellin's "Carte des Cinq Grands Lacs du Canada," in *Petit Atlas Maritime*, 1: 6 ([Paris], 1764); John Mitchell, *A Map of the British and French Dominions in North America,* first published in London in 1755. His reference to the high-quality maps of the Lake Ontario-Lake Erie region must include Lewis Evans, "A General Map of the Middle British Colonies, in America," in *Geographical . . . Essays* (1755).

toways, Mamies, and Potowattomies nations inhabiting the neighbourhood of Detroit have been so well remarkd by others more acquainted with them together with my hasty march through them, I shall pass it over without entering into any particulars on that account.[21]

AUGUST 5, 1766. Took my departure from Detroit. ⟨The same day being the great eclipse of the sun I was at that time about five miles above Detroit on my way to Lake Huron. While I stopd I took the colourd glasses from my quadrant by which I could see the sun with the part eclipsd very plain. A number of Indians being present I gave some of them the glasses and on looking through them on the sun they seemd greatly astonished and made many simple observations on the same to one another — but as I could not then understand but a very little of what they said I could not take any exact account of their opinions, but I observd that they appeard much surprizd.⟩[22]

⟨*Version II Insert 5*

Version II Insert 5⟩

The next day passd Lake St. Clare. This lake is about 30 mile over and about the place where the river (calld by some the Huron [*St. Clair*] River) enters this lake is a great number of small islands, some of which are very pleasant and of a good soil as is also the land about this lake.

AUGUST 8, 1766. Arrivd to the block house [*Fort Sinclair*] commanded at present by Captain Sinclare [*Patrick Sinclair*], who commands the vessel [*"Gladwin"*] which passes and repasses from this place during the summer season with supplies of provisions for Michillimackinac. Very near under the cover of this block house a small creek [*Pine River*] enters the [*St. Clair*] river in which the vessel is careen'd and lies during the winter season. The same day arrivd to where the River Huron has its draught from Lake Huron. The country from Lake St. Clare to this lake has a very good soil and especially near Lake Huron is very

---

[21] Descriptions of the Indians of the central Great Lakes appeared in considerable detail in Rogers, *Concise Account*, 205–253, and throughout Charlevoix, *Journal*. Carver may also have read Rogers, *Journals of Major Robert Rogers: Containing an Account of the Several Excursions He Made Under the Generals Who Commanded upon the Continent of North America* (London, 1765), which described his travels to Detroit in 1760. See Hough, ed., *Rogers' Journals*, 178–202.

[22] This eclipse on August 5, 1766, was recorded by Theodor Ritter von Oppolzer, *Canon der Finsternisse*, 284 (Vienna, 1887). It was total in the eastern part of Hudson Bay.

pleasant open medows. A party of the Chipeway Indians live about here.[23]

⟨*Version II Insert 9*⟩ ⟨On going up the Huron River above Lake St. Clare, after we had stopd at evening and built a camp, one of our party took his gun and went out to see if he could find any deer, but he had not been gone many minutes before he returnd & told us that he had been bit by a rattle snake in the ankle. He had immediatly tyed a garter round his leg at the garter place. I looked and found the incision like the prick of a pin to which we applyd fine salt, giving him somthing at the same time to defend his vitals, and in *Version II* two or three days' time he intirely recovered. Salt is proved to be *Insert 9*⟩ a most extraordinary antidote against the poison of this snake.⟩[24]

⟨*Version II*⟩ AUGUST 10, 1766. Entered Lake Huron on the west shore ⟨in a canoe with Mr. Bruce, a trader.⟩[25]

AUGUST 15, 1766. Arrived at Saganaum [*Saginaw*] Bay. This bay is about 90 [*60*] mile deep; across the chops is about 24 mile, but the common passage for canoes is further, a few miles down in the bay where about the midle of the passage two small islands [*Charity and Little Charity*] serve to fecilitate the traverse.

AUGUST 21, 1766. Arrivd at Thunder Bay, the next day crossd this bay which is 9 [*13*] miles over and ten miles deep. This is calld Thunder Bay by the most ancient accounts that we have had of this country, even from the Indians; I thought for my part it was rightly named for of thirty six hours that I tarried about here I judged 24 was allmost one continued storm of thunder some of which was most amazing hard, and most of the traders and people that I have heard speak of their passing this, say that they seldom pass here in the summer season without extraordinary thunder storms. I have never yet heard any pretend to

[23] On Captain Patrick Sinclair, who was at this time taking Major and Mrs. Rogers to Michilimackinac, and on Fort Sinclair, which stood within the site of the present town of St. Clair, Mich., see p. 15n, above; Cuneo, *Rogers,* 190; William L. Jenks, *St. Clair County, Michigan: Its History and Its People,* 92–95 (Chicago, 1912). A mixed group of Mississauga and Chippewa settled at the northern end of Lake St. Clair in the early 18th century as a result of Cadillac's efforts to induce bands to reside near Detroit. In 1718 the band numbered 60 to 80 men. W. Vernon Kinietz, *The Indians of the Western Great Lakes, 1615–1760,* 320 (Ann Arbor, Mich., 1940); anonymous, "1718 Memoir," in *Wisconsin Historical Collections,* 16:370 (1902). There is still a Chippewa reservation at Sarnia, Ont.

[24] In the same period John Long, *Voyages and Travels,* 150, told of applying salt and gunpowder to a bite and binding it with leaves of the red willow.

[25] On William Bruce, see p. 15, above.

account for this extraordinary incident in nature, but am ready to imagine it must be occasioned by large masses of minerals of a very sulpherous quallity about here, ⟨as I observd some moun- ⟨*Version II*
tains tho very small, yet much the largest I had seen since I had *Insert 6*
left Niagara, which was about five hundred miles, which were *Version II*
about the bottom of this bay.⟩[26] *Insert 6*⟩

AUGUST 28, 1766. Arrivd at Michillimackinac: this is a large stockade garrison containing a number of houses chiefly belong- ing to the merchants, and is defended by four bastions. Each has a platform and mount two or three pieces of small cannon, be- sides two large sentry boxes one over each gate which are sufficient for defence against small arms. The situation of this garrison is on the northern extremity of a large point of land or cape which divides Lake Huron from Lake Michigan, and over- looks the straits between these two lakes which is near six miles over to Cape St. Ignatius [*St. Ignace*], which divides Lake Michi- gan from Lake Superiour, having the Straits of St. Marie's on the east where the waters of Lake Superiour falls into Lake Huron.[27]

The Straits of St. Marie's which makes the junction between the two last mentiond great lakes is about 45 mile long, and very unequal as to its breadth and is very full of islands, two of which the one calld St. Joseph's Isle is very large the other Isle George [*Sugar*] which is not quite so large. Some places has somthing of a hard currant.

The land about Michillimackinac for some miles has a sandy, dry, barren soil, so that the troops and the traders here can scarsly find sufficient for gardens to raise greens on; yet there is spots of tolerable good pasturage for sheep and cattle. ⟨Michili- ⟨*Version II*⟩
mackinack lies in Lat. 45° 15′ [47′].⟩

The lake about here has a great plenty of fish. The most re- markable is the trout some of which has been found to weigh upwards of 70 lb. and are very fat, the other sort are calld the white fish, in general will weigh about 4 lb. and some eight or ten lb. There is another sort of fish [*cisco*] which some call her-

[26] According to the United States Environmental Data Service, National Climatic Center, the port city of Thunder Bay — Alpena — averages 24 thun- derstorms a year. Ralph R. Woodiwiss to the editor, December 10, 1975.

[27] Plans of the fort can be found in J. Jefferson Miller and Lyle M. Stone, *Eighteenth-Century Ceramics From Fort Michilimackinac: A Study in Historical Ar- cheology*, 7–23 (Smithsonian Institution, *Studies in History and Technology*, no. 4 — Washington, 1970). See also p. 9n, above.

ring. Their shape resembles a mackril but their bigness and taste is much like our English herring. These three sorts of fish are to be caught at allmost all seasons of the year and are very servicable to the troops and traders, and what is yet more remarkable they are caught in the winter by cutting holes in the ice where the people set their netts and hooks and take them in plenty.[28]

The land about Lake Huron is very poor and barren and unfit for cultivation excepting some spots at the enterance of rivers, and between Lake Huron and Lake Michigan for near an hundred mile in length is a very high plain lying north & south from which rise several rivers heading near each other that discharge themselves into both of these lakes. The timber that grows here is spruce, pine, hemlock, and fir, some beach, pople [*aspen*], and birch which last is very usefull for the Indians in making their canoes.

The situation of the garrison of Michillimackinac is the most comodious of any fort I have seen in the inland countrys, on account of the peltry and furr trade, as this and the Streights of St. Marie's command the annual passage of near 100d canoes which carry the trade to the west by way of the Green Bay and to the Mississippi &c, and to the southwest to St. Joseph's and to the norwest even as far as Lake Winipeek in the country of the Christenous and Asniboines to Alanipigon [*Lake Nipigon*] and several other places between Lake Superiour and Hudson's Bay.[29]

⟨*Version II*⟩   ⟨A most remarkable circumstance in this strait, and perhaps in some degree extended over the lakes it joins, is the septennial rise of the water being observed to encrease gradually each year till

[28] For the varieties described by Carver, see Samuel Eddy and James C. Underhill, *Northern Fishes: With Special Reference to the Upper Mississippi Valley*, 165–168, 183–189 (Minneapolis, 1974).

[29] On the fur trade traffic at Michilimackinac in the year of Carver's journey, see Charles E. Lart, ed., "Fur Trade Returns, 1767," in *Canadian Historical Review*, 3:352–358 (December, 1922). The Christeno, an Algonquian tribe better known as the Cree, inhabited the land from James Bay to the Saskatchewan River. The Assiniboin, their frequent allies against the Dakota or Sioux, were originally a Dakota tribe, separating from them late in the prehistoric period. They are believed to have lived near Lake of the Woods and Rainy Lake until about 1675 when they started a westward movement which took them as far as Saskatchewan. Both tribes were involved in the Hudson's Bay Company's trade, carrying European goods to more distant plains tribes. See Hassrick, *The Sioux*, 58–61; David G. Mandelbaum, "The Plains Cree," in American Museum of Natural History, *Anthropological Papers*, 37:169–178 (New York, 1941).

on the seventh it exceeds the first by eight feet perpendicular and for the same term of time in like manner falls.[30]

The word Michillimackinac signifies in English a turtle and was at first given to the island lying eastward about eight miles distant at the opening of the strait into Lake Huron and much resembles that animal in appearance above the water at a distance of about three miles.

In 1763 the fort of Michillimackinac was taken by the savages in a manner which might do honor to the most skillful commander. They came in as usual for trade and staid diverting themselves for some weeks till they were ready for the execution of their scheme. When one day being busily engaged in a game much resembling rackets [la crosse], they several times drove the ball into the fort and out again till at length sixteen or eighteen at once entered, dropt their blankets on the parade and flew to the guard which they instantly destroyed with their tomahawks. The commander and other officers being without the garrison were made prisoners. Mr. Jermat [John Jamet] the engineer was the only person who had opportunity to spill the blood of his enemies but being overpowered was barbarously murdered.⟩[31]   *Version II*⟩

SEPTEMBER 3, 1766. Took my departure from Michilimackinac in company with Mr. Bruce, a trader bound for the Mississipi; proceeded along the north side of Lake Michigan.

SEPTEMBER 13, 1766. Arrivd at Little Detroit. This is a small town of the Ottoways situate on an island in the Grand Traverse in crossing the enterance of the Green Bay. The chief of this town and his people recd me very kindly discharging their pieces in a manner which at first a little surprizd me. As I aproached the shore within about 40 rods they began with scattering shotts, firing balls over our heads some of which came very near the canoe I was in, giving at the same time loud whoops and a most

---

[30] The 7-year tide cycle is a common myth with little scientific backing. The levels of Lakes Michigan and Huron vary up to 5 feet over a period of years, but no distinct pattern of fluctuation has been discovered. See Edward L. Towle, "Charles Whittlesey's Early Studies of Fluctuating Great Lakes Water Levels," in *Inland Seas,* 21: 4–7 (March, 1965); W. T. Laidly, "Regimen of the Great Lakes and Fluctuations of Lake Levels," in Howard J. Pincus, ed., *Great Lakes Basin,* 93–99 (American Association for the Advancement of Science, *Publications,* no. 71 — Washington, 1962).

[31] For a contemporary account of the capture of Michilimackinac, see Bain, ed., Henry, *Travels & Adventures,* 77–93. On Jamet, see Thwaites, in *Wisconsin Historical Collections,* 18:249n.

⟨*Version II*⟩ hideous yelling, runing from tree to tree, and squating down as they discharged their pieces. ⟨Being advised by my interpreter that this was their custom, I answered them in like manner.⟩ This they continued till we began to land after which they con-ducted us to their village, gave us plenty of green corn, beans & ⟨*Version II* squash, ⟨and fish with a sort of bread made of the corn in the milk squeezed and pounded together and baked under the ashes. Like wise gave us cake made of whirtleberries [*whortleberries*] full ripe made up in a consistancy like dough dryed in the sun which *Version II*⟩ they frequently carry with them in their travels.⟩[32]

The traverse in crossing the Green Bay is very full of islands, on one of which is plenty of stone of a light gray compleatly fitted for buildings as tho hewn by art. The land on the north of Lake Michigan is much the same with that of Lake Huron. On the banks of this lake as well as the other lakes about here grows a cherry calld the sand cherry which grows on a small bush not larger than sweet fern bushes. The fruit, about as large as a small musquet ball when full ripe, is black and of a very good taste and the best I ever yet saw to put into spiritous liquor. Some other wild fruit grows about here such as whirtle berrys, black berries, ⟨*Version II*⟩ goose berries, and currants. The island of Little Detroit, ⟨about two miles long, not quite so wide⟩ is very good land and not heavy timbered. The Indians raise plenty of corn and other neces-saries of life but in winter they are often a month or two on the march in search of good hunting grounds.

SEPTEMBER 14, 1766. Sett of from Little Detroit after having received the blessings of the chiefe who wished me a fair wind

[32] The 8 islands across the mouth of Green Bay were used as steppingstones for the Grand Traverse between the north shore of Lake Michigan and the Door Peninsula. Bands of Ottawa came to these islands as early as 1650, fleeing from Iroquois attacks farther east. According to "Lieut. James Gorrell's Journal," in *Wisconsin Historical Collections,* 1:32 (1855), 100 Ottawa warriors lived in two villages at Little Detroit and Milwaukee in 1761. See also p. 181, below. *Travels,* 23, said that Little Detroit is "on the largest and best of these islands," which would be Washington Island. Other sources and the paragraph below place it on Detroit Island. The stony island Carver refers to below may have been Rock Island, which has tall limestone cliffs on its north side. Carver's interpreter during this part of the journey may have been Bruce or one of Bruce's men; see p. 77, below. Ronald J. Mason, "Huron Island and the Island of the Poutouatamis," in Elden Johnson, ed., *Aspects of Upper Great Lakes Anthropology: Papers in Honor of Lloyd A. Wilford,* 149, 152, 154 (*Minnesota Prehistoric Archaeol-ogy Series,* no. 11 — St. Paul, 1974); Samuel A. Storrow, "The North-west in 1817," in *Wisconsin Historical Collections,* 6:165 (1872).

and a prosperous voyage and always a clear sky, in a long speech which he delivered with a pathos equal to his vocal force until we were out of hearing.

SEPTEMBER 17, 1766. Arrived at La Bay Fort which is situate on the north side of the entrance of the Sax [Fox] River into the Green Bay close on the banks. This is an old stockade fort very much decayed, being a square of near equal sides having two bastions on the north west and south east corners, a few decayed hutts within where a few traders live, opposite to which over the river on the south side is 3 or four houses belonging to some French people who raise corn and other necessaries of life in plenty.[33]

⟨This place also fell with Michillimackinac in [17]63 but in a ⟨*Version II* different manner. The famous Pondiac, chief of the Miamies, having meditated the extirpation of the English from these posts had engaged all his allies to begin their operations at the same time. But the Chippeways, ambitious of distinction, struck before the time agreed on and thereby gave umbrage to the Menomonies, Ottoways, etcetera, who thereupon took these people in a friendly manner to skreen them from the rest, and at the treaty delivered them safe.⟩[34]   *Version II*⟩

In the Green Bay is caught plenty of sturgeon which is counted here the best of fish. I found them in taste very different from those near the salt water being but very fat and tender. Here is a great plenty of ducks and other fowl, and much Indian rice call'd by the Indians menomonie, ⟨by the English wild rice,   ⟨*Version II* being the grain it most resembles in taste though greatly different in other respects having a kernel above an inch and half in length and very full. This grows spontaneously in moist meadow soil and may be gathered in any quantity desired.⟩ The   *Version II*⟩ soil here is very fertile and yields in abundance. Many thousands of acres of land with scarce a tree which if improv'd would afford excellent pasturage and tillage.

The Indians who at present inhabit about the Green Bay are a nation call'd the Menomonis or rice people. They have two

[33] For a similar contemporary description, see Gorrell, in *Wisconsin Historical Collections,* 1: 26. On the early history of Fort La Baye, sometimes called Fort St. François, see Kellogg, *French Régime,* 292, 295, 374–405, 437.

[34] See Gorrell, in *Wisconsin Historical Collections,* 1: 39–46, for a journal of this occasion. Wild rice, mentioned below, is a grass; see note 80.

villages, the one about an hundred rods west of the fort up the river, and another about 30 miles from the bottom of the bay on the north side. They have hardly 200 warriors and are calld very brave. They are governed by a chief who is heriditary; besides they have a chief of the warriors and a number of other chiefs ⟨*Version II*⟩ ⟨whose advice rather than authority influences public measures as is indeed the case thro all the cantons I have any knowledge of.⟩ This nation like almost all other nations of Indians pay but little respect to any authoritative commands and are principally governed by advice when it best sutes their inclination.[35]

Their native dialect is very different from all other nations. But few traders or travellers that go among them take pains to learn their tongue, it being a very uncouth jargon, hard to express, besides there is but little need for it, as almost all of this nation as they grow up learn to speak in the Chipeway tongue.[36]

This nation is very much attached to their former masters, the French. Several of the warriours of the Menomonies joined the other confederate nations, allies to the French in the time of the last war, and among other acts of barbarity assisted at the unhappy massacre of the garrison at Fort William Henry in 1757, some of which carry apearent marks of their being accessary in that cruel affair which was the occasion of the small pox spreading among the whole of the Indians between these and Canada and some further to the west, and it is common for nations about here even to this day to say that the English are more powerfull in medicine than other nations, and that this disorder was oc-

[35] The Menomini settlement on the Fox River at Green Bay may have been established about 1740 when that area was largely deserted by other tribes. The village Carver mentions 30 miles northward was the ancestral settlement of the tribe at the mouth of the Menominee River in present Marinette, Wis. Gorrell in the 1760s estimated 150 warriors in the two villages; a document of 1777 in the General Archives of the Indies, Seville, agreed with Carver in assigning 200 warriors to them. See Gorrell and anonymous Spanish "Summary of the Indian tribes of the Misuri River," in *Wisconsin Historical Collections*, 1: 32; 18: 364. Estimates of total population in 1764 and 1778 can be found in Albert E. Jenks, "The Wild Rice Gatherers of the Upper Lakes," in Bureau of American Ethnology, *Nineteenth Annual Report*, 2: 1108 (Washington, D.C., 1900). On the chiefs of this village, see Goddard, p. 182, below; Felix M. Keesing, *The Menomini Indians of Wisconsin*, 35–38, 40, 71, 77 (American Philosophical Society, *Memoirs*, vol. 10 — Philadelphia, 1939).

[36] The Menomini were a part of the Central Algonquian linguistic group, and within that group had a distinctive dialect, as Carver indicates. See Leonard Bloomfield, *The Menomini Language* (New Haven, 1962).

casioned among them by medicines of a magical kind, which they say we are well skilld in to destroy our enemies.[37]

This country about Le Bay was formerly possessd by the Saugies which are calld by the French Sacks [*Sauks*]. These people have had hard wars with the French, who with the assistance of the rice people [*Menomini*] drove them from all their settlements about the Green Bay, after which they took refuge up the Fox's River and thereby became united with a nation calld the Ottigawmies [*Fox*], possessing the country between Le Bay and the Ouisconsin [*Wisconsin*] River. These wars I am informed were upwards of sixty years ago (I shall treat further of these nations as occassion may require in the subsequent part of my journal).[38]

SEPTEMBER 18, 1766. Set out from the Green Bay in company with Mr. Bruce a trader who understanding the Indian tongue undertook to interpret for me as occasion might require, there being in company a number of other traders bound to the Mississippi, chiefly French from Michilimackinac. Among other things I cannot help mentioning a scheme that these French traders and people at the Green Bay made use of to prevent the English from going to trade at the Mississippi. They procured some Indians to favour their designs in making reports that the English garrisons at the Illinois and at Aupost on the Ouabach [*Wabash*] were cut off,[39] and that all the Indians on the Mississippi had commenced war against the English, likewise

[37] Carver was among the troops caught in Fort William Henry at the southern tip of Lake George in 1757 by a superior force of French and Indians. See p. 4, above. Smallpox was contracted by the Indians from the English and colonial forces there and carried westward to the Mississippi. The Menomini claimed to have lost 300 warriors to smallpox as a result of this campaign. See Keesing, *The Menomini*, 74.

[38] The Sauk and Fox settled near Green Bay shortly before 1640. The "hard wars" occurred intermittently from the 1680s to about 1738 as the French sought to keep open the Fox-Wisconsin River route to the Mississippi in order to trade with the Sioux. For a summary, see Gilman, in *Wisconsin Magazine of History*, 58: 5–7; p. 81, below.

[39] "Aupost" appears to be the correct reading, but neither this nor any similar place name is found on maps of the period which show the Wabash River. A possible reading would be "au post," referring to Post Vincient (Vincennes), a name that appears both on Thomas Hutchins' map of 1778 and in Hicks, ed., Hutchins, *Topographical Description*, 99, 101. The difficulty here is that the English are not known to have garrisoned this outpost on the Wabash as early as 1766. Possibly it is merely Carver's expression for "outpost."

told us that they had just heard that Mr. Mitchell, an English trader who sett out to go up the Sacks [Fox] River a few days before us, was murdered, his party dispersd and all his merchandize taken by the savages.[40] However terrifying they intended these stories should prove to us we proceeded on our way to the Sax River meeting with no interruption. [passage obliterated] return again to Michilimackinac & they said they greatly feared we might be destroyed yet like true Englishmen we showed ourselves without fear and proceeded up the Sacks River with the same unconcern as tho nothing had been said.

SEPTEMBER 25, 1766. Arrivd at the great town of the Winebaygoes calld by the French Puans, which signifies stinking people.[41] This people were drove of by their enemies from some part of the South Sea near Callifornia upward of a century past. In the time of their emigration it seems they connected themselves and became well acquainted with the Naudauwesse or Sioux, as they call each other brethren to this day.[42]

⟨Version II   ⟨From them the Green Bay was called by the French Bay de Puans, but why the Winebaygoes should be thus nicknamed perhaps no better reason can be given than one I have heard assign'd on like occasions, viz., that the traders might mention the several nations at pleasure before them and they not know

[40] Possibly Thomas Mitchell of whom George Croghan, trader and diplomat to various Indian tribes, wrote on October 18, 1767, from Fort Pitt to General Gage, "I hear one Thomas Mitchell a Trader has been kill'd Lately at One of the Shawanese Towns . . ." See Howard H. Peckham, ed., *George Croghan's Journal of his Trip to Detroit in 1767*, 26 (Ann Arbor, Mich., 1939).

[41] The date of this passage is September 23 in Version II. The "great town" of the Winnebago was on Doty Island at the north end of Lake Winnebago, within the present cities of Neenah and Menasha, Wis. By 1760 some of the Winnebago had moved southward to set up other villages on Lakes Winnebago and Puckaway; see pp. 80, 82, below; Publius V. Lawson, "Habitat of the Winnebago, 1632–1832," in State Historical Society of Wisconsin, *Proceedings,* 1906, pp. 144–166 (Madison, 1907). The term "Winnebago" in the Fox and Sauk language means "people of the filthy water," hence the French usage "Puants," meaning "stinking." For various explanations of the name, see Kellogg, ed., *Charlevoix Journal,* 1: 160–162; Publius V. Lawson, "The Winnebago Tribe," in *Wisconsin Archeologist,* 6: 83–86 (July, 1907).

[42] On the tribe's history, see Paul Radin, *The Winnebago Tribe* (Bureau of American Ethnology, *Thirty-seventh Annual Report* — Washington, D.C., 1923). Naudowessee, variously spelled by Carver, was his expression for Nadouessioux, the name applied to the Dakota by the French. It derives from *Nadoweisiw-eg* (adders), originating with the Algonquian-speaking Chippewa. The term Sioux came to be used as an abbreviation. Frederick W. Hodge, *Handbook of American Indians,* 1: 376 (Washington, D.C., 1907).

what or which they meant.⟩ They roved until they came some *Version II*⟩ where about the Green Bay which was the reason for its being calld at first by the French the Bay of Puans, afterwards La Bay and now by the English the Green Bay.[43]

The town of the Winebagoes is situate on the south east end of an island [*Doty*] at the east end of the Winebago Lake about 36 miles from La Bay Fort. The most part of the way up the Sacks River to this town is hard rapids and several short carrying places. The country here is very pleasant and good land not heavy timberd. They raise plenty of Indian corn, beans, squashes, water melons, Indian tobacco, Indian rice, &c. This town serves as a fine market for traders as they pass this way. They are servd in plenty with provisions. The Winebago Lake is about 30 mile long and seven or eight mile wide and is stored with fish and fowl. This people, was it not for their excessive fondness for spiritious liquors, which they purchase of traders at a most extravagant price with their provisions, would live with that ease and plenty which would be almost envyed by many white people among us.

The Winebagoes are governd by a heriditary chiefe who now is a queen of about eighty years old. A grand son of hers is calld the young prince of Winebago. Their present great counsellor is a near branch of the royal family. To the wisdom of this chief the nation in general adheres more than to any one besides. His name is calld Ekharrimoneyk. He appears like a very good humoured sensible old man.[44]

[43] *Travels,* 21, explained the name "Green Bay" as being due to the early arrival of spring there compared to Michilimackinac. According to Robert E. Gard and L. G. Sorden, *The Romance of Wisconsin Place Names,* 50 (New York, 1968), it was named by the French for the greenish color of the water.

[44] The queen was probably Hopoekaw or Glory of the Morning. In 1729 she married a French soldier turned trader, whose name is usually given as Sabrevoir De Carrie. Their two sons, Choukeka and Chah-post-kaw-kaw (Ladle and Buzzard Decorah) became eminent chiefs and the first of the Decorah (Dekaury or De Carrie) dynasty. "Young Prince of Winebago" is the term Carver uses below pp. 90, 93, and in *Travels,* 66, for the young man who accompanied him to the Falls of St. Anthony. Of at least ten grandsons of Hopoekaw, it is probable that only one was old enough in 1766 to have accompanied Carver — Scha-chip-ka-ka (White War Eagle) or Konoka Decorah, ca. 1747–1836, who succeeded his father Choukeka as chief of his tribe. Carver's Ekharrimoneyk is probably a version of Caromanie (Walking Turtle), the name of a prominent family of Winnebago. The most famous of them was Nawkaw (ca. 1735–1833), who seems to have been the son of the old man Carver refers to here. See "Augustin Grignon's

Their numbers consist of near about 300 warriours. They have two towns one of which is further up the river and but a small village. They have continual wars with the Illinois Indians.[45]

Ekharrimonyk told me that upward of 40 winters past he with a party of his nation sett of from their town with a design of war (perhaps against some of those nations from which they were formerly driven).[46] They pursued their rout towards the setting of the sun and in about 50 days from the Mississippi a little after they had left the river which I suppos'd to be the Missessore [*Missouri*] they lighted on a caravan of the Spaniards with about 80 horses loaded with silver which they intirely distroyd and brought several large masses of silver with them to their own people which the French took care to get from them I suppose for but a trifle, as these ignorant people took it to be no more then white stone of but little value. He like wise said that all the mettle with which the horses were shod and otherways equipd ⟨*Version II*⟩ was of this white stone. ⟨This he might readily conceive from the brightness of an iron horse shoe.⟩ This I suppose to be the land carriage between St. Fee [*Santa Fe*], which has a communication with the Bay of Mexico, and Colorido, a larg river which enters

Recollections," and John T. De La Ronde, "Personal Narrative," in *Wisconsin Historical Collections*, 3: 287; 7: 346, 356, 359 (1857, 1876); Lawson, in *Wisconsin Archeologist*, 6: 136–140, 150–152; Charles P. Hexom, *Indian History of Winneshiek County*, n.p. (Decorah, Ia., 1913); Frederick W. Hodge, ed., Thomas L. McKenney and James Hall, *The Indian Tribes of North America*, 1: 154 (Reprint Ed., Edinburgh, 1933).

[45] For an estimate of Winnebago population in 1764, see Jenks, in Bureau of American Ethnology, *Nineteenth Annual Report*, 2: 1108. Goddard, pp. 183, 184, below, gives much lower figures than Carver for the Doty Island and Lake Puckaway villages.

The major wars between the Illinois and the Winnebago occurred before 1640, when the latter were badly defeated. They were allied with the Fox against the Illinois in the 1720s, but late in that decade were won over by the French in an alliance against the Fox with unfortunate consequences for the Winnebago. See Lawson, in *Wisconsin Archeologist*, 6: 90–99; Hodge, *Handbook*, 2: 958 (1910).

[46] Charlevoix heard an expanded version of the following story from a Winnebago in 1721. It probably refers to the 1720 expedition of Pedro de Villazur, which was annihilated by the Pawnee, Missouri, and Oto on the Platte River. See Henry Folmer, *Franco-Spanish Rivalry in North America, 1524–1763*, 282–284 (Glendale, Calif., 1953). Unlike Carver, Charlevoix stated that the Winnebago did not actually participate in the event, but acquired some plunder from their allies, the Iowa. Kellogg, ed., *Charlevoix Journal*, 2: 59–61. For other accounts received from the Indians by travelers, see Lawrence J. Burpee, ed., *Journals and Letters of Pierre Gaultier de Varennes de La Vérendrye and His Sons*, 416 (Toronto, 1927); Jean-Baptiste Bénard de La Harpe, *Journal Historique de l'Etablissement des Français à la Louisiane*, 249 (Paris and New Orleans, 1831).

into the Gulfe of Californie. I imagine that this silver must be got much further north then the mines of St. Barbe [*Santa Barbara, Mexico*].[47]

The Winebagoes differ in their customs and manners but a very little from their neighbouring nations and those near Michilimackinac & Detroit. For that reason together with my slight acquaintance with them I omit to say any more then that by the best information, their young people are not so lewd as is common among other nations which the French by frequent intercourse had too much corrupted. A few trifling presents in some places would tempt parents to give up their daughters to be debauched. The dialict of the Winebagoes is the most difficult to be pronouncd of all nations. They pronounce very hard from their throats. When they say, "Friend I drink to thee," in their tongue it is *checorarro ukh charrigaugh*. I found the utmost difficulty in pronouncing the last of these words.[48]

SEPTEMBER 28, 1766. Left this town. The principal part of the Winebagoes went with us in order to seek their place for a winter's hunt, determining to travel with us to the carryg place into the Ouisconsin.[49]

SEPTEMBER 29, 1766. Entered a small lake calld the Foxes Lake [*Lake Butte des Morts*]. At this place upwards of 40 year ago the Saugies and the Ottigomis had a castle on the west side of this lake. The French & Menomonies who were at this time at war with these two nations came with an army upon them at unawares in the winter & cut them to pieces in a most cruel manner which nearly destroyed them both.[50]

[47] Santa Barbara was one of the centers of Mexico's silver production. Carver could have been aware of it from Hennepin; see Thwaites, ed., *New Discovery*, 1: 7, 200, 372, 390. Mitchell, *Map of the British and French Dominions* (1755) shows the road leading from the Mississippi toward the mines of "St. Barbe," and Jefferys, *American Atlas*, map 6 (1776) shows the abandoned "mines of St. Barbara" at about 27° north in west-central Mexico.

[48] A more accurate rendering would be *hičakoro* or *čákoro* (friend) *ske^h* (you) *šaráč* (take or have), *gʌn* (drink), *kjené* (future query). What Carver heard may have been "Friend, will you have a drink?" Professor Nancy O. Lurie to the editor, February 11, 1971.

[49] The carrying place is the present site of Portage, Wis. See also p. 82, below.

[50] Carver may have had in mind any one of at least three confrontations at Butte des Morts in 1726, 1730, and 1733. See Louise Phelps Kellogg, "The Fox Indians During the French Regime," in State Historical Society of Wisconsin, *Proceedings*, 1907, p. 172, 174, 177 (Madison, 1908); letter of Pierre Paul la Perriere, Sieur Marin, to Beauharnois, 1730, in *Wisconsin Historical Collections*, 17: 88–100 (1906). "Castle" is a term Carver used frequently, apparently indicating a defensive position.

⟨Version II⟩

OCTOBER 4, 1766. This day passd the upper town of the Winebagoes where more of this nation joynd who were bound for the Ouisconsin. This village is but very small containing eight or ten hutts on the south side of a small lake [*Puckaway*]. This with all other Indian towns is laid down in the ⟨general⟩ map.

OCTOBER 11, 1766. Arrivd at the Great Carrying Place between the Sax's [*Fox*] River and the Ouisconsin. This portage wants a little of being two miles from one of these rivers to the other. One half of the way is a marsh which makes the carriage much more difficult. The other part is very good going, being a

⟨Version II sort of an oak plain. ⟨The Sax River from the Winebaygoe Lake upwards has many windings and turnings, some places a hard current but no rapids. Its length about 200 [*175*] miles in its course, the breadth from five yards at the carrying place to forty

Version II⟩ rods where it falls into the bay.⟩

The country on the Sacks River is very good land and appears to me the best for grass I ever saw. Thousands of acres of grass as high as a middle sized man's head, and so very thick one could hardly walk through it. The uplands have but very few trees, of oak and hickory and some maple, in some places a few pines. The country about this carrying place begins to be somthing mountainous which were the first mountains I had seen since I

⟨Version II⟩ left Niagara. ⟨Perhaps this is the highest ground on this course between the Atlantic and Pacific Oceans, and no mountain appears between this and Niagara.⟩[51]

Here are abundance of rattlesnakes many of which the Indians that pass this way take and make them surprizingly tame even so as to carry them in their bosoms and to come and go when bid.

⟨Version II ⟨[They] are in no ways different from those of other parts in America. If they are tamd here more then in other parts of America 'tis owing to the extraordinary pains the Indians take

Version II⟩ with them more than else where.⟩ The Indians in these parts look upon the rattlesnake as a manatue or god for which reason they seldom kill any, where ever they find them, either in dens or fields for if they do they say they shall have bad luck after it and be unsuccessfull both in war and hunting.

---

[51] The mountains are the Baraboo Range. Carver was here crossing the divide between the Great Lakes and Mississippi watersheds.

⟨The following story of the rattle snake may be mentioned if ⟨*Version II*
the corrector for the press thinks proper. A Frenchman told me   *Insert 7*
that some years ago he was passing this way in company with an
Indian of the Menomonys, he at that time having brought a
rattle snake with him in a box to this carrying place. It being then
late in the fall of the year, the Indian was telling the Frenchman
that as he was going to his winter hunt he designed to leave his
grandfather, for so he cald the snake, at that place till he returnd
in the spring and then designd to call for him again. The French
man told him that he would never see him any more. The Indian
replyd that he would lay a wager of several gallons of rum that
on their return in such a moon in the spring within eight days
after their arrival that his grandfather would come and enter the
box of his own accord. The French man took him up. After the
winter was over they both returnd to the place at the time appointed and waited the number of days mentioned in the wager.
The snake did not come. The Indian acknowledged that he had
lost the wager, but said he would double it if he did not come in
four days more, which was agreed upon. The last of the four   *Version II*
days in the afternoon the snake came and crawld into the box as   *Insert 7*⟩
knowing his former habitation.⟩[52]

OCTOBER 13, 14, 1766. This day put our canoes into the Ouisconsin. Arrived to the town of the Saugies. This is the greatest
Indian village I ever saw containing upwards of three hundred
warriors. The town is somthing regularly built containing
about 80 large buildings, besides a great number of farm houses
in their fields for the conveinance of the squaws while at labour,
for they only till the ground; and men here as well as all other
nations of Indians in these parts disdain to labour and think it
beneath them, so employ themselves only in affairs of war and
hunting. Even the boys who are not of age sufficient to accom-
pany their fathers in that employ will hardly be persuaded to do
anything except learning to shoot with the bow & arrow and to
kill small animals, in which they are always indulged by their

[52] *Travels,* 43, gave an expanded version of this story and identified the author
as "Mons. Pinnisance, a French trader," whom Peter Pond met 7 years later at
Portage, under the name "Old Pinneshon." Pond considered that Carver was
greatly "Imposed apon" concerning the rattlesnake. See Pond, in Gates, ed., *Five
Fur Traders,* 38. The fact that Carver wrote the story, crossed it out, and then left
it up to his editor to decide whether it should go into the published version may
indicate that he also had some doubts about it.

parents, whose fondness for their children exceeds by far that of any white people I ever saw. This town is situate on the north side of the Ouisconsin about 42 [30] mile below where we put in our canoes at the carrying place from the Sax River. The land is extraordinary good here. This people have large fields of Indian corn, beans, squashes, melons, tobacco &c.[53]

As to their government they are subject to a heriditary chief. Their dialect [is] much the same as the Ottowaws and Chipeways ⟨except their frequent use of the L in place of N.⟩[54] Their customs but a little different. This nation hold continual wars with the Illinois nations which to the English is no disadvantage for undoubtedly were they at peace with each other most certainly the French and Spaniards on their side of the Mississipi would have a much fairer opportunity of drawing into their interest not only this but the Winebaygoes and Ottigaumies, their neighbours, which would of consequence deprive us of near all the Mississipi trade, for undoubtedly the Naudouwessie will go where these nations incline as they are seated in their passage either to the Illinois or to Michillimackinac, and are allies to each other.[55]

⟨*Version II*⟩

OCTOBER 17, 1766. Arrived at the upper town of the Ottigaumies which is about 84 mile further down the Ouisconsin, situate on the north side containig about 50 large buildings and some out houses in their fields. They raise plenty of corn and

---

[53] The town was probably on the site of present Prairie du Sac, Wis. It may have been the village founded under the administration of Paul Louis Dazenard, Sieur de Lusignan, in the early 1740s and abandoned before 1786 due to the threat of Chippewa invasion. See memorandum of Richard Dobie *et al.*, to Sir John Johnson, April 13, 1786, and Thwaites, in *Wisconsin Historical Collections*, 12: 80 (1892); 18: 282n; Kellogg, in *Proceedings*, 1907, pp. 143, 181n; and Goddard, p. 185, below.

[54] Professor Timothy Dunnigan to the editor, April 20, 1971, cites two studies by Leonard Bloomfield, "On the Sound-System of Central Algonquian," in *Language*, 1: 130–156 (1925), and in Cornelius Osgood, ed., *Linguistic Structures of Native America*, 85–129 *(Viking Fund Publications in Anthropology*, vol. 6 — New York, 1946), which demonstrate a regular correspondence between the "N" of modern Ojibway and Sauk-Fox. He notes, however, that the protocentral Algonquian source of "N" is in some cases "L," and that the latter may have been retained as a phoneme in early Sauk-Fox. See also p. 88, below.

[55] The strategic importance to the fur trade of Sauk loyalty to England is apparent in Carver's statement. The Sauk ultimately forced the Illinois out of southern Wisconsin and extended their own territory into present Illinois. See John R. Swanton, *The Indian Tribes of North America*, 256 (Bureau of American Ethnology, *Bulletins*, no. 145 — Washington, D.C., 1952); Goddard, p. 185, below.

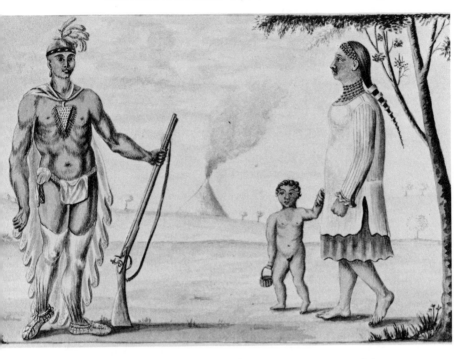

An unidentified Indian family from Version IV. An engraving of this sketch was printed in Travels *as "A Man and Woman of the Ottigaumies." The engraver altered the man's pendant to make it less obviously identical to the Dakota one illustrated on page 96.*

many other necessaries of life, ⟨having a very generous soil to improve, as is most of the land on the Ouisconsin.⟩[56] ⟨*Version II*⟩

This nation is governed by a heridatary chief whose name is Mackidochieck who appears like a sensible, powerfull man and carrys somthing more of distinction among his people then is common among Indians. His common place of residence is in the upper town.[57]

[56] Thwaites, in *Wisconsin Historical Collections*, 18: 282n, placed this Fox village near Muscoda, Wis. Another village was at Wauzeka, 21 miles above Prairie du Chien, according to B. W. Brisbois, "Traditions and Recollections of Prairie du Chien," in *Wisconsin Historical Collections*, 9: 295 (1882).

[57] This name is spelled "Maikidocheek" in Version II, and "Macketochick" by Goddard, p. 186, below; the editor has been unable to locate any further information.

The dialect, manners and customs of the Ottigaumis differs little from that of the Saugies. I found this people in a most unhappy situation. Not long before my arrival among them, the fever and ague at first, afterwards accompanyd by a multiplicity of other disorders which provd mortal like the plague carryd off in a little time near an hundred warriors besides women and children. Many who for some time remaind spectators of the mortallity on seeing the danger of the infection ran into the woods; by that means there was scarcely enough left to bury the dead. For some time, the whole town which was very compact stunk in such a manner that I was under great fears for myself and the party with me on account of the contagion, but by applying our silves to smoking and chewing tobacco it proved a sufficient antidote and we were so lucky as to pass through this country safe, on that account.[58]

On the south side of the Ouisconsin between the two last mentiond towns about one small day's journy, is the famous lead mines where the savages go every year and bring away large supplys of that mettal. Their manner of refining it is to make a fire on the side of the mountain where the ore is and presently procure a load.[59]

⟨*Version II*⟩ A little from this is another mountain where they get lead or matter like lead which is white like chalke. ⟨This information I had from so many credible persons, English, French, and Indians that I cannot scruple it.⟩ About another day's journy inland is a mountain where the Spaniards formerly came and took great quantities of white stone as the Indians formerly calld it which I supposd to be silver which they did till threatned and drove of by the Indians.[60]

[58] Carver's view of the medicinal value of tobacco was not unusual at the time. In his 1779 *Treatise on the Culture of the Tobacco Plant*, 1–9, he urged caution in its use because it was "very powerful in its operations." Chewing it, he said, alleviated the cravings of hunger and the depression of fatigue.

[59] The presence of lead in southern Wisconsin was known to the French from the early 17th century and to the Indians for many years before. Carver here refers to mines in the area of the Blue Mounds in Dane and Iowa counties, Wis.; most mining actually centered farther south, near Galena, Ill. See Reuben G. Thwaites, "Notes on Early Lead Mining in the Fever (or Galena) River Region," in *Wisconsin Historical Collections*, 13: 271–292 (1895); Joseph Schafer, *The Wisconsin Lead Region*, 34, 140 (*Wisconsin Domesday Book: General Studies*, vol. 3 — Madison, 1932).

[60] There are traces of silver in Wisconsin lead, though not enough to make its refinement feasible. Its presence led to numerous early rumors of silver mines in the region. See Moses Strong, "Lead and Zinc Ores," in *Geology of Wisconsin*,

OCTOBER 18, 1766. This day arrivd to where the Ouisconsin joyns the Mississipi.

I cannot but mention here how liable these people are to be deceived. They acquainted me that about thirty or forty years past they had a town near the Ouisconsin about 5 miles from the Mississipi where they lived very well till a spirit appeard on the top of a small rocky mountain and told them that that was his land and that they must immediately move away which they did without any hissitation, really supposing it to be the great manatue's land and that they could never prosper on it again if they continued there; and as a further instance of the reallity of this they say that grass now grows on the top of this hill (that I my self saw) which never grew there before they moved away. As there was very visible appearances of a great town here formerly, the goodness of the land the pleasantness of the situation made me think that somthing extraordinary had induced them to move and quit it, and imagine that it must be some contrivance of the French or Spaniards with design of building forts for the sake of mines, and laid this scheme to get them from thence.[61]

The Ouisconsin River from the carryg place to the Mississipi is full of islands of low land with plenty of maple and elm and some other timber natural to meadow or intorval[e] land. This river has somthing of a hard currant but no rapids, runing all the way in a bed of sand. The country a little distance on each side from the medows is full of small mountains with but a few groves of oak and hickery between, in the valleys. As I was on the top of one of the highest of these mountains,[62] the country round me appeared like a meadow full of hay cocks all covered with grass which made it very pleasant.

<hr>

Survey of 1873–1879, 1:637 (Madison, 1883); Thwaites, in Wisconsin Historical Collections, 13:275, 276; Kellogg, ed., Charlevoix Journal, 2:202–204.

[61] The Wisconsin flows into the Mississippi at present-day Prairie du Chien, Wis. The first area up the river where the bluffs fall back sufficiently to permit an encampment of any size is about 6 miles from the mouth, where Grand Gris Creek flows into the Wisconsin from the north. Numerous Indian mounds can be found on this plain. Any of the river bluffs in this area would fit Carver's description of a "small rocky mountain." Kellogg, French Régime, 329, suggested that the abandonment of the town may have occurred as a result of the conflict, known as the second Fox War, between the French and the Fox in the 1730s.

[62] The highest bluffs in this area are Pike's Peak in present Iowa, across the Mississippi from the mouth of the Wisconsin River, and Wyalusing Peak, on the south side of the Wisconsin. The latter would have been harder for Carver to reach, being farther back from the river.

OCTOBER 19, 1766. Came to the lower town of the Ottigaumies. This town is situate on the east side of the Mississipi
about 4 mile above the enterance of the Ouisconsin, on a large
plain calld by the French Lapraire La Chien or in English the Dog
Plain. This plain is about 6 mile long and 3 [2] mile wide with
neither trees nor stones except a few elms and maple on the bank
of the river. This is one of the most delightsom settlements I saw
during my travels. I could hardly refrain envying these Indians
their pleasant situation. This town contains about forty buildings
with upwards of two hundred warriors. Their governor is
heriditary under the chief [Mackidochieck] of the other village before mentioned. It is reported that the father of the present chief
had eleaven wives by whom he had fifty sons. The old man dyed
about a month before I came to the town, of the mortal disorder
before mentioned. He was much lamented as he was esteemd the
⟨Version II⟩   ⟨father⟩[63] of his people. During his goverment which was a
long time his people had great prosperity for at his first taking
the command he had not above forty warriors, they having been
almost destroyd by wars with the French, the Menomonies and
Naudouwessee with whom this governor made peace and intro-
ducd trade and commerce among the whole nation. His son the
successor told me that some of the last words of his dying father
was charging him that if ever the English should come into his
country by all means to be kind to them for he had heard much
of their power and that they had conquered all that opposed
them, and that he acknowledged the king of Great Britain to be
his father.[64]

All the Ottigaumies speak much the same tongue as the Chippeways except in lieu of the N they for the most part substitute
the L. For instance what the Chippeways call *sauganaush*, they
call *saugalaush* and *quaganee* they call *quagalee* and so in most
other words except when the N concludes the word.

OCTOBER 20, 1766. Went a little further up the Mississipi to
Jaun [*Yellow*] River on the west side where it enters. This in the

---

[63] "Lover" in Version I. On Mackidochieck, see p. 85, above.
[64] The origins of Indian settlement at Prairie du Chien are obscure. There was
no settlement at the site in 1673 at the time of Father Marquette's voyage. La Salle
claimed to have a base there in 1682, and a Fox settlement was recorded as early
as 1732. See Goddard, p. 187, below; Peter L. Scanlan, *Prairie du Chien: French,
British, American*, 9–11 (Menasha, Wis., 1937); letter of Louis Henri Deschamps
Boishebert to Beauharnois, in *Wisconsin Historical Collections*, 17: 151; Coues, ed.,
Pike Expeditions, 1: 35n.

English signifies Yellow River. Here I left the traders having hired a Frenchman and an Iroquois Indian [*Jacko*] to work in a canoe to carry me to the Naudouwessee.[65]

NOVEMBER 2, 1766. Arrived at Lake Pepin calld by some Lake St. Anthony. This lake is near 300 [*125*] miles above the entrence of the Ouisconsin — is about 21 [*28*] mile long and between four & five [*2 to 3*] mile wide. This lake begins the teretorys of the Naudouwessee. It was calld the Lake of Tears first by Father Lewis Hennepin, the first white man that ever travelled this way, as he in his journal says that in this place the Naudouwessee who had taken him prisoner intended to burn him to death and according to their custom of weeping previous to the execution of their prisoners they weepd and made a great outcry. He afterwards being rescued by one of their chiefs in his favour calld this the Lake of Tears.[66]

The French had formerly a trading house or factory on the plain east of this lake till the late [*1763*] treaty of peace. As this is a proper lake of dead water having no currant I could not help but look upon it as the most proper head of the Mississipi. The river below this lake is very full of islands some of which are very large and good land. On each side is several large open plains covered with grass. On each side of the river at a distance is a row of mountains some of which have prodigious precipices and several rocky clifts like pyramids almost perpendicular for near 200 feet. These mountains are covered with grass with here and there a small tree. The valleys have some groves of trees, chiefly oak & walnut.[67]

---

[65] On Jacko, see p. 93, below. The editor has been unable to identify these men.

[66] Carver's usage of the names Lake St. Anthony here and St. Anthony River two paragraphs below is unusual. The editor knows of no other published 18th-century reference. The name is obviously borrowed from that given by Father Hennepin to the Falls of St. Anthony in the Mississippi River in present-day Minneapolis. See Thwaites, ed., Hennepin, *New Discovery*, 1: 223; Upham, *Minnesota Geographic Names*, 5, 10, 226.

[67] French posts existed on both sides of Lake Pepin in the 17th and 18th centuries. For summaries, see June D. Holmquist and Jean A. Brookins, *Minnesota's Major Historic Sites: A Guide*, 91–93 (St. Paul, 1972); Mildred Mott Wedel, "Le Sueur and the Dakota Sioux," in Johnson, ed., *Aspects of Upper Great Lakes Anthropology*, 160. *Travels*, 56–59, referred in more detail to a post on the east shore probably established in 1736 by Jacques le Gardeur, Sieur de St. Pierre. See Louise Phelps Kellogg, "Remains of a French Post near Trempealeau: Historical Sketch," in State Historical Society of Wisconsin, *Proceedings*, 1915, p. 121 (Madison, 1916).

The explorer's reference to Lake Pepin as "the most proper head of the

NOVEMBER 8, 1766. Came into the river calld by some the Mississipi and by others the river St. Anthony.

NOVEMBER 10, 1766. Arrived at the first band of the Naudowessee calld the Nehogotowannah band. The 11th had a counsel with this band, delivered a belt, and a kegg of rum, and a ⟨Version II⟩ prick of tobacco, with a speach from Major Rogers.[68] ⟨This speach was delivered in five dialects: English, French, Ottaway, Winebaygoe, Naudowessie.⟩[69] In this counsel the young prince of the Winebago was very helpfull who had been with me the most part of the way from their castle.

The country below this and about Lake Pepin is very dangerous to travel in on account of a party of Chipeways calld the rob[b]ing people.[70] The traders when they pass here go in large parties for fear of being cut off. It was impossible for me to take this precaution for the traders had passd before me and I had with me only my two hired men. The evening before I came to Lake Pepin I encampd near the bank of the river. After having finished our hutt and dressd something to eat my men lay down to sleep. I set up a while after them to do some writing by firelight. When I had finished I stepd out of my hutt, imediately saw a number of Indians creeping towards my canoe under the bank which at first I supposd to be wild beasts. But when I perceived they were Indians I ran into my hutt, waked my two men, took our arms and gave a loud shout and run down upon them. They on seeing our resolution soon began to retreat. We pursued them till we came to the woods. I was not certain as to their numbers but supposed them to be about eight or ten. Afterwards each of us took turn about to keep watch through the night.

Mississippi" is erroneous; Lake Itasca in north-central Minnesota is the river's source. The "prodigious precipices" of the Mississippi River bluffs in this area vary from 500 to 600 feet above the river level.

[68] Swanton, *Indian Tribes*, 282, and Hodge, *Handbook*, 2: 53, identify the Nehogatawonah as a band of Dakota living near the St. Croix River in Minnesota or Wisconsin. Hodge referred to them as one of three river bands of Dakota. The ceremonial use of the wampum belt was described in *Travels*, 362. See also Long, *Voyages and Travels*, 47.

[69] The text in Version I reads: "This speach I delivered in four dialicts, viz., the French to the Ottoway, the Ottowaws to the Winebagoes, the Winebagoes to the Naudowessee."

[70] The Chippewa band of Pillager who lived farther north on central Minnesota's Leech Lake were often known as "the robbing people." See William W. Warren, *History of the Ojibway Nation*, 256–262 (Reprint Ed., Minneapolis, 1957). On the story below, see Carver's letter to his wife, p. 200, below; *Travels*, 51–53.

The next day my men advisd me to return, urging the great danger we should be in on account of these barbarians who they said would undoubtedly murder us in our sleep or kill us as we was going up the river in our canoe and overpower us with numbers which if we should fall into their hands we might depend on being burned to death. But I told them we would proceed with good caution, that I would be ashamd to return on that account, and persueaided them to comply on condition that I should arm my self in the best manner I could and march on ye banks of the river and serve as an outguard, that if I was killd they would have an opportunity to escape and return to the traders with my papers & goods, and give them an account of my fate, as they urged that if we was all killd no one would ever hear what became of us — this for fear of mutiny I was obligd to comply with.

The morning after having delivered the belt and presents I took my leave of the chief of this band who wished me well. The same day arrived to where the river St. Croix joyns the Mississipi or St. Anthony's branch. This river is almost as big as the other.

NOVEMBER 14, 1766. This day arrived to the great stone cave calld by the Naudowessee *Waukon Teebee,* or in English the house of spirits.[71] This cave I found to be a great curiosity, in a rocky mountain just by the bank of the [*Mississippi*] river. The mouth of the cave fronting the river [is] ⟨on an ascent near 45°,⟩ ⟨*Version II*⟩ the enterence about ten feet broad and three feet high. I went in and measured the room upwards of thirty feet broad, and about sixty feet from the enterence of the cave [to] where I came to a lake. As 'twas dark I could not find out the bigness nor the form

---

[71] Carver's *Waukon Teebee* corresponds to *tipi wakan,* a term later applied to churches. Appendix 2, J36, 47, below; John P. Williamson, *An English-Dakota Dictionary,* 32 (New York, 1902).

On "Carver's Cave," now marked by a plaque at Mounds Boulevard and Cherry Street, St. Paul, see *Travels,* 63, 86; Sue E. Holbert and June D. Holmquist, *A History Tour of 50 Twin City Landmarks,* 16 (St. Paul, 1966). Though often confused with other caves in the area, Carver's Cave was a point of great interest to subsequent explorers. About 1885 the cave entrance was blocked by debris resulting from railroad construction, and was not reopened until November 5, 1913. It remained open at least until 1958, but is now again closed by fallen rock. It is on property owned by the Burlington Northern Railroad, east of the St. Paul Union Depot. Charles T. Burnley, "Case of the Vanishing Historic Site," in *Ramsey County History,* Fall, 1967, pp. 8–12.

⟨*Version II*⟩ [of it]. ⟨The roof was about 20 feet high at the greatest elevation, the bottom clean white sand a little descending to the water from the mouth.⟩ I cast a stone which I could hear fall at a distance and with a strange hollow sound. I tasted of this water and found it to be very good.

The Indians say that several have attempted to go with a light and a canoe on this water but have been detered by some frightfull appearances of lights shining at a distance and strange sounds which makes them give it the name of *Waukon Teebee,* or in English, the house of spirits. As I found the Naudowessee very credulous to believe everything that cannot most easily be accounted for in nature to be somthing supernatural, made me suppose that those appearances of light was only the reflection of their torches upon some smoth chrystal like stones which are in many places in these parts, and the strange sounds was only the echo of their own noise reverberating against the hallow rocks at a distance, for I perceived a small noise would sound like thunder.

The rock at the enterance of the cave is of a lightish gray colour and very soft like the grit of a grindstone. I found many strange hieroglyphycks cut in the stone some of which was very a[n]cient and grown over with moss. On this stone I markd the arms of the king of England.

Near this cave is the burying place of the Mottobauntoway band of the Naudowessee. A few months before I came here dyed and was buryed the chief of this band. I went to see the grave. It is impossible for me to describe all the hieroryglyphicks and significant marks of regard and distinction this people had paid to the memory of this deceased grandee, much more than I had ever seen of the kind among any nations I had passd before.[72]

NOVEMBER 14, 1766. Arrived to the place where the river St.

---

[72] In *Travels,* 60, this band is called Mawtawbauntowahs. Another variation is Motobauntoway, a name Carver gives to a river between the Chippewa and St. Croix, probably the Trimbelle, on the map published with *Travels.* Hodge, *Handbook,* 1:819, identified the Matabantowaher as the Matantonwan, one of two early divisions of the Mdewakanton Sioux. See also Roy W. Meyer, *History of the Santee Sioux,* 16 (Lincoln, Neb., 1967).

Carver is here probably speaking of the Kaposia band, which was found near the site of present St. Paul as early as 1700 by French explorer Pierre Le Sueur. Its chiefs were members of the Little Crow dynasty from the early 18th century. Though Mdewakanton genealogy is uncertain before 1800, the chief buried just

Pierre [*Minnesota*] joyns the Mississipi.[73] On the morning of the 15th I found my canoe froze hard in the ice of which the river was full continually coming down. I judged it intirely impossible to go up any further by water, concluded to leave Jacko the Iroquois with the canoe and baggage and to take the Frenchman along with me and the young prince of Winebago who arrived at this place about the same time I did to go to the Falls of St. Anthony [*by land*] or further if I could.

The same day I arrived at the falls and measured the cascade which I found to be about 29 feet. About the middle of the fall is a small island and a little below is another small island [*Spirit*] containg about an acre of land with several oak trees on which are a vast many eagles' nests. It is judged the reason of such a resort of this fowl at this place is occasiond by the great numbers of fish that is killd in attempting to get up and down the falls. The great quantity of ice on the banks and about prevented my being so nier as I should have been had it been otherwise. The portage I measured and found it 220 rods of level land except some rising ground between the small meadow below the falls and the plain which is much higher land. I had heard before I came to see these falls that they was sixty feet perpendicular. I don't believe that the whole of the rapids above and below the cascade including the hole could be equal to that. The land about these falls is a level spacious plain with a very few small trees of oak and hickery. I could not but remark how different the land is about these falls when I had always taken notice that land about such a large cataracks was very rough and uneven.[74]

before Carver's visit could have been the first Little Crow. See Henry R. School-craft, *Summary Narrative of an Exploratory Expedition to the Sources of the Mississippi River*, 160 (Philadelphia, 1855); Coues, ed., *Pike Expeditions*, 1:85n.

The burial grounds referred to were probably in Indian Mounds Park, St. Paul. See Holmquist and Brookins, *Minnesota's Major Historic Sites*, 17; Long, in *Minnesota Historical Collections*, 2:30.

[73] The St. Pierre, now the Minnesota River, joins the Mississippi within present-day St. Paul. It appears as "Ouatebamenisouté" on Guillaume de l'Isle's map of the Mississippi (1702) reproduced in Johnson, ed., *Aspects of Upper Great Lakes Anthropology*, 168, and as "Rivière St. Pierre" on De l'Isle's map of Canada and New France published in Paris in 1703. In *Travels* and on its accompanying map, Carver also called the stream Wadapawmenesoter or Waddapawmenesotor. See Upham, *Minnesota Geographic Names*, 2–4; Appendix 2, J79, below.

[74] *Travels*, Plate 1, is the earliest published sketch of the falls located in present Minneapolis. Its vertical fall was later more accurately established at 16½ feet. The drop of the falls and the rapids below is about 75 feet. Carver's plate shows Spirit Island, which divided the cataract at the time of Hennepin's visit in 1680, in

[NOVEMBER 17, 1766–APRIL 25, 1767.][75] This day as I could not persuade my people to travel further north with me by reason of the coldness of the climate and season, I returned to my canoe, cut it out of the ice, concluded to take my rout up the river St. Pierre, as I judged that this river came from the west in its general course. Of consequence I supposed that it would be later in the fall before it would be shut up with ice. After having entered the mouth of the river, which cost us no little trouble by reason of the thickness of the ice which we were forced to cut away with our axes, I proceeded up the river.

On the 20th of Novemr arrived at the Grand Encampment of part of five bands of the Naudowessee.[76]

This day gave a speech in counsel to the river bands which came to hunt among their breathren of the plains. As I was doubtfull whether this country of the Naudowessee of the plains could be calld within the limits of the Brittish Dominion, thought it most prudent not to give any offense to the Spaniards

the river below the falls because they had since receded. N. H. Winchell and Warren Upham, *The Geology of Minnesota*, 2: 329–333 (St. Paul, 1888), discuss the recession and Carver's description in *Travels*, 69–71, concluding that the small island at the brink of the falls, which was also noted by Pike in 1805, was a rock outcropping that collapsed before 1817, surviving only as debris in the river channel. The rock shown in the crest on the east side of the falls was "the toe of Hennepin Island . . . the intervening portion of the foot being still submerged." John G. Shea, ed., Hennepin, *Description of Louisiana*, 200 (New York, 1880), recorded the falls' height as "forty or fifty feet"; Thwaites, ed., Hennepin, *New Discovery*, 1: 223, as 50 or 60 feet.

[75] At this point Carver abandoned dated entries, resuming them on April 26, 1767 (p. 116, below). His "Survey Journal," p. 159, below, records an 8-mile excursion beyond the falls unmentioned here. *Travels*, 71–74, claimed to have continued the journey northward until November 21, arriving at the St. Francis (Elk) River, 60 (really 35) miles above the falls, and then returning by canoe to the mouth of the Minnesota on November 25, at which time the Winnebago prince left him. The journal text for this period seems more likely to be truthful, for there could be no plausible reason to omit a 4-day journey. Such an excursion might have been added to the published version to enhance Carver's reputation and make his acquaintance with the area seem more comparable to Hennepin's.

[76] On p. 160, below, Carver estimates that he had traveled 67 miles from the mouth of the Minnesota River, or a little less than half the distance to the Green (Blue Earth) River, by November 20, when he came to the "Grand Encampment." Since he overestimates the distance to the Blue Earth River almost by a factor of two, this would place the "Grand Encampment" near Belle Plaine in present Scott County, Minn., a spot traditionally known as the site of a Dakota village. See Samuel W. Pond, "The Dakotas or Sioux in Minnesota as They Were in 1834," in *Minnesota Historical Collections*, 12: 321, 322 (1908); Babcock, in *Minnesota Archaeologist*, 11: 137–141.

by giving belts and presents to those who they might think was their allies, tho at the same time I did not think that Spanish Louisiania by their first charter could extend so far north as to the river St. Pierre.[77] In this counsel I made a present of a belt, a quantity of powder and balls, and a few dozen of knives and some vermilion &c. The speech I gave to them and their answer is in manuscript by itself.[78]

The country of the Naudowessee of the plains about the river St. Pierre exceeds for pleasantness and richness of soil all the places that ever I have seen. On each side of the river which is very full of windings, is large medows with scarcely any trees. Here grows plenty of wild baum [*mint*], hopps, angelica, nettles, and all sorts of herbs of a most aromatick smell. The banks of the river and many other places covered with vines hanging full of heavy clusters of grapes which I found as late as November. The juce of these grapes was very rich and imagine 'twould make the best of wines. For a space (all the way when I was on this river) between the medows and the plains is thousands of acres of marshy land where grows vast quantitys of Indian rice where the Naudowessee get their supplys and cannot gather the hundredth part[79] which is a great means of a vast resort of all sorts of water fowl in spring and fall: ⟨swans, geese and ducks, storks [*herons?*], cormorants, a few parrots and many other species.⟩ A great many geese and ducks lay eggs and hatch their young in these marshes ⟨on bogs and small islands in which nature seems to direct for safety and hatch in May. The marshes are so continually covered with water among the rice that a small canoe may go all over where it grows, as is the manner of the natives. About three weeks before it ripens the squaws paddle in among it and tie bunches of the heads together to keep the wind or fowls from shelling it, and when thorough ripe bring their canoes again under the bunch and beat the grain out which falls all into the

⟨*Version II*⟩

⟨*Version II*

---

[77] According to *Articles Préliminaires de Paix entre le Roi, le Roi D'Espagne et le Roi de la Grande-Bretagne, Signés à Fontainbleau le 3 Novembre 1762*, 13 (Paris, 1762), the boundary was to run through the middle of the Mississippi River to its source. Carver's statement concerning Spain's "first charter" must refer to the grant of the territory west of the Mississippi to Spain by France prior to the actual Treaty of 1763.

[78] These speeches have not been found. They are not in the journals, nor were they published in *Travels*. For other speeches, see pp. 118–120, below.

[79] Version II reads "the thousandth part."

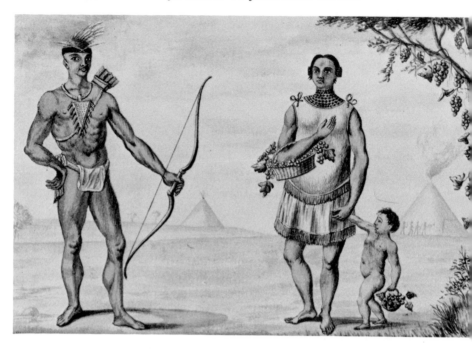

An unidentified Indian family from Version IV. This group was later engraved and printed in Travels *as "A Man & Woman of the Naudowessie."*

canoe and fills it several times in a day. The remaining labor is no more than to dry it and bury in the ground what they reserve for future occasions.)[80]

Version II)

The plains back of these marshes afford a very beautifull prospect of gradual ascents and descents with here and there a grove of trees some of which are neat as tho planted by art, large groves of maple sutable for the sugar manufacture, plenty of [*crab*] apple trees which bear an apple much better than the common crab apple on the Mississippi, and plumbs of a very good taste.

[80] On parrots, see Kellogg, ed., *Charlevoix Journal,* 2: 190. Carver probably did not witness a wild rice harvest, for it normally occurred in September, as he noted in *Travels,* 524. The Minnesota River Valley is no longer a wild-rice-producing area. For a thorough discussion of Indian methods of gathering and processing this grass, see Jenks, in Bureau of American Ethnology, *Nineteenth Annual Report,* 2: 1019–1137.

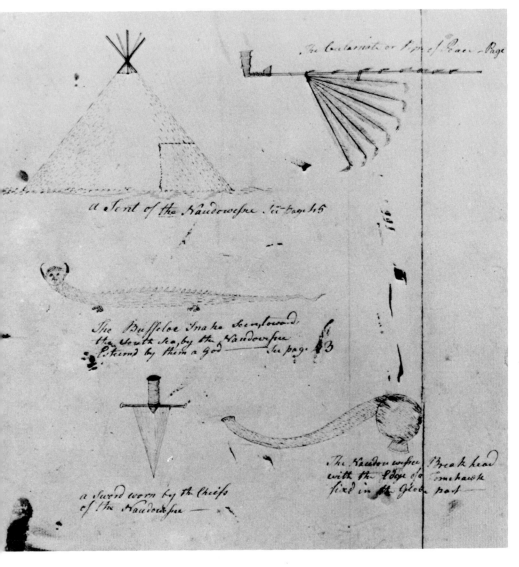

Sketches intended to illustrate Version I of the journals. The pictures of the pipe, dagger, and club were used in Travels, *Plate 4.*

The Naudowessee get wild potatoes very sweet much like the Carolina potatoes only somthing more ⟨dry and⟩ mealy. I thought them to exceed those in the provinces. In short almost every necessary of life grows here spontaneous. ⟨And could salt be easily had of which the Indians say there be several springs whose water tasted like the salt I had with me, this country might alone suffice its inhabitants.⟩ The plains which extend to the western ocean by accounts from the savages teem with large droves of buffaloe, elk, deer, bear, and other game, also tygers.[81]

⟨*Version II*⟩

⟨*Version II*

Version II⟩

The Naudowessee have made the figure of a serpent of a monsterous shape and size which they call *Tautongo Omlishco* which signifies in English the buffeloe snake,[82] it having horns (and four feet and claws like a bear) they say 'tis three fathoms long near as big round as a buffaloe with a black head and tail; the middle from neck to tail is red having somthing like fins on the back. The chief of the warriours of the Mottobauntoway band[83] who was my particular friend told me he saw one of

---

[81] The only apples native to this area are crab apples, called by the French *pomme sauvage*. See *Travels,* 503. Wild potatoes could be one of several roots used by the Indians of the region: *Psoralea esculenta,* called *tepsina* by the Dakota, or the ground nut or Indian potato, *Glycine apios.* On the uses of these plants, as well as wild plums and maples, by the Dakota, see Melvin R. Gilmore, "Uses of Plants by the Indians of the Missouri River Region," in Bureau of American Ethnology, *Thirty-third Annual Report,* 86, 87, 92, 94, 100 (Washington, D.C., 1919).

Salt springs existed near Belle Plaine in nearby Scott County, and unsuccessful efforts were made to develop them commercially in the 1870s. See Folwell, *Minnesota,* 4:480; *Minneapolis Tribune,* May 29, 1870. Others were located farther west in the Red River Valley. See Keating, *Narrative,* 2:39; Newton H. Winchell, *Report Concerning the Salt Spring Lands,* 12 (St. Paul, 1874). The "tygers" could have been either lynx or puma. See *Travels,* 442.

[82] Figures outlined in boulders are known to have existed in Murray County, Minn. Among them was a buffalo with "two lines (trails) of small stones 2½ feet asunder and running toward what has apparently been a stone heap or cairn," according to Theodore H. Lewis, in Winchell, *Aborigines,* 107. See also *Aborigines,* 199, for recorded mounds and piled stones in the Swan Lake area, where Carver may have wintered (p. 17, above). It is interesting to note that the name of the chief, Ottahtongoomlishcah, in *Travels,* 380 (spelled Otohtongoomlisheaw on the Carver grant), is similar to that given here for "buffalo snake." In 1867 an investigator of Carver's Cave reported finding an Indian petroglyph of a snake there; he suggested that this was the "autograph" of Ottahtongoomlishcah. See *St. Paul Pioneer,* January 31, 1867. On the etymology, see Appendix 2, J14, 27, 75, below.

[83] The chief of the warriors has not been firmly identified, although the Mottobauntoway, more usually called the Matantonwan, were one of the two early primary divisions of the Mdewakanton Sioux, according to Hodge, *Handbook,*

The Buffeloe Snake Seen towards the South

Carver's sketch of the buffalo snake from Version IV.

these serpents on the plains with a young one which was in the
crotch of a large tree by which he suppos'd that the old ones often
climb up on the trees. The figure of this serpent I have annex'd to
this journal.

The Naudowessee in their manner of goverment differ in
some respects from the other nations of Indians and may more
properly be call'd a common wealth or republick. They are divided into bands to each of which they have given distinguishing
names as we do to regiments. The chiefs of these bands are
hereditary in their families. Besides these every band has a chiefe
who is call'd the chief of the warriors whose office does not
decend to him in his family but is chosen by the people or
ascends to it by merit. He never goes out to war but orders all
the departments destind against the enemy and gives them their
routs and particular instructions as far as is needfull. There is
another chief in each band who is call'd the second chief of the
warriours. He goes out with the party and they obey him as their
commander. This officer governs the soldiers in camp. These
soldiers are always kept up and are arm'd in readiness to go at a
minuts notice on any emergency whatever.[84]

1:819. The man usually regarded as the hereditary chief of the Mdewakanton
during this period, and sometimes associated with the Matantonwan band, is
Wabasha I (1718–99), who may have been living at this time at Tetankatane or
"Old Village" on the Minnesota River. On this chief, see Winchell, *Aborigines*,
540–543, and pp. 115, 117, below.

[84] Carver's description of the political and military structure of the Dakota is a
concise sketch of a subject treated at length in Ruth Landes, *The Mystic Lake
Sioux: Sociology of the Mdewakantonwan Santee*, 28–94 (Madison, 1968); Hassrick,
The Sioux, 11–31.

The names of the bands of the Naudowessee that are under connections to each other are as follows

Mottontoway [*Matantonwan?*]	1
Mottobauntoway [*Matantonwan?*]	2
Minewantonko [*Mdewakanton?*]	3
Wahpeentowah [*Wahpeton*]	4
Shahsweentowah [*Sisseton*]	5
Nehoggotowannah [*Nehogatawonah*]	6
Tetowah [*Teton*]	7
Shyanawh [*Cheyenne*]	8
Osracuttah [*Wazikute?*]	9
Ohah [*Omaha?*]	10
Mahtahn [*Mandan?*]	11

Besides these eleaven bands there is another calld the Assnibboils which some years passed revo[l]ted from the others on some dispute between them and ever since have been at war with these bands. The Assnibboils live near Lake Winipeek and are much connected with the Christenoes and trade chiefly to Hudson's Bay.[85]

These bands of the Naudowessee are some of them 300 strong. They hold continual wars with the Chippeways and the Illinois Indians and the Pawnees on the Missure and the Asnibboils.[86] From the two last they bring a great many slaves every year which they exchange with the traders for such things as they want. They have been known to give a slave for one gorget made only of sea shells. This is done by the more remote bands who have no knowledge of Europeans and only trade with their brethrean [of] the river bands who of late years have opened a trade with the French and English.

On the manners and customs of the Naudowessee I shall be as particular as possible, as I was six months among them & had

[85] On the first three bands, see Hodge, *Handbook,* 1:819, 826–828. On the others, see Meyer, *Santee Sioux,* 15; Swanton, *Indian Tribes,* 276, 278, 282, 286; note 29, above; and *Travels,* 59, 80, 109. The Cheyenne, an Algonquian language group, were not Sioux, although the two tribes at times were allies and often intermarried. The Omaha and Mandan spoke a Siouan language, but were not bands of the Dakota. See Hodge, *Handbook,* 1:251, 257, 796; 2:119.

[86] For Dakota population estimates, see note 88, below. The primary home of the Pawnee was the Platte River. See note 147, below.

oppertunity to learn somthing of their dialect. These people live in tents of leather taken either from the elk or buffaloe. Their tents are fixd on poles in form of a pyrimid or cone, open at the top for the smoke to pass up, ⟨some of them 20 feet wide & near ⟨*Version II* as high. They have also canoes of skins made a little pliable.[87] These they pack up and carry with them and when they wou'd cross a water cut sticks to stretch them on and quickly fit them for passage. Even their bark canoes differ from all nations.⟩ *Version II*⟩ They are continually on the move, seldom remain more than a month in one place, in summer never so long as that. They pride themselves much in being good soldiers and brave warriours and truly they are much dreaded as such by all their neighbours for they are not only esteemd great warriours but the most numerous of any nation known in North America, for they told me they could count six thousand warriors and that they knew not how many bands they had to the westward which they was not acquainted with for they say that the people as far as the great waters, pointing to the west, spake their tongue.[88]

They are very fond of prying into futurities. They have several juglers among them who easily impose on their belief. For instance I saw one of these jugler who they took and bound fast both hand and foot and over that they bound cords several times round even from his shoulders to his feet and after that rolld him up in a buffeloe skin and bound cords several times round the whole and then laid him between a number of stakes drove firm in the ground on each side and then all stood at a distance. The jugler after some jargon peculiar to himself would begin to be in a great agony and sweat after some convulsive throws and dis-

[87] Carver is here referring to the bullboat of the plains Indians. On its construction, see Edwin T. Adney and Howard I. Chapelle, *The Bark Canoes and Skin Boats of North America,* 220 (U.S. National Museum, *Bulletins,* no. 230 — Washington, 1964).

[88] A late 18th-century estimate quoted by Jenks, in Bureau of American Ethnology, *Nineteenth Annual Report,* 2: 1108, placed the number of Dakota warriors in 1764 at 4,300 out of a total population of 21,500; Hutchins' estimate in Hicks, ed., *Topographical Description,* 137, is 10,000 total in 1778; Swanton, *Indian Tribes,* 283, quotes James Mooney's estimate of 25,000 Dakota of all divisions in 1780. Carver's 6,000 figure could reflect quite a different grouping of "allies" than the other computations. On the importance of the Dakota and their distribution westward to "the great waters," possibly meaning the Missouri River which was at this time the approximate western boundary of the Dakota, see Hassrick, *The Sioux,* 22, 57, 62; Swanton, *Indian Tribes,* 283.

tortions of body. He in the space of an hour left all his incumber-
ances behind and protended to foretell whatever he had a mind
to. I knew some things they foretold very exact but whether by
chance or magick I am not able to say but am rather apt to think
'twas chance. These juglers protend to great skill in medicin.
They commonly sit by the sick patient with a *quicapoo* or rattle shell for whole nights together making a noise with the rattle
and singing to drive away the *Shejah Waukon* as they call it (in
English the bad spirit).[89]

⟨*Version II Insert 8*   ⟨As to the story of the cunjurer page ye 12 [*101*] I can only add
that those instances are certainly frequent among several of those
western nations, and I imagine it to be somthing of the same
kind which was frequently taken notice of among the first plant-
ers of America who imagined that in these nocturnal revels
which are commonly held in night calld by the Indians pow-
wows the divil was raised and that they invokd some infernal
spirits to inform them into futurities, as it was then and is now
believed by many that they could by such magical machinations
fortell any thing relating to the common affairs of life. But this
custom among those nations more acquainted with Europeans
seems to be generally exploded in proportion to that acquaintance.

As to my own opinion concerning what I see among those
remote nations, tho I acknowledge that some things which I
have known them fortell has hapened according to their predic-
tions, yet in every instance apearantly so extraordinary I imagin
it to be only a deception by frequent practicing whereby they
impose on the vulgar, for as the author on the natural history of
Gu[i]ana justly observes that the vulgar of all nations are lyable

---

[89] Insert 8, which follows, was marked by Carver to be inserted at the beginning of this paragraph. Here it follows the paragraph in order to improve the
sense of the passage.

Both James W. Lynd, "History of the Dakotas," and Pond, in *Minnesota Histor-
ical Collections,* 2: 158; 12: 421, ascribe similar abilities to Dakota jugglers, and the
former notes that such escapes were considered "in the highest degree *wakan.*"
Carver here combines the functions of the juggler, medicine man, and shaman.
For earlier and later discussions, see Shea, ed., Hennepin, *Description of Louisiana,*
284–287; E. D. Neill, "Dakota Land and Dakota Life," in *Minnesota Historical
Collections,* 1: 218–223 (Reprint Ed., 1902); Landes, *Mystic Lake Sioux,* 48–66.
Carver's use of the word *quicapoo* may refer to *iċakoka,* the Dakota word for
rattle. Charlevoix called it *chichikoué;* on this and medicine men, see Kellogg,
ed., *Charlevoix Journal,* 1: 299; 2: 153–159. On *Shejah Waukon,* see note 103, below.

to be deceived and the Indians are all vulgar.[90] Yet I never see tho I have often been within twenty feet of these conjurers in the time of their being bound as aforesaid, any thing whereby I could possetivily account for the manner they are let loose.⟩

⟨They lay great stress on dreams and things they dream esteem portenteous. The crow, raven, and owl are looked upon as ominous birds, the wolf the same. This last they never kill with their bows and arrows as they say the same bow or gun will never kill anything afterwards. They will, however, take them in snares, or with their dogs if they can.[91]

They bury the bones of the beaver and elk very carefully after eating the flesh, thinking that the spirits of these animals have influence on the living ones and will inform them how they have been treated, which if ill will afterward be detrimental to their success in hunting.

When they have bad dreams they will black themselves all over and fast sometimes for two or three days in proportion as they conceive the premonition may affect them.

On discovering any malicious design against a friend such as laying in wait &c. they think it enough to inquire which way he intends that day which being informed they only say, "Take care, friend, there is a dog on the wayside that may hurt you." The informer need not be more explicit.

When a band have resided any considerable time in a place and determine to leave it they kill a dog and lie him on a pelt with his face to the sun at noonday. They do the same when they come to the place where they intend any considerable stay for hunting. This I imagine is a sacrifice to the sun for good hunting weather.⟩[92]

Version II
Insert 8⟩

⟨*Version II*

Version II⟩

[90] This is a reference to Edward Bancroft, *Essay on the Natural History of Guiana, In South America,* 310–317 (London, 1769) describing witch-doctor techniques used in Dutch Guiana. In its treatment of plants and animals, Bancroft's book is similar to the natural history section of Carver's *Travels.* In view of their common interests, Massachusetts backgrounds, and their arrival in London about the same time, it is likely that Carver and Bancroft knew each other. See *Dictionary of American Biography,* 1: 563 (1928).

[91] On the significance of dreams, see Kellogg, ed., *Charlevoix Journal,* 2: 144–149; Hassrick, *The Sioux,* 229–239. In Dakota belief, the black wolf and the white crow were thought to drive away buffalo. Refusal to kill the wolf may be a reflection of a totem or a taboo upon an animal. See Lynd, in *Minnesota Historical Collections,* 2: 153, 161, 163n, 164.

[92] On the sacrifice of dogs and other animals as votive offerings by the Dakota, see Pond, in *Minnesota Historical Collections,* 12: 420.

When anyone of this nation dies their nearest women relations begin to cry and make a loud lamentation and cut gashes in their legs and feet untill the blood runs in streams. This from day to day they provoke by pricking and squeazing till it either gets well or kills them. 'Tis often that they with grief and by their manner of wounding themselves lose their lives and follow their friends which they seem to be very fond of, especially if they regard them much. I knew a man of this nation while I was with them who lost a son of about 5 years old. The child being dead the father, according to the custom of the men in mourning, pierced arrows through his arms till by the loss of blood he contracted a fever and dyed in about a month's time. The bereaved widow after the death of her husband seemed to dry up her tears and cease her mourning by taking comfort with the thought that her child had its father in the other world to take care of it, for they hold to a future existence in some other world. These imaginations are attended with very imperfect ideas in these ignorant people. The men seldom are heard to weep aloud. The women are extraordinary on that account. I could but take notice how that the mother of the child I just mentioned would sing to the corps of her son telling over in a sort of a singing tone how it had slain its enemies and taken prisoners, gained laurels fit for a chief, and how it had killd the buffaloe, outrun the deer, chased the elk, taken the beaver with his craft, inriched it self with the otter, cloathed it self by its valour and dexterity with the quills and feathers of the woodcock, the duck, and the porcupine and many other such like harrangues.[93]

By these elegies they mean to signifie no more then what they think probable the child might have performed had it lived to mature years. They likewise tell the corps how they will raise a number of warriors who shall go and fall upon and kill some of its enemies to revenge its death, which they frequently do the first oppertunity that presents, and if they take any prisoners they distribute them among the bereaved till their loss is made up, ⟨tho they still retain the barbarous custom of roasting their ⟨*Version II* prisoners alive, especially those advanced in years who will not sell well for slaves, never practicing this cruelty on women or

---

[93] Expressions of grief among the Dakota discussed by Neill and Pond respectively, in *Minnesota Historical Collections,* 1:225; 12:478–485, in general substantiate Carver's description. See also Landes, *Mystic Lake Sioux,* 153–160.

children. When they design to torture one to death they black him all over and crown his head with the skin of a crow or raven. Thus they lead him to the stake where they make him sing and dance and invite him to tell over all his war exploits in which he spares not to recognize what he has formerly done to his now tormentors, which often hastens his death by them justly esteemed the greatest favor he can expect. 'Tis worth observation that all the while they are preparing their victim for execution they one and all weep and make loud lamentation.)[94] *Version II*)

It is common for these people especially the women whenever they dream of their deceassd relations to rise immediately out of their beds tho in the middle of the night and dark and go at a distance from the camp and make a very bitter outcry. I have often been disturbed with their weeping in the night. This they will do tho it be ten years after. I have heard them weep for relations that had been dead for many years.

Tho this nation like the roving Arabians or Tarters continually move yet they have burying places where they take the utmost pains possible to enter all their dead in those places.[95] When they have occasion to wander far from such places, as is often the case in winters when they are out a hunting and any of their band dies, they then role him or her up in a skin and make a scaffold on some strong tree and their repose their dead till they have occassion to return to their burying ground. If it be in the sum-

[94] The Chippewa name for the Dakota was *Ab-boin-ug* (with variations), meaning "roasters" for their supposed custom of roasting captives, according to Warren, *History of the Ojibway*, 36; but in the French period Nicolas Perrot, in Emma H. Blair, ed., *The Indian Tribes of the Upper Mississippi Valley and Region of the Great Lakes*, 1:169 (Cleveland, 1911) reported that the Dakota burned captives only in retaliation when their own warriors had been burned. Carver did not specifically ascribe these torture customs to the Dakota in *Travels*, 331–348, where his account is similar to that on Iroquois customs in Kellogg, ed., *Charlevoix Journal*, 1:354–356. The roasting of captives would seem to suggest cannibalism, a practice ascribed to the Dakota in Shea, ed., Hennepin, *Description of Louisiana*, 315, and Edwin James, ed., *Narrative of the Captivity and Adventures of John Tanner*, 380 (New York, 1830). Later writers report more kindly treatment of prisoners; see Lynd, in *Minnesota Historical Collections*, 2:168; Keating, *Narrative*, 1:397–403.

[95] A relationship between the Tartars and the American Indians was suggested as early as 1614, and mentioned with particular reference to the Dakota in Kellogg, ed., *Charlevoix Journal*, 1:17n, 18, 262; Coues, ed., *Pike Expeditions*, 1:350; and *Travels*, 212. Carver's observations on burial customs below conform to those of Pond, in *Minnesota Historical Collections*, 12:478–485; minor differences in detail were recorded in Winchell, *Aborigines*, 509–517.

mer season, then they only carry back the bones after the flesh is so as to fall from them. I have been informd that some of the bands burn their dead and preserve their bones till they have occasion to return to their burying ground. The relations of the deceasd while they are thus lodged on a tree go daily and weep under them, cut of their hair and leave it scattered about under-

⟨*Version II*⟩ neath. I have seen a beaten path round such trees ⟨like a high-way⟩ which I supposd to have been done some years before. It is surprizing to see how these people afflict themselves in mourn-ing for their dead.

Their marriage customs are very peculiar. When two young people are about to joyn in wedlock they walk out both together on the parade which is generally in the middle of the camp where a number assembles to assist in the ceremony. Among these is one of their underchiefs who in a short speach informs the spec-tators that them two, calling over their names, are come there that the whole may witness that they love each other that he takes her for his wife (which they call *takshedigo*) to get wood, dress his victuals, take care of the tent both while he is at home and out a hunting and at war, after which they take hold of each others' hands, and the whole of the spectators discharge their arrows over the heads of the bride and bridegroom, after which the man turns his back to the bride. She gets on him and he carrys her to his tent. The spectators give a loud cohoop and wish them happy all their days. Thus ends the ceremony.[96]

The Naudowessee are great poligamists. It is common to see the men have three wives at once and some chiefs have five or six. These live like sisters in the same house together and never are jealous of one another. 'Tis often that they marry two or three sisters for they hold that such will agree best in the same house. These women are no other then slaves to their husbands who when they are with their wives scarsly ever untie their shoes, they being always willing to do the meanest offices of

[96] This marriage ceremony is similar to those described in Landes, *Mystic Lake Sioux*, 131; and Mary Eastman, *Dahcotah; or, Life and Legends of the Sioux Around Fort Snelling*, 108 (Reprint Ed., Minneapolis, 1962). See also Pond, in *Minnesota Historical Collections*, 12: 453–456. The expanded passage in *Travels*, 373, based on this paragraph, was, however, criticized as "fabulous" in Keating, *Narrative*, 1: 324. Carver reversed the Dakota words for sister and wife; *takshedigo* means sister. See Appendix 2, J82, 99, below.

kindness without ever finding fault. It is common for those who are so well stored with a plurality of wives to be very kind in oblidging strangers that come among them which they will do and oblige their women to comply however unwilling they may be. The women of the Naudowessee are much handsomer then the more eastern nations some of which have very fair hair and a skin but a very little inferiour to white people. I have seen some of the women very freckled which is very uncommon among our Indians. They seem to have a modesty beyound what is common among other nations, tho their soldiers are very great debauchees. For fear of them the women never dare to walk in a dark night without having company and a torch.[97]

Women with their monthly disorders retire from all company and live by themselves in a tent kept for that purpose and suffer none to come near them till they are thoroughly puryfied. The common time for maids' retirement the first time is 40 days. The men will not so much as look into these tents nor light a pipe by any fire they have used, as they look upon it unclean.[98]

The Naudowessee are a very merry sociable people full of mirth and good humour. They spend whole nights in feasting and dancing. The men dance with out any great matter of motion, which is not so common among other nations of Indians who use a great many distortions of body. They step with both feet alike and keep time very well with the musick which consists of a skin streatchd upon a hallow tub like what we call a Negro's banjo upon which one well skilld in musick striks with a stick to proportion the time. At the same time they sing and

[97] Although later writers confirm most of Carver's observations, they expressed the view that, while polygamy existed, it was not general among the Dakota and disagreed somewhat concerning the position of women. Pond, in *Minnesota Historical Collections,* 12: 456–458, 463–469, wrote sympathetically of the sexual morality of the Santee as he knew them in 1834, noting that Dakota women were "not the right material to be made slaves," that "adultery was not rare," but that chastity was expected of unmarried women. On these points, see also Keating, *Narrative,* 1: 394, 404; Landes, *Mystic Lake Sioux,* 111, 129, 139; Neill, in *Minnesota Historical Collections,* 1: 234–236. McGee, in Bureau of American Ethnology, *Fifteenth Annual Report,* 185, described the skin of the Dakota as "the usual coppery cast characteristic of the native American."

[98] The use of menstrual lodges by the Dakota was mentioned in *Travels,* 236, and confirmed by Hassrick, in *The Sioux,* 41. The latter gives the period of confinement as 4 days rather than 40.

rattle with a shell like a goad [*gourd*] shell with some carnels of corn in it.[99]

They have perticular feasts which resembles very much the customs of some ancient heathens calld feasts or sacrifices to the goddes Venus. This is a feast made by anyone of the female sex of any note who is a mind to distinguish herself in such rites and ceremonys. The manner of the ceremony is as follows: the young woman invites a great number of men, commonly the principle part of the most respectable of the band, prepares a dish of rice inrichd with bear's greese. The reason of this feast being of rice is its being esteemd a sort of female food which they more commonly eat then the men, and another reason is its being a sort of provision that they more perticularly have the charge of gathering and preparing more then any other sort. After each one has finishd his dish and some time spent in dancing she retires to one side of the tent where is a bed prepared on purpose where she is followd by one at a time till the whole of the guests have known her, after which they all retire. She is esteemd the heroin of the band and seldom fails of geting a husband of distinction. I knew a woman who they told me gave her body to 40 stout men at one feast. She had after that a good man for her husband and was counted a virtuous woman by all her acquaint-

⟨*Version III*⟩ an[ces.] ⟨But if at any other time the woman should be found in adultery with any of these her former guests or any other she is looked upon as a whore.⟩[100]

They have among this people a particular society into which a member to be admited requires a great deal of ceremony. This is calld the medicin society. Their method of admiting is as follows. After some time is spent in dancing it is common for the great chief of the warriors who is commonly a man greatly respected by the populace with his attendance of women and servants to enter within the circle where there is rails put up round to keep the spectators from the members. He comes in

[99] Pond, in *Minnesota Historical Collections*, 12:387, 399, found many of the Santee "entertaining in conversation, full of wit, good sense, and good humor, with a great relish for jokes and quick at repartee," and described the drums and rattles in use among them in 1834. Frances Densmore, *Teton Sioux Music* (Bureau of American Ethnology, *Bulletins*, no. 61 — Washington, D.C., 1918) discussed and illustrated traditional Dakota instruments in detail.

[100] The bear's grease feast was a part of types of cousin conflict described by Landes, *Mystic Lake Sioux*, 119–127. This story is in *Travels*, 245.

with a rattle in his hand shaking it as he walks and singing. He with his attendends are all members otherwise they would not dare to enter within the rails. He is conducted round the whole circle each one taking the members which are already seated by the hand saying as they pass round, *"Waukon washta kitchewaw che,"* which is in English, "God bless you, my good friend," after which they seat themselves in their places. When they receive the above blessing they say nothing but hold up their hands and look very solemn which here is a token of thanks.[101]

The member that is to be admitted is seatd on a cushion of skins or blankets if any they have, on his knees, with a member behind him to support him as he is supposed to be in danger of fainting under the opperation, after which a principle member streatches out his hand and makes a speach with an audable voice informing them that there is a member to be admited, reminding of them at the same time of the solemnity of the occasion, exhorting them to pay respect to order & decency, after which two members skillfull in the science each having a skin calld *wawkon chee* (which is either a martin or a squirrel skin or somthing like it which are ornimentded with curious workmanship by their women which is by them esteemd as sacred, for they the members of this society seldom go to war without these), these 2 members pass three times round the ring, each time as they pass are more & more agitated with convulsive motions, which they say is caused by the being possessd of the medicin which they are about to communicate to the new member, after which they spring of a suden to the new brother, lay their *wawkon* skins on him ⟨at which he⟩ immediately faints and lies for dead. ⟨*Version II*⟩

At this time they take care to put somthing in his mouth by slight of hand unknown to the spectators after which he presently begins to revive. They then take him up and then strike on

---

[101] The Medicine Dance Society was not peculiar to the Sioux, being found also among the Chippewa, Winnebago, Fox, and other tribes. The social and political significance of the society is discussed in Landes, *Mystic Lake Sioux,* 57–59, 87, 159. Descriptions of the similar initiation ceremonies among the Dakota and Chippewa, confirming the essentials of Carver's account, can be found in Pond, in *Minnesota Historical Collections,* 12:409–412; Martha C. Bray, ed., *Journals of Joseph N. Nicollet . . . 1836–37,* 200–209; W. J. Hoffman, "The Midé wiwin or 'Grand Medicine Society' of the Ojibway," in Bureau of American Ethnology, *Seventh Annual Report,* 149–300 (Washington, D.C., 1891). The ceremony is described in *Travels,* 272–278.

his back. He at the same time, appearing as one rising from the dead, vomits up the medicin which these officiating members receive into their hands, which I saw look like a large white bead or wampam which one of these members took in his hand and went round the circle of members by the power of which they seemd to be thrown into convulsive motions. Each member on seeing it protended to receive a shock like the electricity, after which they throw the medicin the second time at the new member which again has the same effect on him as it had the first time. Then they take him and strip of his old cloaths and dress him in new and clean garments which was never before put on, and then he is esteemd by the society as a compleet member and is then saluted by the whole brotherhood and sisterhood.

The remainder of the day they spend in dancing and communicating their medisons which has the same appearant magical effect as before mentiond. I have seen a dozen of them on the ground at once, for when they dance round in the circle making a strange noise, they all of a sudden put the *wakon* skin in to the face of a brother or sister. He or she instantly falls as tho they was dead but soon recover. There is neither brother nor sisters admited into this society but those that bear the best of characters among them. After this is all ended they having a number of sacrificed dogs boyld which is servd out in portions to each, they eat, make themselves merry, and return to their tents, for dogs are eat by them in all extraordinary feasts.

The Naudowessee worship or esteem all extraordinaries in nature as gods, viz., the sun and moon, the earth in general, the greatest of rivers such as the Mississippi, the largest lakes, cataracks, mountains, rocks, or stones that by any means resemble in shape either men or beasts. They have to each of these perticular gods that preside over those extraordinaries to whom they pay homage by giving presents such as tobacco and beads and wampam. I observd that when some of them came down with me from the river St. Pierre to the Mississipi that they made a speach to the god of this water praying for good weather and good success at the same time made an offering of tobacco &c. When I came to the Falls of St. Anthony one who was with me [*Scha-chip-ka-ka?*] who had never seen such falls before made an extraordinary address to the god of this falls, stripd himself of his wrist clasps, neck beads &c. and cast them into the cascade.[102]

They hold that there is two superiour spirits in perpetual opposition to each other, the one being infinitly good and kind, the other they hold to be a composition of evils from which all the calamities that befalls either whole communities or individuals they imagine do proceed, and that all the misfortunes in life are in his sole power to either inflict or prevent. For this reason when any is sick or in any other trouble they pray and make use of such customs as they are use to to divert the evil spirit and are fully of the opinion that offerings of tobacco &c. will mittigate his anger. They give out as a reason for this that the good spirit being unalterable so never seeks to harm anyone, so that they look upon it to be labour in vain to pray to a being to do them good who they never thought would do them any hurt. However incoherant this principle may be yet I imagin 'twould not be an easey matter to bring them from it.[103]

In the counsels of the Naudowessee the pipe is much made use of. This pipe which they call *shandnuapaw* is adorned with ten or twelve large hawk's feathers, the quill ends fastened together. The feather ends hang like a fan opened. The upper feather is fastened along to the stem of the pipe. This pipe feathered is esteemed sacred by all nations in these parts and is carryed in truces as a flag. It is common to paint it of a sky colour to signifie a clear sky or peace and tranquillity.[104]

[102] Sacrifices at the falls were also described in Thwaites, ed., Hennepin, *New Discovery*, 1:277, and many sources confirm the Dakota identification with objects in nature. See, for example, Gideon H. Pond, "Dakota Superstitions," and S. W. Pond, respectively, in *Minnesota Historical Collections*, 2:215–255; 12:401–409; J. Owen Dorsey, "A Study of Siouan Cults," in Bureau of American Ethnology, *Eleventh Annual Report*, 361–500 (Washington, D.C., 1894). Carver's account of the young Winnebago at the Falls of St. Anthony is expanded in *Travels*, 66–68.

[103] On the Dakota religion, see *Travels*, 380–384. Keating, *Narrative*, 1:391, saw the two deities as co-eternal, with *Wahkan Tanka*, the Great Spirit, having more influence but by no means complete control over *Wahkan Shecha*, his adversary. See also Vernon D. Malan and Clinton J. Jesser, *The Dakota Indian Religion*, 9 (South Dakota State College, Rural Sociology Department, *Bulletins*, no. 473 — Brookings, 1959).

[104] On *shandnuapaw*, see Appendix 2, J70, below. Carver's drawing of the calumet (p. 97) differs from his description here only in the number of feathers. The 7 feathers shown in the journal drawing became 8 in the *Travels*, Plate 4. See also *Travels*, 359. Carver's observations here and below concur in general with those of many other travelers. See George A. West, *Tobacco, Pipes and Smoking*

When they sit in counsel one takes this pipe and after having lighted it, he holds the stem (which is commonly four feet in length) with the bowl down and the end of the stem upward, moving it slowly round three times for the sun and moon and other of their celisteal gods to smoke, after which they turn the stem down and the bowl up for the gods of the terristeal ellements to smoke, moving it gradually three times round. Then the master of this ceremony gives every one a short smoak in turn about till the whole members in counsel have taken a whiff. Then the pipe is placed in the middle of the circle till the counsel ends. When ever they hold a council on any public affairs in this republic the chiefs of the several bands with their aid dee camps and some others seat themselves in a place fitted for that purpose. Theose chiefs have each of them a sort of a wreath which they wear on their heads with four feathers fixed cross ways in front over their forehead. This seems to resemble Ceasar's soldiers. This badge their chiefs wear on all public occassions. They put them on when they met me on my first arrival among them.

As to the laws of the Naudowessee, they have nothing more to govern them by then the advice of their chiefs and the customs handed down from one generation to another. In case of murder the nearest relations take revenge. Adultery is punished by the husband when commited without his consent by cutting of the nose which I have seen done. Theft is punished in no other manner than by the disgrace and guilt it of consequence brings upon the offender when discoverd, who is despisd and hated among all his former friends and often is the means of his running away and seeking new acquaintances. These people pass their life without prisons almost without trouble in a state of sweetness and tranquillity and I beleave enjoy a happiness that ⟨*Version II*⟩ the ⟨more refined⟩ [105] are strangers to, living quietly under the laws of instinct that wise nature has imprinted upon their minds ⟨*Version II*⟩ from their cradles. ⟨In commerce they are strictly just; in general conduct, open, generous, and beneficient, in social duty exemplary to a prodigy.⟩ In their sentiments they seem to observe an exact conformity, are kind and benevolent to each other, the aged, the criples, naturals, and all indegents by natural

Customs of the American Indians, 231–270 (Milwaukee Public Museum, *Bulletins,* vol. 17 — Milwaukee, 1934). On the Dakota use of a ceremonial headdress below, see Hassrick, *The Sioux,* 267.
[105] "English" in Version I.

misfortune are well taken care of. Those that are idle and lazy are not taken notice of but are despised.[106]

The principle dialict to the west of Canada after you pass the Iroquois nations is the Chippeway, which is as much esteemd among the Indians from Canada to the Mississippi as the Greek and Latin is in Europe, and all nations endeavour to get some spicimen of this tongue by which they may travel as far west as the Naudowessee who are not at all understood by the nations to the east of the Mississippi. They are calld by some nations the hissing people as they speak with a less accent then other nations. That language that was formerly calld the Algonkins [*Algonquian*] is much the same as is now calld the Chippeway tongue and is spoke in much the same manner by the Ottowaw nation at present. As to the Naudowessee dialect, their being unacquainted with and are strangers to arts and sciences, with the laws of ceremony and complement, and that infinity of words that the Europeans use to embellish their discourse with all, their speach is only adapted to the necessities and conveniences of life, and their is not one useless or superfluous word in the whole language. I have for the satisfaction of the more curious added a short dictionary of what words I could gather from this people.[107]

As I was six months among the Naudowessee of the plains on the river St. Pierre I can't but take notice of the season while I was in those parts, which was from the latter end of November to the begining of May. For near four months of the first part of

---

[106] Carver's concept of revenge, the punishment of adultery and theft, and his admiration for the Dakota (which may owe something to Jean-Jacques Rousseau's "noble savage" concepts) are both echoed and modified by such earlier and later observers as Shea, ed., Hennepin, *Description of Louisiana*, 296; Kellogg, ed., *Charlevoix Journal*, 1:263; Neill and S. W. Pond, in *Minnesota Historical Collections*, 1:278; 12:392, 464, 498; Perrot, in Blair, ed., *Indian Tribes*, 1:160n; Hassrick, *The Sioux*, 43–52; and Landes, *Mystic Lake Sioux*, 111.

[107] From "Canada to the Mississippi" refers to the area from the St. Lawrence to the Upper Mississippi valleys. Carver was aware that he was on a frontier between two major linguistic groups — the Chippewa, originally an eastern tribe of Algonquian linguistic stock, who were dominant from the northern shores of Lake Huron to the Turtle Mountains of North Dakota, and the Sioux, who controlled the major rivers to the south of that region. The economy of the Dakota language is discussed by Stephen R. Riggs, *Tah-koo Wah-kan*, 10–12 (Boston, 1869); and by S. W. Pond, in *Minnesota Historical Collections*, 12:393. For Carver's dictionary, see Appendix 2, below.

the time I never knew two hours stormy weather at one time. The sky for the most part being continually serene and clear, and during the whole winter had not more then one or two inches in depth of snow at a time and that but very seldom tho 'twas not much odd of ⟨above⟩ 43 degrees of north latitude. The west winds and those from the southwest are much the warmest ⟨and most constant for the fore part and after a short intermission in the depth of winter again returned till spring. From the beginning of January for about 5 weeks the weather was pretty sharp, the wind northwest, sometimes pretty high and very dry.

⟨Version II⟩
⟨Version II

This course of the wind and superior degree of warmth to any place on the eastern part of the continent even at 40° north exactly confirmed to me the conjecture of some persons, in perticular, one of my acquaintance in Boston,[108] who sailing in the West Indian Seas for 6 months together, noticed the current of air into the Bay of Mexico to be infinitely greater than its sensible return, therefore concluded it took an oblique course upwards along the high lands stretching from the bay northwestward and coming into higher latitudes condensed and afforded the almost constant stream of northwest wind so troublesome over all the provinces. The north and east winds bring storms and cold weather, the south wind much colder than the southwest. The people on the Ouisconsin said that they had frequently snows knee deep the same winter.⟩

Version II⟩

*⟨Version II
Insert 10*

⟨About the middle of April all the water being clear of ice and my presents for the Indians being all expended could see no probability of making any further advances toward the South Sea tho assistance had been frequently offered me by the Naudowessie. I found my self under the necessity of returning again to Michilimackinac.[109] The Naudowessie bands at that time being much scattered about on their vast plains employd in hunting, only a few remain in the camp where I was, among whom was

[108] Carver supplied the name "Dr. Thomas Young" in a note at the bottom of the page. Young (1731–77) moved to Boston from Albany in 1766, became prominent in the Boston Committee of Correspondence, and subsequently served under Dr. Benjamin Rush as a physician in Philadelphia during the American Revolution. His earlier career contains an interesting parallel with Carver's. In 1760 he purchased a tract of land in what is now Vermont, the title to which was based on Indian deeds. It was subsequently proved fraudulent, to Young's considerable financial loss. *Dictionary of American Biography,* 20:635 (1936). On the mild weather, see Goddard, p. 187, below.

[109] See Carver's commission from Rogers, p. 192, below.

my very good friend the chief [*Wabasha I?*] of the warriors of the Mottobauntoway band who for his wisdom and abilities in the art of war among them was lookd upon a chief of chiefs of the other bands of that nation. He always appeared of a lively aspiring genius and very obliging. He delighted much in hearing me tell of the customs of the English, and especially in war affairs and seemd hardly inclined to bleave that the king of England could raise several hundred thousand warriours in his dominions.

And here I cannot omit mentioning somthing of an extraordinary circumstance of his regard for me as a sort of an embassadore from the English (for in that light I was esteemd by them). My canoe being somthing out of repair I had drawn it a little up from the water one day in order to mend it. At evening a couple of young men who had been out that day a hunting came on the opposite side of the river to our camp and calld for a canoe to bring them over. A couple of young women in great hast to oblige their sweethearts ran to my canoe with a design to take it to cross over with. As it was but partly finished I forbid them taking it and they were obligd to get another which took them some time longer. This delay greatly affronted the young men who demanded of their doxes the cause. ⟨They⟩ readyly made   ⟨*Version IV*⟩ answer that the white man would not let them have his canoe (without mentioning the cause) at which they were greatly affrontd and as soon as ever they came on shore one of them in a great passion ran to my canoe and with his hatchet gave it several strokes which greatly damaged it. I was instantly informd of what the Indian was about and ran with a stick designing to chastize him, but on his seeing me he ran and entered the tent of the chief of the warriors. I followed him and went in soon after him, told the chief that the young man had abused me and I would have satisfaction by beating him. The chief begd of me to tell him the story and promised me satisfaction which I did and after hearing me he calld the young man and tho a relation of his banishd him from the camp and ordered him to some remote part of their dominion and made him depart at that instant least as he said I should treat him as he deserved.

About this time I was informed that near the great [*Carver's*] cave on the Mississipi the chiefs of their several bands were assembling in order to hold a sort of an annual council according

Version II
Insert 10⟩

to their custom. By the invitation of the great chief of the warriours and another chief I determined to see what passd in this council.⟩

APRIL 26, 1767. This day took my departure from the Grand Encampment of the Naudowessee. Fell down the river about 30 mile, waited there with a number of traders for the return of the Wahpeentoah band who was out on the plains to the northward on their spring hunt. At this place one of the men I had hired returned to me. My other man, the Iroquois, I was informd had deserted and gone and joyned the roving Chippeways and had been down with a war party against the Naudowessee on the Mississippi, which I perceived had much inraged the bands that I was with, for not long before that some party of the Chipeways had sent a belt and a beaver blanket in order to settle a peace. The beaver blankit is an emblem of peace and signifies that those that send it are inclind to peace that those that receive must ly down and rest easy on it.[110]

APRIL 30, 1767. This day arrived to where the St. Pierre enters the Mississipi. Here I found part of two or three bands of the Naudowessee and a number of chiefs both of the plains and river bands which I had invited to meet me here in order to consult how I should provide for their passage to Michillimackinac where they were a going to visit Major Rogers. Several of these chiefs had never been among the English which made me the more urgent for their proceeding in hopes that it might be of service to promote trade among these people that seemd inclined at present to favour the English more then any other white people on the continent. Some of these chiefs could not be prevaild upon to tast any spiritious liquors on any account as they lookd upon it as a bad medison. The Naudowessee of the plains have scearsly any knowledge of spiriteous liquor and are not at all inclind to it.

⟨*Version II*
Insert 11

MAY 1, 1767. ⟨May the first I arrived at the great cave a little before noon. The council was then sitting. A messenger was sent and acquainted them that I was come. Three chiefs were soon

[110] On the possible location of this Grand Encampment, see note 76, above. If Carver is referring to the same place here, then his rendezvous farther down the river would perhaps have occurred near present-day Shakopee.

For examples of the use of the beaver robe as a seat of honor or with ceremonial significance, see Long, *Voyages and Travels*, 46, 111; Peter Pond, in Gates, ed., *Five Fur Traders*, 52; Clements, ed., in American Antiquarian Society, *Proceedings*, 28:235.

sent from the council who came to the tent where I was and invited me to the council. I went with them. They took me into the tent which was very spacious. The members who were in general very old with gray hair made a venerable appearance. The great solemnity which appeard in each member's countenance I thought might well become the most polite nations. When I entered not an eye turnd so much as to look on me. Every one appeard in a deep thought and meditation as tho the burden of a nation lay on his shoulders. All was in a profound silence till I had taken my seat which was opposite the president or speaker who was a chief heridatery of the Mottobauntowah band [*Wabasha I?*] and appeared to be about sixty years of age. I had been well acquainted with him and had I not heared before great encomiums on his elloquence, I should have thought by his extraordinary taciturnity at all other times in whatever company that he never could have confidence sufficient to open his mouth in this assembly. However, according to what little knowledge I have of elocution I thought such an orator would becom any assembly in the more polite nations. In several speaches I heard him make he delivered himself with great energie, in particular I observd when he came to mention the necessity he thought there was of maintaining and opening a corispondence with the English. He refered them to the accounts which I had given of their power and grandure and abilities to supply them in articles of trade and especially in fire arms which was so necessary being much sperior to their arms both for war & hunting, likewise some other articles such as tobacco, beads, and paint and cloaths of several sorts. Likewise observed the great safety there was in going to request traders from the English at Michilimackinac, and on the other hand the danger there was of contracting the fever & ague (a disorder which the[y] greatly fear) in their going to Louisiania among the French to which the whole council seemd to listen and but one chief spoke in favour of going to the French at Louisiania.[111]

In this council they thanked me for the visit I had made them and wishd I would encourage the English to come among them and trade and settle near them and insisted upon my returning

[111] The possible implications for British western policy of Carver's success in getting the chiefs to agree to go to Michilimackinac rather than New Orleans are obvious; see pp. 10, 11, above. Note that the "Carver grant," supposedly dated May 1, 1767, is not mentioned here.

again to their country and bring fire arms & tobacco. I complyd with their request on conditions that the great king of the English would let me with which they appeared contented.

The same day I took my leave of this people. The chiefs of the council accompanied me down to the water's edge. One of the eldest in a short speach wishd me a safe return to my native country and after their figurative manner of speaking wishd that my road might be plain and strait, the sky without clouds, and the sun to shine clear, and all the lakes and waters smooth with many such like enigmattical expressions which they most commonly use in their councils and speeches on particular occasions, and presented me a pipe and some tobacco to smoke on the way with some other trifling presents. Finally, I had no occasion to complain of the treatment of these Indians to me, but on the contrary for near seven months that I was among this people I *Version II* experienced of their kindness beyound what I could expect from *Insert 11*⟩ barbarians.⟩ Here I gave several presents to assist them in the voyage to Michilimackinac. Tho the Indians are great travelers yet this is esteemd a very long journey and but few care to undertake it.

⟨*Version IV*   ⟨Speeches interchanged between Capt. Carver and the cheifs of the several bands of the Naudouwessee in council at the great cave near the Falls of St. Anthony, in the Mississippi in North America, when he was adopted a cheif in their bands May 1st 1767.[112]

My brothers, cheifs of the numerous and powerfull Naudowessee, I rejoice that, by my long continuing among you, I can now speak (though in a broken manner) in your own tongue like one of your own children, and that I have had opportunity so often to acquaint you of the glory and power of the great king of the English and other nations who descended from a very ancient race of kings as old as the earth and waters whose feet stands on two great islands, greater then any you have seen,[113] amidst the greatest water in the world whose head

[112] Similar speeches appeared in *Travels*, 87–91. In the journals, these were placed at the end of Version IV, but we have printed them here for the reader's convenience.

[113] On a separate sheet in Version IV, Carver added the explanation: "Two islands are, Great Brittan an[d] Ireland. The country of the Naudowessie contains only small lakes & rivers."

reaches to the sun, and his arms clasp round the whole earth, the numbers of whose warriors are like the trees in the valleys or like the stalks of rice in yonder marshes, or spires of grass on your great plains, who has hundreds of his own [canoes] of such a bigness that all the waters in your country would not suffice for one of them to swim in. Each of these have guns (not small like mine which you see here) but of such a magnitude that a hundred of your stout men could but with difficulty carry one, and are equally surprizing in their operation against the king's enemies when engaged in battle, the terror of which your language wants words to express. You may remember not half a moon since when we were in camp at Wadawpawmenesoter, the black clouds, the fire, the noise and horible cracks, the trembling of the earth, and the wind, you then said you thought the gods were very angry.[114] Much so is the warlike emplements of the English when fighting under the greatest king in the world.

Several of the cheifs of your bands have often tould me in times past, while I dwelt among you in your tents, how much you wished to be counted among the children of the great king my master. You may remember how you have desired me when I return again to my own country to acquaint the great king of your good dispositions towards him and his subjects and that you wished for traders to come among you. And now, as I am about to take my leave of you and return to my own country a long way towards the rising sun, I ask you to tell me if you continue of the same mind as when I spoke to you in council last winter and as their is several of your cheifs here who came from the Great Plains towards the setting of the sun who I have never spake with in council before, I ask you to let me know if you are all willing to acknowledge yourselves the children of my great master the king of the English and other nations, and I shall take the first opportunity to acquaint the king of your desires and good intentions. I charge you not to mind nor give heed to any bad report, for there is bad birds [115] flying and may soon be here who may whisper evil things in your ears against the English

---

[114] On a separate sheet in Version IV, Carver added the explanation: "A great storm of thunder and rain which are encamped on the river St. Peirre called by them Wadawpawmensoter." See *Travels,* 85.

[115] By "bad birds" Carver, of course, means French traders. See also his reference to "bad people," p. 128, below.

contrary to what I have told you. You must not mind them for I have told you the truth.

And as to the chiefs who are a going to Michillimackinic I shall take care to make for them and their sute a straight road, smooth waters, and a clear blue sky, that they may go there, smoke in the pipe of peace, and rest secure, and sleep on a beaver blanket allready spread for them under the great tree of peace. Farewell.

The answer by a cheif their greatest speaker.

Good brother: I am now about to speak to you with the mouths of those my brothers, cheifs of eight bands now in council. We beleive and are satisfied in every thing you have tould us about your great nations, and the great king our greatest father, for whom we spread this beaver blanket that his fatherly protection may ever rest easy and safe among us his children the Naudowessee. Your colours and arms and every thing you have brought with you convince us of the truth of every thing you say. We desire that you will on your return acquaint the great king how much we wish to be counted among his good children. You may depend on what we say, that we will not hear to any who may dare to speak against your great king or your people. We thank you for what you have done in making peace between us and our enemies the Chippeways and hope you will not forget to make such representations to our great father as that he may not forget us, but send traders continually among us with such things as we need that the hearts of our young men, wives, and children may be made glad, and may peace last among us as long [as] the sun, moon, earth, and waters shall *Version IV*⟩ endure. Farewell.⟩

MAY 3, 1767. Passd Lake of Tears or Lake St. Anthony [*Lake Pepin*], came to the enterance of the Chipeway River. Here I found two chiefs of this [*Chippewa*] nation, a trader from Louissiania, and one from Michillimackinac. At the evening a number of their young men came to give me a dance. Their ceremony began with a sort of a drum and rattle shell at some distance, advancing slowly and stoping now and then to dance, each being dressd with short leather breeches like a highland kelt with the edges very beautifully figured with quills and long feathers on their heads. When they came to the door of my tent I was informd that the dance was intended for me. I stepd to the door and bid them welcom.[116]

They entered and soon began their dance, each one of them having a tomehawk in his hand or a club calld breakhead which every now and then they would strike upon the tent poles over head and make a short speach on somthing extraordinary that they have done before, either in war or hunting, after which they gave a loud coohoop with their hands on their mouths interupting the sound with a sort of tremour attended with such postures and motions of body as appeared both hostile & terrible, which I was informd by the French with me was their constant custom when they gave a dance to any strange chief that came among them. I was informd by people with me that they expected some presents, which I was very willing to bestow in order to get shot of my guests. Here I gave some vermillian and a few shirts and some powder.

MAY 6, 1767. Arrived at La Prairie Lachien [*Prairie du Chien*] or the Dog Plains. Here I found Capt. James Tute, Mr. James Stanley Goddard, and a party with some goods in order to proceed from this to find out the great river Ourigan that runs into the South Sea and a northwest passage if possible. These orders was from Major Robert Rogers commandent of Michillimackinac who sent orders by Capt. Tute for me to joyn this party as a draughtsman. Here we took leave of the English and French traders.[117]

[MAY 11, 1767.] After my arrival here and the arrival of the several chiefs of the Naudowessee and a number of other chiefs of the nations about the Ouisconsin, May the eleaventh, Capt. Tute held a counsel with the Ottigaumies [*Fox*] on account of their chiefs going to Michillimackinac. The next day had a counsel with all the chiefs that was present on the same occasion. The Ottigaumies require Monsr. Calvin, a Frenchman that inhabits

[116] The meeting place of traders near the Chippewa River may well have been the spot later known as Grand Encampment on the present site of Wabasha, Minn. See Coues, ed., *Pike Expeditions,* 1: 59n. According to Bray, ed., *Nicollet Journals,* 258, this dance, traditionally performed for strangers in the Chippewa country, was called *ogitshida nimmiwin,* or strike-the-pole dance. See also William E. Culkin, "Tribal Dance of the Ojibway Indians," in *Minnesota History Bulletin,* 1: 83–93 (May, 1915); *Travels,* 279.

[117] For the movements of Goddard and Tute during the winter of 1766–67, see pp. 186–188, below. On "Ourigan," see p. 13n, above.

with them, to go with them as their interpretor to Michilimackinac. Capt. Tute is obligded to hire him at which they are
content.[118]

It is much surprizing to see how intent the French from Louissiania are in endeavouring to draw the Indians on the Mississipi
from the English interest, offering them large presents, inviting
them on our side of the Mississippi to come over and settle on
their side. And I was credible informd they had sent belts and
presents to Indians on the English teretories and had taken all
possible means to sower their minds against the English goverment and make them appear contemptable by telling them
the English were coveteous and stingy and would give them no
presents or nothing comparable with what their French fathers
usd to do, and that their French father the great king was not yet
dead but thought much of them and would yet recover all that
the English had stole from him while he was looking another
way, and that he was now preparing a great many great canoes
for that purpose, and that Vaudeville [*Vaudreuil*], former governor of Canada, their very good friend, would once more grow
great tho he was now but small, that the English were a quarel-
ing people and always divided among them selves, and a
thousand such like meliceous reports to make the English ode-
⟨*Version II*⟩   ous in their sight. ⟨The disadvantage of our competition with
our restless neighbors in the trade and business with the Indians
is inconceivable.⟩ These traders from Louissiana affirmd that
there would shortly be a fort built on or near the river Audan
[*Turkey*] about forty or fifty miles below the Ouisconsin on the
west side, on purpose to draw the Indians, our allies, into their
favour and had invited all the Ottigaumies to come and settle on
their side. In short I am not able to relate half the intrigues this
people make use of to possess the Indians with the belief that
they will yet be masters of North America notwithstanding the
superiority the English have at present over them.[119]

[118] Calvin is probably Joseph Calvé, a trader on the Mississippi who was
subsequently employed by the British as a military agent among the Sauk and
Fox. During the Revolutionary War, he was accused of betraying the British
interests in favor of the Americans. See "Gautier's Journal of a Visit to the
Mississippi, 1777–78"; Patrick Sinclair to Frederick Haldimand, July 8, 1780; and
Haldimand to Sinclair, August 10, 1780, all in *Wisconsin Historical Collections*,
11:108n, 156, 161.

[119] Pierre Rigaud, Marquis de Vaudreuil, was governor of New France at the

Had we any ways become masters of the country ownd by the French on the west of the Mississippi we might now have the advantage of the trade of more Indians then double the number that at this time is our right or that are within the English dominions. Besides, it would put an intire check upon any attempts that these people might make had not they some place to draw the Indians too. It is most certainly made use of for the worst of purposes, I mean for them to put bad things into the Indians' heads. Even some of the inhabitants of Canada while they are abroad among the Indians can set very quietly and hear the English goverment rideculd in a shocking manner and rather then hold their peace would help a word or two. However they may flatter and cringe and protend to a deal of honesty when they are where they must submit to goverment, yet these creatures being ignorant and not naturally well inclind are only fit tools for very bad purposes among the Indians. And I wish I was certain that no belts are yearly sent among these nations even from some persons of distinction in Canada who are yet in their hearts well wishers to their former masters.

These discouragements, given out by those who were very understanding in their tongue, would have had a very disagreeable effect on their minds had not Captain Tute and Mr. Goddard and myself exerted ourselves by giving large presents to keep them in the English interest, and after all perhaps would not have obtaind our end among them had it not been for the great influence Mr. Goddard had over the king of the Ottigamies together with the interest I had made with the Naudowessee bands by presents I had given them.

I humbly prosume that anyone well acquaintd with the circumstances ⟨temper and situation⟩ of the Indians ⟨on account of   ⟨*Version II*⟩ the general decline of the English interest among them, especially those toward the Mississipi⟩ in the beginning of the year 1767 will say that they are of the opinion that if it had not been

time of its loss to the British in 1762. On French and Spanish activity along the Mississippi River boundary, see Phillips, *Fur Trade,* 1: 586–603; Abraham P. Nasatir, "The Anglo-Spanish Frontier on the Upper Mississippi, 1786–1796," in *Iowa Journal of History and Politics,* 29: 155–164 (April, 1931). The Turkey River was a common meeting ground for traders and Indians; the French had a post near there in 1753. It was also Goddard's intended wintering place. See p. 186, below; Grace Lee Nute, "Marin versus La Verendrye," in *Minnesota History,* 32: 235 (December, 1951).

⟨*Version II*⟩

for the pains taken by Capt. Tute and Mr. Goddard and myself by loading of them with presents beyound what would need have been given in any other case, ⟨and every argument in our power to create and propagate the importance of their being in the English interest,⟩ that we should have lost two if not more very valuable nations, viz., the Saugies and Ottigaumies, which if we had lost them it would have intirely ruined the Mississipi trade with the English all above the Illinois, besides cutting of the communication and turning the Naudoweissees and a large part of the Chipeways about St. Croix River and the Ottowaw Lakes. I am very certain that the Naudowessee would have gone

⟨*Version II*⟩

to the Illinois ⟨and opened a trade with the French and Spaniards at Louissiana⟩ if I had not laboured hard with them both by urging and presents by which means I turnd their course to Michillimackinac, excepting one chief who being peculiarly connected with one La Vern a Frenchman went with him to Louisiana.[120]

I can but remark again that these difficulties would never have risen if the French had not any place to invite the Indians to. I say the French tho I am sensible that country belongs to the Spaniards by a cession from the French king, yet the French inhabitants remain there and are allowd to monopolize as before. Had the Spaniards only been sent there and the French sent of, we should have been before hand with them for our English traders had begun to push out among these nations of Indians that I just mentioned and to trade and learn their tonges and customs before this cession was made by the French to the Spaniards, or at least before it was known in these parts.

⟨*Version II*

⟨Perhaps some would ask in what manner the Indian trade is so very profitable to us and especially in Great Britain. I answer it is

[120] On p. 204, below, Carver estimates that Tute, Goddard, and himself gave gifts worth £500 sterling here. This was a large amount, especially in view of the economy the British government was trying to enforce in Indian relations. Carver's defensive tone may be explained by the fact that both Rogers and Sir William Johnson, British superintendent of Indian affairs, were displeased; see pp. 17, 18, above.

Travels, 98, said that 10 chiefs went southward on the Mississippi, perhaps an exaggeration to magnify the problem of French competition. William Bruce had similar trouble with a French trader Le Vorn from the Illinois River in 1764. He may have been Joseph Lavergne, a courier for Marin in 1753–54. See the deposition of Garrit Roseboom, Tunis Fischer, Cummin Shields, and William Bruce, in *Wisconsin Historical Collections,* 18: 268; Nute, in *Minnesota History,* 32: 235.

most essentionally profitable to us on two accounts: the first is the vast consumption of the woollin and hard ware manufactures, ribands and beeds, paint, and a variety of other articles made only in Great Briton. The second is the great duty which the return of these articles when imported to Great Britain pays yearly to the Crown. The duties on the peltry and furr trade only at the distant post of Michilimackinac are computed to be no less then [blank in mss.] which is a sum I think well worth considering under our present difficulties.⟩[121]   *Version II*⟩

MAY 21, 1767. Took my departure from the Ottogaume town in company with Cap. Tute, commander of the party, Mr. Goddard, a lieutenant, Mr. Guiltier [*Charles Gautier*], interpreter, and Mr. [*Joseph*] Reaume, having two cannoes and eight working people, one Chipeway chief, our guide. With these we proceeded up the Mississippi with a determination to winter at a place calld by the French Fort Lapraire, not far from Lake Winepeek, it being the furthest trading post the French ever had to the northwest.[122]

[MAY 26, 1767.] The night of the 25 while we was the most of us asleep there came a party of Ottigaumies who was returning from hunting. These Indians on seeing our fires supposd us to be a party of Indians going to war. They came privatly upon us and undoubtedly would have done us mischief if one of the Indians of our party had not just before awaked and set up smoking his pipe discoverd and challengd them before they struck shore. Thay perceiving we was friends came to us. They told us the reason of their coming down in the night was their having taken

[121] According to Lart, ed., in *Canadian Historical Review*, 3:353, goods worth £38,964, 6s., 11d., were sent out from Michilimackinac to the west, and 124,695 pelts were received in return between June and October, 1767. Rogers estimated that if a free and open trade to the west were allowed, it would justify an annual outlay of £60,898 in merchandise, wages, canoes, etc. If confined to Michilimackinac, £6,089 would be adequate, the balance being lost to the French. Rogers' estimate is in American Antiquarian Society, *Proceedings*, 28:261.

[122] Charles Gautier de Verville was an interpreter and soldier in the French and Indian and Pontiac's wars. Joseph Reaume was a member of a large family of Green Bay traders. See Goddard, below, p. 188; Kellogg, *British Régime*, 13; Elliott Coues, ed., *New Light on the Early History of the Greater Northwest: The Manuscript Journals of Alexander Henry and of David Thompson, 1799–1814*, 1:164n (Reprint Ed., Minneapolis, 1965); Grignon, Gautier, and Michel Curot, "A Wisconsin Fur-Trader's Journal, 1803–04," all in *Wisconsin Historical Collections*, 3:231, 237; 11:100n; 20:400n (1911). On Fort des Prairies, see p. 16n, above. Carver does not name his guide, but Goddard, p. 189, below, calls him Acopewine.

fright at a war party of Chipeways near the Lake Pepin or Lake of Tears. Tho the Ottigamies are not at war with the Chipeways yet it is common among all these nations of Indians when they go out in parties for war that they kill all they light on, friends or foes. For they say blood they seek and blood they will have let it run in whose veins it will, except their own party, or when the pipe of peace is carryd, which, if seen, they will not ⟨Version II⟩ destroy what they generally look ⟨upon so⟩ sacred.

MAY 28, 1767. This day came to where the Chipeway River joyns the Mississipi. The same evening we was given to understand that the guide and the rest of the Indians with us declind going any further up in the Mississipi. Capt. Tute calld a counsel to consult upon what methods would be most expedient. In that case it was genererally agreed to take our course up the Chipeway River, the reasons was first that we had not with us prasents sutable for to pass through the Naudowessee with, and secondly that as Major Rogers had by letters informd us that he would send us a supply by the way of Lake Superiour and the Grand Portage[123] of such goods for presents to the Indians when we should have occasion to pass as we should stand in need of, ⟨Version II⟩ thirdly ⟨the Indians gave⟩ as a reason for their not being willing to go by the way of the Naudowessee was for fear of war parties towards the head of the Mississipi which often pass there in the summer season. The 29 of May we set of up the Chipeway River.

JUNE 4, 1767. Came to the great medows or plains. Here I found excellent good land and very pleasant country.[124] One might travel all day and only see now and then a small pleasant groves of oak and walnut. This country is coverd with grass which affords excellent pasturage for the buffeloe which here are very plenty. Could see them at a distance under the shady oaks like cattle in a pasture and sometimes a drove of an hundred or more shading themselves in these groves at noon day which ⟨Version II⟩ ⟨afforded⟩ a very pleasant prospect for an uninhabited country. We killd several of these buffeloes, one of which we all judgd would weigh fifteen hundred weight and if the same could be fed as is common to fatten our tame cattle undoubtedly would weigh three thousand, they being by far the largest creatures in bulk

[123] On Grand Portage, see pp. 17n, 130.
[124] This area is between Lake Pepin and Eau Claire in western Wisconsin.

that I ever saw. Their meat is very good and tender, and their fat is but a little inferiour to butter, there marrow is equal to the best of butter. As these beasts have extraordinary large bones a large quantity is taken from one which the Indians (who often come here to hunt the buffeloe) git and put into bottles made of bladders and skins for that purpose.

Here is a great plenty of elk, the largest that ever I had seen. As it was after they had shed of their horns, they apeard at a distance on the plain like droves of horses. A hunter might get very near to these as they was very tame and would hardly move out of our way till fired upon.

About as far as this the traders generally come from the Mississipi. The numerous hard rapids further up this river prevents them going further up. The Indians that live at the Ottowaw Lakes [*Lac Court Oreilles*] meet them here where they find good hunting. These Indians often come here the latter part of summer to hunt the buffeloe. The Naudowessee with whom they are at war watch the oppertunity and send out war parties and often fall upon them and cut them off.[125]

The manner these war parties take to discover the hunters is to find a large oak tree on the plains on which they build or place a parcel of small sticks in form of an eagle's nest of which there is a great many about here. One of the party gits into it and is concealed here. He lys as a sentry whole days looking out on the plains while the rest of the party are conceald near in the grass in some valley. These sentrys thus conceald on a tree will see at a great distance any parties that are moving and make discoverys of smoke at a great way from them. For that reason this is calld the road of war and 'tis seldom there is much hunting in the summer season here abouts. I could but take notice of the excessive hard thunder we had during our voyage up this river. Scearsly a day without several showers accompanyd with one clap after another like volleys of cannon.

JUNE 22, 1767. Arrivd at the Chipeway town [*at Lac Court Oreilles*]. After we left the plains till we came to this town for upwards of an hundred miles is a most dreary wilderness of trees

---

[125] On the route, see pp. 161–166, below. See Warren, *History of the Ojibway*, 191, 305–314, on the Lac Court Oreilles band, the village mentioned below, and the frequent warfare between the Dakota and Chippewa in this region in the years after Carver's passage.

or timber of all sorts, but principally birch and uneven land, tho no mountains, all the way from the Mississipi. Here is hardly any game excepting a few deer. This town stands on a neck of land where is a small channel of about ten rods between two small lakes. This channel is about four rods wide and runs very swift. Their houses stand on each side of this junction. These lakes are calld by some the Ottowaw Lakes by others the Lakes of ye Deserts.[126]

JUNE 23, 1767. Held a counsel with the chiefs of this town at which Cap. Tute gave a belt and several presents, and some strings of waumpum to the captain of the warriors to prevail with him to rest peacable in his town, for on our arrival we was informd that he was about to set of with a war party against what nation I could not learn but supposed against the Naudowessee, but they promissd us that they would rest quiet in their village. Our coming at this juncture was very happy for us on two accounts, first because if these partys had met us before we arrivd to their village undoubtedly they would have fallen upon us as their customs is to fall on all parties they light of as I mentiond before. The second is that if this party of warriours had gone and fallen on the Naudowessee or any other nation in alliance with the English and they had known of our party passing that way they would most certainly be jealous that we had prompd them to go against them. This with bad people among them might put very bad things in their heads against the English.[127]

⟨*Version II*⟩   ⟨JUNE 24, 1767.⟩ This day the chiefs of this town calld a counsel. Their speaker made a long speach in which he in behalf of his whole people thankd us in that we had shown them so much charity as to call and see them in their town, we being the first

---

[126] According to both Warren, *History of the Ojibway,* 193, and p. 189, below, Ottawa Lake was so named because an Ottawa Indian was buried there. Lake of the Deserts may be a confusion on Carver's part with Lac Vieux Desert in Vilas County, Wis.

[127] Goddard, p. 189, below, identified the chiefs as Andickweas, Megose, Ochick, and Acopewine. The "bad people" (French traders) could take advantage of the precarious peacemaking of Carver's group with both the Dakota and the Chippewa, traditional enemies in precisely the fur-trading area Rogers hoped to develop. Sir William Johnson was not pleased with the party's peacemaking role, writing that discord between the Dakota and Chippewa "should have been in good policy connived at." See Johnson to the Earl of Shelburne, October 26, 1767, in O'Callaghan, ed., *Documents . . . of New-York,* 7:989.

white people they had ever seen there.[128] Likewise thankd us for the presents, and made particular remarks on what they calld my goodness in advising and keeping the Naudowessee while I was with them last winter from sending war parties against them, as they said they had been truly informd of what I had said to them while I was there.

This town contains about fifteen houses and about seventy warriours. On our arrival we was recd with great demonstrations of joy. On seeing the pipe of peace as we approachd the town they fired of all their pieces and put fire to a large ⟨parcel⟩ ⟨*Version II*⟩ of powder they had put into somthing hollow in the ground which made a great noise and explosion.

JUNE 29, 1767. This day took our departure from this town, crossd several small lakes [*Grindstone, Windigo*] between the waters of the Mississipi and Lake Superiour. From thence in to a branch of river St. Croix [*Namekagon R.*] down as far as the forks and then up another branch of the same till we came to the head of St. Croix. Near the head of St. Croix is a small lake calld Sturgeon Lake [*St. Croix Flowage*] where we caught a plenty of the best sturgeon I ever tastd. After we left this river we had a carrying place about two miles, then came to the head of a river [*Brule*] which leads to Lake Superiour. This has a course almost north. Here we put in our canoes, the stream not large enough for a small mill, was forced to make dams to raise the water for passage. In a few days arrivd to Lake Superiour west part on the south shore.[129]

JULY 12, 1767. Arrivd at a small Chipeway village on the entrance of the river St. Louis at the wistern extremity of Lake Superiour. This village is a most dirty begarly village I ever saw ⟨containing about 12 families.⟩ Capt. Tute held a counsel with ⟨*Version II*⟩ their chief, made him some presents. The next day tarryd to

[128] The date of this passage is June 23 in Version I. Goddard, p. 190, below, similarly claimed that they were the first white men to travel to Lac Court Oreilles, although there has been speculation that Radisson and Groseilliers may have reached this far in 1659. See Grace Lee Nute, *Caesars of the Wilderness*, 61 (New York, 1943).

[129] See *Travels*, 62; Goddard, below, p. 190. Carver named the Namekagon for Tute and the Brule for Goddard, but neither name persisted. As elsewhere in his journey, Carver is here following what later became a well-established fur trade route. The Lac Court Oreilles-Namekagon and the Brule-St. Croix portages are still marked and preserved.

supply our selves with fish as our provisions was near gone.[130]

July 14, 1767. Took our departure from this town. The 19 arrivd at the Grand Portage. The country from the west end of the lake is rocky and very uneven all the way. Near shore the lake seems to ly in a bed of rocks. Our general course being north and north east for two months we keepd pace with the season. Strawberries that we left in the blossom at Lapraire Lechien we found much the same at the Grand Portage though sixty days odd.

⟨Version II
Insert 13

Here we found the king of the Christenoes and several of his people encampd who was glad to see us, ⟨and several tents of the Assinipoils which I mentioned before was a revolted band from the Naudowessee and speak their language. These two nations seemd much connected together by fraquent intermarrying and inhabit the country between the Chipeways tereteries on Lake La Plue [*Rainy L.*] and Lake Winipeek and trade chiefly to Hudson's Bay, but came here in search of traders from Michilimackinac with a design if possible to git some of them to go into their country and winter with them. The reason they give for their coming here after traders is that they say that at Hudson's Bay they are forced to give much more for their goods then for those they purchase of traders from Michillimackinac or Montreal.[131]

I could not but wonder at this extraordinary account which these honest people gave of their treatment at the places they had been at of the companies trade. When I consider that the transportation of goods from England to Hudson's Bay cannot be attended with but a little more expense then from England to Montreal when the companies people do not carry their good[s] beyond their factories to which is a free navigation on ships, and

[130] The name Fond du Lac was applied to various Indian villages and later trading stations at the west end of Lake Superior. On the Chippewa community there and its chiefs, who were members of the marten clan, see Warren, *History of the Ojibway*, 129, 130. Goddard, p. 190, below, notes that the chief was their guide's brother, but does not name him.

[131] On the Indians at Grand Portage, see p. 191, below. In adding Assiniboin to the population, Carver is confirmed by James, ed., *Tanner Narrative*, 144, who noted the intermingling of the three tribes in this area. For the beginnings of competition between the Montreal traders and the Hudson's Bay Company, see E. E. Rich, *History of the Hudson's Bay Company, 1670–1870*, 2:31, 39 (London, 1959); Rich, *Montreal and the Fur Trade*, 62–98 (Montreal, 1966); and Harold A. Innis, *The Fur Trade in Canada*, 169–183, 192–202 (New Haven, 1930).

the people of Montreal carry their goods seventeen hundred miles beyond that place up rivers in small canoes where is many carrying places, a voyage which can scearsly be performed in a year, and yet these voyages from Montreal are esteemd well worth undertaking, I have often wondered that the Hudson's Bay Company should be allowed thus to impose on any people who in any manner bear the resemblence of humane beings. A factory set up at the Great Carrying Place on the north of Lake Superior and well supplyed with articles for the Indian trade would in a little time draw a great part of those innocent people who are *Version II* thus treated like brutes by the company at Hudson's Bay.⟩ [132] *Insert 13* ⟩

We procured some rice of this people and a plenty of fish. Otherwise we must have starvd to death, for we had not for the space of a week more than a quarter allowance. The country very destitute of all sorts of game, our hunters returnd dayly without success. The country at the Grand Portage is ownd by a chief of the Chipeways who has a large house and a few warriours here.

⟨The bay at the Grand Portage is about a mile and a half deep ⟨*Version II* and about so broad almost to the bottom, being nearly square. In *Insert 12* the chops of this bay or where it communicates with the lake is a very pleasant [*Grand Portage*] island lying in the middle, leaving a little opening to the lake on each end. On this island and landing at the bottom of the bay is some of the best land on all the north *Version II* of Lake Superiour.⟩ *Insert 12* ⟩

JULY 20, 1767. This day held a counsel with the king of the Christenoes, smoakd with him in the pipe of peace.[133]

These people I perceived according to the general custom of these heathen nations in counsel first gave the gods of the elements to smoke and after that those in counsel. The last whiff each one took especially the chiefs they blowd the smoke up into

[132] On the fraudulent practices of traders, see, for example, Bain, ed., Henry, *Travels & Adventures*, 334. Carver's criticisms of the Hudson's Bay Company are more restrained in *Travels*, 110. His observations on the merits of Grand Portage as a trading location were justified within a decade. The intense rivalry among traders there, among other things, brought about the formation in 1779 of the Montreal-based North West Company, which challenged the Hudson's Bay Company in the late 18th and early 19th centuries. See Woolworth, in *Minnesota History*, 44: 201, 207; Holmquist and Brookins, *Minnesota's Major Historic Sites*, 152–156. The Chippewa and Cree chiefs in this period mentioned below have not been identified.

[133] For a longer account of the council, see *Travels*, 123–129.

the air holding their faces up at the same time till 'twas exausted. These ceremonies were performd just as the king of the Christenoes began his speach. In this counsel Capt. Tute gave a belt and several presents.

JULY 23, 1767. This day the king of the Christinoes calld us to a counsel with him. We smoked with him in the pipe of peace. He gave Capt. Tute a beaver blanket and several other presents. The same day six canoes came in from Michilimackinac. These were the Lake La Plue Indians. Their chief [*Nittam*] appeard a great friend to the English. They had been to Michillimackinac to see Majr. Rogers. The weather so cold I could ware a coat and jacket and a cloak in the middle of the day.[134]

JULY 27, 1767. Began to be in great want of provisions. Capt. Tute sent the interpreter with some other hands to meet the traders from Michilmackinac and to hurry them on as fast as possible for fear a mutiny would break out among the people which we expected every day on account of our being in want of provision.

AUGUST 2, 1767. Came two canoes in the morning, in the afternoon four more, these being some traders bound to the northwest. Of them we procurd some supplys till the succours expected from Majr. Rogers should come.

⟨*Version II*⟩   AUGUST 7, 1767. This day Mr. Francis ⟨La Blonc, a trader from Michilimackinac⟩ bound to the northwest, came in and brought some letters from Major Rogers by which we understood we was to have no supplys this year from him, at the same time desired us to push on for our discoverys. The same day Capt. Tute calld a counsel to know what was to be done in our then unhappy condition, no provision nor goods to get any with, when it was universally agreed to return to Michillimackinac and give over our intended expedition. Accordingly the next day took our leave of the king of the Christenoes, came round on the north and east side of Lake Superiour and arrivd to St. Mary's August the 27th.[135]

[134] In his testimony at Rogers' court-martial, Goddard said that the Rainy Lake Indians led by Nittam brought the news that Rogers himself was planning to travel to Grand Portage in the spring of 1768. Armour, ed., *Treason?*, 55. The Lac la Pluie Indians could have been either Chippewa or Cree, for Rainy Lake was the approximate border between these groups. Rogers' journal in American Antiquarian Society, *Proceedings*, 28: 253, recorded the arrival of unnamed Chippewa chiefs at Michilimackinac on June 10.

[135] François Le Blanc, also known as "Mr. Franceways" or Le Blancell, took 6

Lake Superiour from the western end which is properly a bay from the islands calld the 12 Apostles westward round on the north north east and east to the Straits of St. Marie's it seems to lye in one continued jangle of rocks, the land very mountaneous for thousands of acres together in many places a firm rock except some chasms where grows some small scruby trees.

The land about St. Mary's is tolerable good. The fort consists only of some old stockades round a house, the whole very much decayd and gone to ruin since the French lost the command. At the Falls of St. Mary's is calld the best place in all these lakes on account of the white fishery, especialy in the fall when any supply might be had.[136]

AUGUST 29, 1767. This day arrived at Michilimackinac,[137] ⟨after [having] performed a travel of upwards of three thousand miles including the circuit of Lake Superiour, during which time I never tasted bread or any other liquor then water except sometimes during the spring time when I had a little sugar made of maple sap which dissolvd in water made an excellent drink. After having suffered hardships by hungar and cold in danger of being destroyd by savage beasts and men more savage then they, exposd to sickness and other desasters, without physicion or surgeon, yet I never enjoyed a greater degree of health during the whole course of my life than in these travels for which I am bound in duty and gratitude to acknowledge my self indebted to the allwise protecting hand of almighty God whose tender mercies are over all his works for this his kind preserving hand of providence over me during my travels.

⟨Version II Insert 14

canoes from Michilimackinac to Forts Dauphin and Des Prairies in 1767, according to Lart, ed., in *Canadian Historical Review*, 3: 353. Some conjectures on his travels in this period can be found in Innis, *Fur Trade in Canada*, 192–194; Wallace, *Pedlars*, 6, 7. Marjorie W. Campbell, *The North West Company*, 7 (New York, 1957) identified him as a business associate of Isaac Todd and James McGill of Montreal and as the first trader to reach Lake Winnipeg after 1763. For Rogers' letter of July 20, 1767, see p. 198, below.

136 The decayed condition of the fort was due in part to a fire that occurred on December 22, 1762, while Alexander Henry was at Sault Ste. Marie. See Bain, ed., Henry, *Travels & Adventures*, 60–65.

137 *Travels*, 148, stated that Carver arrived at Michilimackinac "the beginning of November." This later date enabled him to avoid any reference to Rogers' conflicts there with Benjamin Roberts, Sir William Johnson's agent. Goddard, p. 191, below, confirms the August arrival. In a letter of October 1, 1767, Roberts referred to the return of "Major Rogers's Band . . . in the expectation of more Merchandize." He added that they "have found Out the River that Runs from Lake Superior to the Mississippi . . . it seems they have Quarreld for Rank & precedance." Flick, ed., *Johnson Papers*, 5: 711 (1927).

My arrival at Michilimackinac being so late in the year as would not conveiniently admit of my returning to New England before winter was by that means obliged to remain at that place untill spring. As this place is almost surrounded with three great lakes [*Huron, Michigan, and Superior*] and no mountains 'tis extreemly exposd to blustering winds which during the winter are almost continual, attended with snow storms of a long continuence, which with the extraordinary depth of snow prevents any exercise abroad, but little company, all manner of communication stopd for about six months, makes this place very disagreable during the winter. However the great supply of trout caught here daily at this season makes some amends for the want of a market of fresh meat, tho 'tis common that in February the Indians bring in a plenty of elk, moos, and beaver which bears a very high price at first. In the month of April here is commonly a prety good market for sugar made of maple sap which is often bought of the Indians for three pence pr. pound sterling. A pound of this sugar will not do the service equal to the same quantity of West India suger yet 'tis esteemd much more wholsom and four times as cheap as the other by reason of the long caryage.[138]

'Tis commonly about the tenth of May before the lakes are clear of ice. At that time the people generaly begin to keep a look out for the vessel from Detroit which comes here every spring as soon as the season will permit. About the same time the Indians begin to come in from their winter's hunt with large packs of peltry & skins in order to barter for such articles as they stand in need of, both for cloathing and accommodating themselves for fishing and hunting during the approaching summer.

May 23d arrivd the schooner Gladwin at Michilimackinac and on the 27th I embarqud for Detroit and saild the same eveng, but by being retarded by contrary winds for two or three days on Lake Huron we did not arrive at Detroit till the fifth of June. The distance between these two posts is about three hundred & sixty miles [*323*], three hundred [*316*] of which is on Lake Huron.

At Detroit Captain [*George*] Turnbull of the Royal Americans

---

[138] The importance of trout and maple sugar in the diets of residents of Michilimackinac and Sault Ste. Marie during the winter and early spring is confirmed by many travelers, including Henry, in Bain, ed., *Travels & Adventures*, 66, 70.

who commanded there kindly assisted me with provisions for my way to Fort Pitt on the Ohio, for which and other favours I had the hapiness to receive from that good gentleman I think my self bound in gratitude to make mention of him in my journal.[139]

The 17th of June I set of from Detroit in company with Doctor Prentice, a gentleman belonging to Carlisle in Pensylvania.[140] With him I went in a battoe round on the east end of Lake Erie to Sinduskie [*Sandusky*] Bay where horses being provided for our journey across the woods to Fort Pitt, not two days after we left Lake Erie we found such excessive heavy rains as laid all the savannahs under water, so that for hours together we rode to our horses' girts in water and often swim over creeks of several rod in width on horseback, by which means we lost all our provisions except a little salt pork which with some venison which an Indian who overtook us in the wilderness suplyd us with sarved for a tolerable supply till the fifth of July, when we arrived at Fort Pitt, which stands nigh in the forks at the junction of the Allegena and Monongahala rivers, after which 'tis calld the Ohio or Pleasant River which windes through a pleasant teretory of rich and most fertile lands for eleaven hundred miles where it falls into the Mississipi.

On the 15th I arrived at Carlisle, a small but beautifull town in the province of Pensylveinia. The 20th I arrivd at Lancaster in the same province. This is one of the finest inland towns I ever saw. It is situate in a valley. The groves of trees of a natural growth on eve[r]y side stand within a few rods of the ends of the streets.

July 24th arrived at Philadelphia the capital of the province of Pensylvainia, a very beautifull city. August the first I came to

---

[139] Turnbull appears to have become commandant at Detroit in the autumn of 1766. For an outline of his career, see Thwaites, in *Wisconsin Historical Collections*, 18:312n. For an account of Fort Pitt, now Pittsburgh, at about this time, see David Jones, *A Journal of Two Visits Made to Some Nations of Indians on the West Side of the River Ohio*, 20 (New York, 1865).

[140] Possibly Robert Prentice, who is listed in U.S. Census, *Heads of Families at the First Census of the United States 1790: Pennsylvania*, 76 (Washington, D.C., 1908). A Dr. Prentice appears in Pennsylvania frontier history in April, 1756, when Fort McCord was attacked by Indians. See Thomas L. Montgomery, ed., *Report of the Commission to Locate the Site of the Frontier Forts of Pennsylvania*, 1:544, 556, 578 (Harrisburg, 1916). His presence in Detroit in 1768 was perhaps occasioned by the fact that John Prentice, a trader, was believed to have been killed or taken prisoner by the Indians in 1763. See Charles A. Hanna, *The Wilderness Trail*, 2:378 (New York and London, 1911); William A. Hunter, *Forts on the Pennsylvania Frontier, 1753–1758*, 460 (Harrisburg, 1960).

New York and from thence soon after to Boston where I com-
pleated my journal and here concludes my travels.[141] Soon after I
came to New York where I found my self in great want after so
long a march, but was releavd by the truly kind and benevolent
John Small Esqr., major of brigades at headquarters,[142] so that I
was able to proceed on my return to New England and on the
Version II   first of September arrivd in Boston under the kind auspices of
Insert 14⟩   the indulgent hand of providence.⟩ Here ends this attempt to
find out a northwest passage.

⟨*Version II*   ⟨Having in the foregoing pages described the countries and
inhabitants somewhat concisely and barely as a journalist from
minutes taken as I travelled, the design I went upon and the
natural importance of this vast tract of continent seem to require
a publication of the information I was favored with from others
with some further and more general observations on theirs and
my own discoveries. The Naudowessie who extend indefinitely
westward speak familiarly of the South Sea as the great water to
the sun setting. They call the inhabitants that way the red men
and say they speak their language. They say a war party of their
nation in their excursions near the salt water coasts laid an am-
bush for a party of these red men which they saw coming towards them; but on their near approach hearing them speak loud
to each other and understanding them they discovered themselves and contracted a friendship with them. Here they tarried
several days and were curiously entertain'd with accounts of
many things they had never known before; and in particular of a
people who they called the bearded men which came often to
their country in very large canoes and in lesser canoes wou'd
come in great numbers on shore, cut down and carry away a sort
of stinking wood and load their great canoes with it, that sometimes they had wars with these bearded men and other times had
traded with them for knives, hatchets, &c. But what they gave in
exchange they cou'd not or wou'd not tell, pretending they did
not know.[143]

[141] This sentence was crossed out by Carver.

[142] Small was born in Scotland in 1726 and came to America with his regiment
in 1756. He served in the French and Indian War and in the Revolution, became a
major general in 1794, and died in 1796. See *Appleton's Cyclopaedia of American
Biography,* 5: 552 (New York, 1888).

[143] The material included from here to p. 142, below, from Version II of the

The Killistenoes and Assniboils living about the lakes DuBois [*Lake of the Woods*], Winepeek &c. in upwards of 52° north informed me they cou'd go in seventeen days from their country to Hudson's Bay, it being all the way down stream but that it required fifty days to return. From these I had hopes of much information and had it been possible to have staid so long with them as to become a little intimate we might doubtless had more satisfaction. But such is the nature of an Indian that one must wait for his story till he is pleased to tell it. Shou'd any presume to urge them all is over perhaps forever. They said that in their passage to Hudson's Bay there was plenty of buffaloe but smaller than those southward. Not far from the countries of these nations a little south of the west is a nation called Mahahs [*Mandan*] who raise plenty of Indian corn which the two former who never raise it purchase from them for a few European trinkets as knives, hatchets, &c. The white people as yet have never opened a trade with them. The Indians say that near this nation are some very bright shining mountains like bodies of christal stone.[144]

A little west of the Mahahs is a tribe called the Shyans [*Cheyenne*] who are scarsely known by any. Some war parties from the Naudowessie say they have been among them and

journals represents Carver's first attempt to enlarge his manuscript. It is, of course, much briefer than the additions which appeared in the published *Travels*. This very vague hearsay information might pertain to Spaniards on the California coast or on the coast of Texas. La Vérendrye obtained similar information about whites in the west around 1740; see Burpee, ed., *Journals and Letters*, 369–372.

[144] In 1767 William Pink made a journey from the Lake Winnipeg area to Hudson Bay in 21 days, and returned to The Pas in the same time. Other travelers reported similar timing. J. B. Tyrrell, ed., *Journals of Samuel Hearne and Philip Turnor*, 6, 32, 156n (Toronto, 1934). On the routes in this area, see Morse, *Fur Trade Canoe Routes*, 37–43. Although Mahah is the name frequently given to the Omaha by early travelers, Carver's account of this tribe, both here and in *Travels*, 80, 109, suggests that he was referring to the Mandan. See note 85, above.

Carver's description of the Shining Mountains in *Travels*, 121, which portrayed them as part of the height of land dividing the watersheds of the Gulf of Mexico and the Gulf of California, leaves no doubt that he was aware of the Rocky Mountains of which his Shining Mountains were a part. Although there is considerable controversy concerning this name in the La Vérendrye literature, it was commonly used later to designate the Rockies. See, for example, Edwin James, *Account of an Expedition from Pittsburgh to the Rocky Mountains . . . under S. H. Long*, in Reuben G. Thwaites, ed., *Early Western Travels, 1748–1846*, 17: 149 (Cleveland, 1905).

report that they live in villages and raise Indian corn. They think them smaller in stature than other Indians and say they have horses on which they fight in a very singular manner. The horse equipt in their fashion, they mount, having for defence a target in the bridle hand, to the right arm a little above the elbow joint is a string about five or six feet long fastened by one end. To the other a stone of about two pounds' weight something curiously wrought is suspended. This they shorten at pleasure by winding round the arm or lengthen by letting off, and being exercised from their childhood in this sport they will strike a deadly blow on full gallop & seldom miss their aim. 'Tis thus they hunt the buffaloe. When these people overtake any parties of enemies on the plains they are sure of destroying them all unless they come to water and enter their canoes when their horses can pursue no longer.[145]

Near this nation I learned is a river rising from mountains in their neighbourhood and running north of the west till it falls into salt water, enlarging much in its course.[146] On enquiry after a passage from the Indians they wou'd speak and make signs of great waters to the north west but whether salt or fresh, straits, rivers, seas, or inland lakes is hardly to be gathered from people whose way of life leads them into no such researches. There are many bands or cantons in these parts who have no commerce with the white people.

Southward of this and of the Naudowessie plains on and about the head of the Missouri are many Indian bands called in general Pawnees or Pawnanes signifying slaves. War parties from the Naudowessie bring from hence abundance of slaves as noticed before.[147]

On the plains between the river St. Piere and Missouri is a large mountain of red marble where all the neighbouring nations

[145] On the Cheyenne, see note 85, above. The buffalo-hunting technique here described is similar to that attributed to the Assiniboin by Henry, in Bain, ed., *Travels & Adventures*, 304. It may be a refinement of the *cassé tête* illustrated in *Travels*, Plate 4, and p. 97, above. See also Kellogg, ed., *Charlevoix Journal*, 1: 320.

[146] The stream is mapped as "River of the West" and called Oregon River in *Travels*, 76, and p. 121, above.

[147] Carver gives the Pawnee a more northwestwardly location than the traditional Kansas-Nebraska area. He may have been following De l'Isle's maps, which place the "Panis" on the Missouri. Carver's *Pawnanes* relates to *Padani*, the Dakota word for the Pawnee. See Hodge, *Handbook*, 2: 199; p. 100, above.

resort for stone to make pipes of.[148] Even those who hold perpetual wars in all other parts meet here in peace. The pipe being
the symbol of peace, it shews the prevalence of custom when
people of so cruel and implacable a disposition can so far bridle
their impetuosity as to be diverted from revenge by any means.

A little further south of the head branches of the Missouri on
the heads of some rivers falling into the Gulph of California is a
great number of bands called the Greater and Lesser Macques
[Hopi], the former about 40° N., the latter more southward are
pretty well known to the Spaniards who have sent some
missionaries among them but what trade or commerce is carried
on with them I have not been able to learn.[149]

To the southeast of those nations rises from some mountains
(a chain of which runs northward a great length) the Rio del
Nord [Rio Grande], or North River, which runs in a very straight
course and falls into the Bay of Mexico near its western extremity. On this river stands Fort St. Fee [Santa Fe], built for the
protection of the parties employed in transporting silver from
the mountains on Colorado River hither, whence it goes by
water to the Havanah [Cuba]. This land carriage is said to be
about three hundred miles. The Indians from the northward
have frequently made incursions on these Spaniards and
doubtless furnished themselves with the first breed of horses
now so plenty in very remote nations.[150]

The country between these parts and the Mississippi with the
great extent from the Mississippi to the Apalacheon Mountains

[148] The quarries of catlinite to which Carver refers are located near Pipestone,
Minn., and are now preserved as a national monument. Their mention in *Travels*,
101, brought them to the world's attention.

[149] "Moqui" or "Moki" was the name given to the Hopi on French maps of
the west. Their first contact with the Spaniards was in 1540. See De l'Isle,
"L'Amerique Septentrionale," in *Atlas Nouveau*, map 45; Hodge, *Handbook*,
1:560.

[150] Comparing the map of North America in *Travels* with Jefferys, "New and
Correct Map of North America with the West India Islands," in *American Atlas*,
5, it is evident that the River of the North or Rio Grande is what the *Travels* map
calls the Nuces River. "Nuces" may be an error for Nueces, another river which
flows into the Gulf of Mexico at present Corpus Christi, Tex. See also Florence J.
Scott, *Historical Heritage of the Lower Rio Grande*, 1 (San Antonio, Tex., 1937). A
more common name was Rio Bravo del Norte or Rio Grande del Norte. For the
dispersion of the horse in North America, see Frank G. Roe, *The Indian and the
Horse* (Norman, Okla., 1955).

having been more immediate subjects of the inquiry of the ingeneous Mr. Thomas Hutchins, lieut. and engineer formerly at Fort Pitt now at Illinois, I refer to his description.[151]

This vast tract of country now in great part under the dominion of our sovereign, capable of subsisting inconceivable numbers of inhabitants, abounding in variety of soils, climates, and natural productions, must afford many articles of commerce, and notwithstanding the difficult communication, take off millions in the light articles of British manufacture even so as to render the trade of Britain very respectable in her own territories. It has long been talkd that a very respectable province might [be] erected in the neighbourhood of Detroit of which this might be the capital.[152]

From the Green Bay up the Sax [Fox] River to the carrying place into the Ouisconsin is as the river runs about an hundred and ninety miles, and perhaps on a right line a hundred and ten containing the cantons of the Menomonies, Winebagoes, and part of the Saugies, wou'd make a good province. The climate is moderate, the soil rich, having about a sufficiency of timber for the use of the inhabitants and no more. Thousands of acres are perfectly clear and fit for agriculture, pasture, or mowing, and the interval[e]s abounding with grass which might feed cattle enough for a kingdom. Game of most sorts [is] in great plenty.

The country on the Mississippi from a little below the entrance of the Ouisconsin as far up as Lake Pepin being about two hundred and fifty [125] miles contains many fine ilands, large meadows, and plains. Many of the rivers which enter in this space have fine intervals on one or other of their banks, it frequently happening that there is found a mountain on one side and interval on the opposite. These intervals often terminate in large plains covered with grass and herbage on which are seen vast droves of wild cattle, deer, elk, and other game, besides fowl in plenty. This might well contain to sixty or eighty thousand settlers.

[151] Hicks, ed., Hutchins, *Topographical Description*, 71–121. See also p. 28, above.

[152] The proposed province with Detroit as its capital, and the subsequent suggestions below for provinces in present Wisconsin and Minnesota are the beginnings of a plan elaborated in *Travels*, 531–538, for the division of the upper Mississippi region into 11 provinces, based upon the availability of suitable water transportation for each.

The mountains upon the Mississipi abound with a kind of stone as easily wrought as wood when newly taken out of the ground but hardens in the air. Much of it is white as snow and wou'd serve for building in the best manner. Others have the color and quality of grindstone. The vast quantity of maple here will afford sugar. The Indians tell of some springs of salt water near the great river which may probably also supply that important article, salt, by boiling as is now practiced in the Illinois and Seneka countries. The rivers contain plenty of fish such as sturgeon, sword-fish of about lb. 20, catfish from 50 to 100. These are pretty good eating.[153]

The navigation of this great stream of water tho impracticable for large ships is doubtless much more important than is commonly thought, and a good acquaintence with the set of the current, eddies, &c. wou'd much facilitate the passage upwards. It is in its whole length very full of islands which must make much dead water and afford great safety in bringing up such open vessels as must use it.

Northeastward of this upon and about the St. Croix and Chippiway rivers is a tract sufficient for another very good province, the qualities of soil, climate, and productions very similar to the parts above described. One thing well worth notice in these parts is the wool of the buffaloe which is long and fine and cou'd certainly be manufactured into cloth. Whether these crea-

[153] The soft white stone is probably St. Peter sandstone, which underlies the area between the Mississippi and Minnesota rivers from their junction as far south as Northfield. The grindstonelike rock was probably the gray limestone which commonly overlays the sandstone. George M. Schwartz and George A. Thiel, *Minnesota's Rocks and Waters: A Geological Story*, 135, 136 (Minnesota Geological Survey, *Bulletins*, no. 37 — Revised Ed., Minneapolis, 1963).

This is an unusually early mention of the salt of the Onondaga country of western New York. Carver may be referring to salt works of the Indians or individual settlers. Though salt springs were discovered there in 1654, no salt works were established until 1787. See Harry B. and Grace M. Weiss, *The Revolutionary Saltworks of The New Jersey Coast*, 62 (Trenton, N.J., 1959). The salt source for the Illinois country was a saline spring near present Ste. Genevieve, Missouri, which was being worked by the French inhabitants of that town in Carver's time. See Hicks, ed., Hutchins, *Topographical Description*, 111. See also note 81, above.

Sturgeon and catfish are native to the Great Lakes-Mississippi Valley, but swordfish is an ocean species. Professor Lloyd L. Smith of the University of Minnesota identifies Carver's swordfish as either the paddlefish or the long-nosed gar. See Eddy and Underhill, *Northern Fishes*, 120–124, 126–129, 133, 297–301.

tures might be rendered quite tame is doubtful, but as they are, those who inhabit where they keep find no difficulty in coming at them. A bull of them when wounded but not disabled is very apt to turn and pursue the hunter.[154]

On the north or west side of Lake Superiour I cannot find much encouragement for cultivation. The fishery is considerable all round it but quite respectable at the Straits of St. Mary where seems also a better soil. The great quantity of virgin copper oar found on its southwestern shore is sufficient to render it worth *Version II*⟩ attention.⟩[155]

To the Reviser

⟨*Version II*   ⟨Concerning currents, rapids, according to the general accep-tation of the word in the author's country, is taken for a quick swift stream of shallow water breaking over rocks which emerge near the surface of the water. It is common for us to mention runing or river water under four denominations: first, a smooth gentle current; second, a hard strong current where the water is deep and no breaking occasiond by rocks near the surface; thirdly, rapids as before mentioned; fourthly, catarects or falls where water has a perpendicular descent. But as I don't know that the reader in general will take the deffinations of the words as I have mentioned them, I must refer this with all other phrases in my journal that are any ways doubtfull or ambiguous to the better judgment of the reviser, and further beg the favour that when he finds any accounts so unconnected as that he cannot adjust them well, that he the reviser will be so good as to let the

[154] Many early authors suggested the use of buffalo wool for cloth. Kellogg, ed., *Charlevoix Journal,* 2:206, and Jefferys, *Natural and Civil History,* 1:141, both attributed to the Indians a skill for spinning buffalo wool "to an equal perfection with the *English* wool," and Charlevoix, 2:219, suggested taming the animals for food. Several 19th-century attempts to produce buffalo wool proved economi-cally unfeasible. See Martin S. Garretson, *The American Bison,* 165–168 (New York, 1938).

[155] The presence of copper in the Ontonagon region of Michigan was known as early as 1659. Rogers promoted the first mining attempt, possibly because he claimed to own the Ontonagon region via an Indian land grant conveying the area to him on December 23, 1760. Alexander Henry, who participated in the first mining attempt, was one of the witnesses to the Rogers grant. See p. 19n, above; deed of December 23, 1760, in Rogers Papers. On the promotion of mining in the area and on Henry's role, see Kellogg, *British Régime,* 107–113; Bain, ed., Henry, *Travels & Adventures,* 220–229. Later mining is summarized by Bald, *Michigan in Four Centuries,* 231–237.

author know by Mr. Pain and every information shall be given that the author is capable of. And any thing that the reviser shall see fit to add to embellish or give better sence to the journal will I dare say be very agreable to the publishers and to the author. ⟩ [156]   *Version II* ⟩

⟨Explanation   ⟨*Version IV*

1st   A Naudowessie chief delivering a belt of wampum with a speech.

2nd   A Chippeway cheif (according to their customs) represented in form of a deer, receiving the belt and speech.

3d   An Englishman they always distinguish by a hat on their heads.

4th   A Frenchman by a handkerchief tyed round their heads.

5th   Indians have feathers on their heads.

6th   The pipe or cullimate of peace.

7th   The English colours.

8th   The heads of the canoes are set as going up the Chippeway River which is the only passage from these parts of the Mississippi to Lake Superiour.

9th   Six tents or houses signify that six days passed or six

[156] See p. 29, above. The reference to the author's country indicates Carver's awareness of the differences in language between England and the emerging United States. "Mr. Pain" may have been Henry Payne, a bookseller in Pall Mall, who was one of the publishers of the 1781 issue of the *Travels* and could have been involved in an editorial capacity earlier. *Dictionary of National Biography,* 44:110 (1895).

encampments the Naudouwessee cheifs had delivered this belt with a speech requesting the cheifs of the Chippeways through whose country we had to pass, to give me every protection and assistance I might stand in need off, and the party with me who are all particularly signifyed in the above hieroglyphicks which was drawn by our pilot (an Indian of that country) with coal on the bark of a large tree in a place most likely to be seen by travelling partys.

N.B.   This was a sufficient protection for me from all war parties of what nation soever.

The prickd line from mouth to ear of each cheif signifies hearing and answering each other, the upper being the first speech the under being the second or answer.[157]

Version IV⟩

Jonathan Carver⟩

[157] According to *Travels,* 418, this drawing was executed by the party's guide as they started up the Chippewa River. Its meaning was "that one of the Chipéway chiefs had received a speech from some Naudowessie chiefs at the town of the Ottagaumies, desiring him to conduct the Englishman . . . up the Chipéway river; and that they thereby required, that the Chipéway . . . should not be molested by them on his passage." For a later commentary on Chippewa picture writing see Bray, ed., *Nicollet Journals,* 266–275.

❧ Chapter Two ❧

SURVEY JOURNAL

BY JONATHAN CARVER

Weeks Days	Months Days	Course	Distance Miles	Remarks &c
				Survey Journal from Detroit to Michillimackinac in the Year 1766
Tuesday Augst. 5		NE	2	From Detroit up the [*Detroit*] river.
		N	1	
		NE	2/1	
		N	1	
		E	4	To Grand Pt. on the left hand.
		NE	2	This is in the south of Lake St. Clare [*Clair*]. A small bay on the west shore.
Wednesdy	6	NE	11	Here I came to Pleasant Island, on our right a little.
Thursday	7	NE	9	Here I passd through a great no. of islands on both hands [*mouths of St. Clair R.*].
		SE	3	At the end of this came to the beginning of River Huron [*St. Clair*] after I left Lake St. Clare.

Weeks Days	Months Days	Course	Distance Miles	Remarks &c
		NNE	2	The river in general sixty rods wide.
		N	3	
		NNE	3	Here is a small island [*Fawn*], and Bell[e] Rivr [*at Marine City, Mich.*] from the west: small.
		NE	2	
		N	1	
		NNE	1	Here comes in from the east Rivr Autronch [*Clay Creek?*], small.
Fryday	8	N	1	
		NW	2	
		N	2	To block house [*Fort Sinclair*]. A creek [*Pine R.*] comes in from west, 3 rod wid.
		NE	2	
		NNE	1	
		N	3	Passd an island [*Stag*] a mile long.
		NNE	2	To Birch Creek on west shore [*near Marysville, Mich.*].
		NNE	1	
		N	1	To Baubee's sawmill on a creek, west shore.[1]
		NE	3	
		NNE	1	
		NW	1	

[1] According to Jenks, *St. Clair County*, 363, 364, Duperon Baby had a sawmill on Bunce Creek near present Marysville, Mich., in 1780, and there was a tradition that a sawmill had existed there since 1690. The sawmill is marked on the "Riviere au Sapine" on Thomas Hutchins' map in Hicks, ed., *Topographical Description*.

Weeks Days	Months Days	Course	Distance Miles	Remarks &c
		ENE	1	This last 2 mile widens west, formes a bason much wider [*Sarnia Bay, at Port Huron, Mich., and Sarnia, Ont.*].
Saturdy	9			Lay by to mend our canoes.
Sunday	10	N10°W	3	This is in Lake Huron, west shore.
Monday	11	N	12	To a small river [*Mil-waukee or Birch Creek?*].
		N	26	Indented with small points [*between Lakeport and Richmondville, Mich.*].
Tuesday	12	N	17	
Wednsy	Augt. 13	N10°W	32	To Rogers's Point.
		NNW	10	To an island near shore. Very shoal water along here [*near Harbor Beach, Mich.?*].
		NNW	5	A small pt. of land.
		NNW	12	
Thursy	14	SW	14	To a large pt. calld Sugar Point.[2]
		SSW	3	To the enterance of Sugar [*Pinnebog*] River, pritty large.
Fryday	15	W	7	To a pt. [*Oak*]. This forms the mouth of Saganaum [*Saginaw*] Bay.
Saturday	16	NW	9	Across part of Saganaum Bay to a small island

[2] It is impossible to identify the islands and points Carver mentions here with certainty. James Duane Doty speaks of a Sugar Loaf Point apparently just south of Flat Rock Point, near present Port Austin, Mich. Doty, "Official Journal, 1820," in *Wisconsin Historical Collections*, 13:171.

Weeks Days	Months Days	Course	Distance Miles	Remarks &c
				[*Charity*]. Has anothr very near to the west [*Little Charity I.*].
Sunday	17	NW	6	Across the remaining part of the bay to a great point [*Pt. Lookout or White Stone Pt.?*].
		N	8	
		NE	7	To a great point [*Au Sable?*]. Forms the beging of the north part of Saganaum Bay.
Mondy	18			Stormy weather.
Tuesdy	19			Do.
Wednsy	20	NE	4	
		E	2	
		N10°E	5	To River Ausable [*Au Sable*] which is a large river.
Thursdy	21	N10W	38	To Thunder Bay River.[3] Passd a small island 3 mile back or south.
Frydy	22	NE	9	This is across Thunder Bay. An island a little way out on the south part.
Saturdy	23	NNW	4	To island in a sort of a bay [*Misery*]. Against the north pt. of Thunder Bay is 5 small island [*Thunder Bay, Sugar, Gull, Crooked, and Round*].
Sundy	24	N	3	To an island near shore.

[3] Normally, traders would traverse the mouth of Thunder Bay, so the river Carver mentions here may not be the present Thunder Bay River, which flows into Lake Huron at Alpena. He may have mistaken the Black River for the Thunder Bay River.

Weeks Days	Months Days	Course	Distance Miles	Remarks &c
Mondy	25	NNW	8	To Prequisle [*Presque Isle*]. A large peninsula on a narrow sand beach joyns th[e] shor[e].
Tuesdy	26	W	10	To a point [*Adams?*].
		WNW	10	To a large point [*Forty Mile?*].
Wednsy	27	NW by N	25	Across a bay six or seven mile deep [*Hammond Bay to Cheboygan Pt.?*].
		WNW	15	Across a bay [*Duncan?*].
Thursdy	28	N	3	
		NNW	12	This pt. is near east from a small bay lying south.
		NW	1	To [*blank in mss.*]
		W	1/2	To Michillimackinac.

In Lake Michigan to the Green Bay, Sepr., 1766

Wednsy	Sepr. 3	N	6	This is over the channel to Cape St. Ignatius [*St. Ignace*].
		NW	4	Against this end of four mile is the Isle St. Helens [*St. Helena*].
		NW	1	Small pt.
		NW	1	To a pt.
		NW	3	To a great point [*Pointe aux Chenes?*].
Thursdy	4	NW	15	Two small rivers comes in at a great pt. (at the end of this) [*Pt. Epoufette?*].
Frydy	5	WNW	3	To a pt. when comes in a small river.[4]

[4] The description below does not resemble the topography of the area closely enough for firm identification.

Weeks Days	Months Days	Course	Distance Miles	Remarks &c
		W10°N	6	To a pt. and two small islands near shore.
		W10°N	5	To a pt. when comes in two small rivers near each other.
Saturdy	6			Had stormy weather. Lay by.
Sundy	7	SSW	10	To a great point [*Seul Choix?*].
		WSW	7	
		W	5	
		S	3	To a pt.
Mondy	8	W	3	To a river [*Manistique?*] somthing large.
		SW	4	To a river.
		S	1	
		SE	1	To a point.
Tuesdy	9	NNW	5	
		WNW	3	
		W	3	This gt. bay I calld Elisabeth Bay.
		WSW	4	
		SW	13	
		S	5	To a great point [*Pt. aux Barques?*] in form of a crown.
Wedy	10	W	2	This is round the extremity of the last namd pt.
		SSW	2	To a pt.
		WSW	4	Very indented shore along here.
		SW	9	To River Au Sable, pretty large.
		SSW	5	Here is a large pt. [*Pt. Detour*] a little round,

Weeks Days	Months Days	Course	Distance Miles	Remarks &c
				begins the Grand Travers.
		WSW	3	To the first island [Summer] in the Grand Traverse across the Green Bay.
Thursdy	11			Stormy weather, lay by.
Fryday	12			Ditto.
Saturdy	13	S	7	Some islands all the way, referd to a rough draught taken on the spot [Poverty, Gull, Little Gull, St. Martin, Rock I.].[5]
		S10°W	14	To an Indian town on an island, referd to rough draught.[6]

To La Bay or Green Bay, 1766

Weeks Days	Months Days	Course	Distance Miles	Remarks &c
Sundy	Sepr. 14	SW	6	To Cape Townsend [Door Peninsula], south of the Grand Traverse.
		SW	15	Here I passd 11 islands near shore in the Green Bay [Sister, Horseshoe, Pirate, Jack, Adventure, Strawberry, Chambers, and Hat I.].
Mondy	15	SSW	26	To Sturgeon Bay. A small river [Sturgeon Bay?] comes in here. Indented shore.
		WSW	10	This ten miles is very indented full of narrow pts. and bays.

5 This rough draft is not with Carver's journals in the British Museum.
6 On the location of this town, see p. 74n, above.

Weeks Days	Months Days	Course	Distance Miles	Remarks &c
Tuesdy	16	SW	3	To a pt.
		SSW	18	Here is four small points near each other [N.W. Brown Co., Wis.].
		W10°S	6	
Wednsdy	17	SW	10	To the La Bay Fort [Green Bay, Wis.].[7] In this ten mile passd two points & two islands.

This Is a Survey up the Menomony or Sax River or
More Properly the Winebaygo [Fox] River, 1766

Thursdy Sepr. 18		W	1/2	Up the Sax [Fox] River, 40 rods wide, somthing deep at the mouth.
		S	2	
		SW	3	
		S	1/2	
		SSW	2	
		SW	1	Here the river is some wider for about a mile [below De Pere, Wis.].
Frydy	19	SSW	11	This 11 mile is very crooked.
Saturday	20			Lay by. Carryg our baggage by the carryg place [near Kaukauna, Wis.].[8]
Sundy	21	W	1	Two small islands in ye rapid at the carryg place.
Mondy	22	SW	1	Rapids all the way.
		NW	1	Do.

[7] On Fort La Baye, see p. 75n, above.

[8] The series of rapids mentioned here were named the Grand Kakaling, where the river fell 52 feet in the course of a mile. Below Carver notes his passage through rapids named Little Chute, the Cedars, and Grand Chute before he stopped near Appleton, Wis. See Lahontan's description of the Fox-Wisconsin waterway in Thwaites, ed., *Voyages*, 1:173–178. Among many other travelers who described this route were Hennepin, in Thwaites, ed., *New Discovery*, 1:305–307; Pond, in Gates, ed., *Five Fur Traders*, 35–45.

Weeks Days	Months Days	Course	Distance Miles	Remarks &c
Tuesdy	23	SW	7	Rough water and crooked.
Wednsy	24			Lay by to mend our canoes [*near Appleton, Wis.*].
Thursdy	25	S	5	The 3 last of this five miles is somthing wider [*Little L. Butte des Morts*].
		SE	3	This 3 mile is an island [*Doty I. at Neenah and Menasha, Wis.*] all the way on the uper end of which is the Winebago castle.[9] The river is 21 rod wide. The other branch on the other side of the isld is not so wide.
Fryday	26			Lay by.
Saturdy	27			Do.
Sundy	28	S10°W	5	This is on the west side of Lake of the Winibaygoes [*L. Winnebago*]. This lake is twenty mile long and 8 mi. wide.
Monday	29	S10°W	10	At the end of this came to a river [*Fox R. at Oshkosh, Wis.*].
		NW	5	This is up the Sax [*Fox*] River.
		W	5	This 5 mile is in the Sacx or Rice Lake [*L. Butte des Morts*].
Tuesdy	30			Had high winds, lay by.
Wednsy	Octr. 1	W	4	This four mile in the

[9] On the Winnebago "castle," see p. 78n, above.

Weeks Days	Months Days	Course	Distance Miles	Remarks &c
		SW	18	above lake which is 9 mile long and 3 broad. This [*Fox*] river is very crooked, 20 rod wide (it comes in a mile south of west e[n]d).
Thursdy	2	SW	14	Short crooks all the way [*N.E. corner of Green Lake Co., Wis.*].
		S	4	Do.
		W	3	Do.
Frydy	3	NW	2	Do.
		W	2	Do.
		SW	6	Do.
		W	4	Do.
		SW	7	Do.
Saturdy	4	SW	11	Do.
Sundy	5	W	4	
		E	1	A point of land just so as to turn [*near Mecan, Wis.*].

Continued up the Sax River, 1766

Weeks Days	Months Days	Course	Distance Miles	Remarks &c
Sundy	Oct. 5	W	2	
		S	2	
		E	3	This last 12 mile is round a neck of land. Come almost to the same place agan [*south of Princeton, Wis.*].
Mondy	6	SE	4	
		W	3	To a small lake [*Puckaway*]. A little below this lake comes in a small river [*Fox*] from no.
		W	2	This is in a small lake [*L. Puckaway, western end*].

Weeks Days	Months Days	Course	Distance Miles	Remarks &c
Tuesdy	7			Lay by at this lake opposit the town of Puans [*Winnebago Indians*].
Wednsdy	8	W10°N	3	This lake is about 5 mi. long and 3 broad, a town of Puans on the south shor.
		W10°N	7	This is in a river [*Fox*], at the end of this came to another small lake.
Thursdy	9	W10°S	6	This is in a narrow lake [*Buffalo*].
		S	1	A narrow place [*near Packwaukee, Wis.?*].
		S	3	Over another small lake about a mile wide [*Buffalo L., southern end?*].
Frydy	10	SE	8	
		SSE	3	Here comes in a small river from the north.
		SSW	5	At the end of this comes in another river [*Neenah Creek?*].
Saturdy	11	S	12	This is very full of short turns and windings.
Sundy	12	W	1	This is part of the cary place to the Ouisconsin [*Wisconsin R. at Portage, Wis.*].
		SW	4/3	To the Ouisconsin River.

A Survey down the Ouisconsin River, 1766

Mondy	Oct. 13	S	8	In the Ouisconsin River. At the end of this 8 mi. come in a small river [*Baraboo*] from NW.

Weeks Days	Months Days	Course	Distance Miles	Remarks &c
		S	4	All the way this four mi. is an island [*Lib Cross I.*], pritty narrow.
		SW	10	Small islands all the way.
Tuesdy	14	SW	14	
		S	5	At the end of this is the town or castle of the Sawgies [*Sauk Indians*], on the NW side on a large plain [*at Prairie du Sac, Wis.*].[10]
Wedy	15	W	7	At the end of this is a high mountain near the river [*Ferry Bluff*].
		WSW	27	
Thursday	16	SW	5	
		N	1	Here the road goes from the river to the lead mines.[11]
		W10°N	9	
Frydy	17	W10°N	11	
		W	24	At the end of this is the first town of the Otto-gomies [*Fox Indians*] on the north shore.[12]
		W	11	
Saturdy	18	WSW	40	
		W	5	
		SW	5	Here the Ouisconsin joyns the Mississipi.

[10] On the Sauk town, see p. 84n, above.

[11] R. W. Chandler, "Map of the United States Lead Mines on the Upper Mississippi River," in *Wisconsin Historical Collections*, 11:400, shows an old trail leading from the lead mines in the Blue Mounds area to the Wisconsin River at Arena.

[12] On the location of this town, see p. 85n, above.

Weeks Days	Months Days	Course	Distance Miles	Remarks &c
				Survey Continued up the Mississippi River from the Entrance of the Ouisconsin, 1766
Sunday	Octr. 19	N	10	This ten mile is up the Mississpi to Jaun [*Yellow*] Rivr on the west. The Mississi at the enterance of the Ouisconsin is half a mile wide.
Mondy	20			Lay by. Four mile above the mouth of the Ouisconsin is the second town of the Ottogamis on the east side of the Mississippi, situated on a large plain [*at Prairie du Chien, Wis.*].[13]
Tuesdy	21			Do.
Wednsdy	22	N10°E	8	
		N	3	
Thursday	23d	NNW	30	Passd some small rivers falling in on both sides [*Paint Creek, Village Creek, Upper Iowa R., Ia.; Copper Creek, Sugar Creek, Rush Creek, Wis.*].
Fryday	24	N10°W	25	
Saturdy	25			Lay by. This day had stormy weathr.
Sunday	26	N	11	Here I came to the Golden [*Bad Axe?*] River, not very large, on east side.
Mondy	27	N	27	At the end of this come in a river [*Root?*] from the west, not large.

13 On Prairie du Chien, see p. 88, above.

Weeks Days	Months Days	Course	Distance Miles	Remarks &c
Tuesdy	28	NW	30	
Wednsy	29	WNW	14	Here is a very large plain on the west side [*near Winona, Minn.*].
Thursday	30	WNW	21	
Frydy	31	NW	14	A very large plain. Very high land on west shore [*near Kellogg, Minn.*].
Saturdy	Novr. 1	N	4	
		NW	2	
Sundy	2	WNW	11	At the end of this comes in the Gibway [*Chippewa*] Rivr about half a mile below the Lake of Tears [*L. Pepin*].
		W	5	This five mile is in the Lake of Tears or Lake St. Anthony on norwest side.
Mondy	3			Had stormy weather.
Tuesdy	4			Do.
Wednsdy	5			Do.
Thursdy	6	NW	8	On the norwest of the above lake.
Frydy	7			Had stormy lay by.
Saturdy	8	WNW	8	Here [*near Bay City, Wis.*] ends the Lake of Tears, 21 mi. long four mile wide in the middle, more narrow at each end.
Sundy	9	W10°N	15	The beging of this is when I came into the river again. At the end of this 15 come in a sml R-W [*River from the west — Cannon R.*].
		NW	8	

Weeks Days	Months Days	Course	Distance Miles	Remarks &c
Mondy	10	NW	7	A small river [Big] entrs on the east.
Tuesdy	11	NW	3	
		WNW	4	At the end of this joins the great Rivr St. Croix from the NE [at Prescott, Wis.].
		W	2	
Wednsdy	12	W	18	
		N	3	

Continued up the Mississippi, 1766

Thursday	Novr. 13	NNE	2	
		NNW	6	
		W	3	
Frydy	14	NNW	2	At the end of this come to the Great Cave, one of the greatest rarity the country affords [Carver's Cave, St. Paul, Minn.].
		W	2	
		SW	6	
		W	2	At the end of this joins the great River St. Pierre [Minnesota] from ye SW.
Satury	15	NW	1	
		N	2	
		NW	2	
		NNW	1	
		NW	2	
		N	1	
		NW	1	To the Falls of St. Anthony of Padau [at Minneapolis, Minn.].
		NNW	8 [14]	

[14] Apparently an excursion beyond the Falls of St. Anthony, not mentioned in the journals.

Weeks Days	Months Days	Course	Distance Miles	Remarks &c
Survey up the River St. Pierre in the Country of the Nauduwesse or Sioux of the Plains, 1766 [15]				
Sunday	Novr. 16	S	10	This is up the River St. Pierre, a large isld [Pike] where it enters ye Missp.
		SSW	5	
Mondy	17	SW	4	At the end of this is a small village of the Nauduwesse. [16]
		WSW	4	
		W	4	
Tuesdy	18	W 10°S	20	
Wednsdy	19	W 10°S	12	All the way is full of very short turns & windings.
	20	S	8	
		N	5	
	21	W 10°N	18	
	22	SW	4	
		NW	2	
		W	2	
		SW	8	
		W	4	
		WSW	20	To the enterence of Green River [Blue Earth R., Mankato, Minn.?].
		WN	40	
		SW	8	This river [Minnesota] is all the way from when it joyns the Mississippi, full

[15] Carver's map does not indicate so great a distance from the Green River to his wintering place as the 82 miles logged here, and it is doubtful that he traveled so far since he does not seem to have been aware of the Cottonwood River, which meets the Minnesota at New Ulm.

[16] If Carver's mileage were reliable, this village would probably be the traditional Sioux encampment at present Shakopee. Considering his exaggeration of distances, however, it is more likely to be the village at the mouth of Nine Mile Creek, or some less permanent camp. See Babcock, in Minnesota Archaeologist, 11:138-140.

Weeks Days	Months Days	Course	Distance Miles	Remarks &c
				of short crooks and turns. I only observed the general course and this distance to the best of my judgment.
		W	24	
		NW	10	

Survey Journal up the Chippeway River [*Wis.*] and on to the Heads of St. Croix, down Another River into Lake Superiour and to the Great Carryg on the Nor West of the Lake, and to Michillimackinac, 1767 [17]

Weeks Days	Months Days	Course	Distance Miles	Remarks &c
Fryday	May 29	NNE	I	This is from the entrenc[e] of the Chippeway [*Chippewa R.*] into the Mississippi half a mile below Lake of Tears [*L. Pepin*].
		N	I	The river when it joins the Misspi is about 70 rod wide.
		NE	3	
		NNE	2	
		N	I	
		N10°W	I	Here comes in a small river [*Little Bear Creek*] from ye west.
		N	I	
		N10°W	I	A few scattering islands all the way [*Wahcoutah, Battle, and Plum I.*].
Saturdy	30	NNE	2	To a great island [*Dead Lake or Buffalo I.?*].
		NE	I	
		N	I	
		NE	3	
		N	3	

[17] On Carver's tour up the Chippewa River, see pp. 126–129, above.

Weeks Days	Months Days	Course	Distance Miles	Remarks &c
Sunday	31	E	2	Some small islands a long here.
		NE	1	To a small lake about a mile round the whole [*near Nine Mile Slough?*].
		NW	1	
		NE	2	At the end of this comes in a large branch from ye N [*Red Cedar R.*]. This is calld the forks.
		E	1	
		NE	2	
		N	2	
		NE	2	
		N	1	
		E	1	Here came to the buffelo's plains [*near Meridean, Wis.*].
		SE	1	
Mondy	June 1			Lay by to kill buffelos.
Tuesdy	2	NE	1	Here is a small bay & a small rivr comes in from SE [*near Meridean Slough*].
		NW	1	Came to high sand banks.
		NE	1	
		SE	1	
		E	1	
		S	1	
		E	2	Here is a very large island [*part of Happy I.?*].
		SE	1	
		N	1	
		E	2	
		N	1	
Wednsdy	3	E	1	Very high plains on ye north side [*entering Eau*

Weeks Days	Months Days	Course	Distance Miles	Remarks &c
				Claire Co., Wis., from the west].
		SSE	1	
		E	3	
		SSE	2	
		N	2	
Wednsy	June 3	NE	2	
		E	1	
		N	1	
		ENE	2	High sand bank or high plains on ye north.
		NNW	2	
Thursdy	4	N	1	Hard rapids & high ledges of rock on each side [Eau Claire, Wis.].
		E	1	
		S	1	More moderate currant.
		E	1	The traders from ye Mississippi seldom go further up then here.
		NW	3	
		N	1	
		ENE	1	
		N	1	
		NE	1	
Frydy	5	E	3	
		N	2	More hard rapids.
Saturdy	6			Stormy weather, lay by.
Sundy	7	N	1	Hard rapids.
		E	2	Here is an island [Gravel].
		NE	3	To the falls [Chippewa Falls, Wis.], a carrying place 128 rods over.
		NE	2	More moderate water.
		NNE	1	
Mondy	8	ESE	2	Hard rapids. A river comes in from ye south

Weeks Days	Months Days	Course	Distance Miles	Remarks &c
				calld Virmillian [*Paint Creek*].[18]
		ENE	1	
		NE	3	To a pretty large river [*Yellow*] from ye NE.
		NW	1	
		W	1	To an island.[19]
		W	2	
		N	2	Hard rapids.
		N	1	
		NE	1	
Tuesdy	9	E	1	To the [*Jim*] falls. Two carryg places near each other.
		NE	3	
Wednsdy	10	NE	1	To some more falls, a short carryg place.
Thursdy	11	NNE	12	Some hard rapids in this [*to Cornell, Wis.*].
Frydy	12			Stormy weather.
Saturdy	13	N	1	An island [*Brunet*].
		NNW	1	This is all the way a carryg place or falls.
Sundy	14	NNE	6	
		N	1	
		W	1	This last 2 mile is all the way a carryg place or falls [*at Holcombe, Wis.*].
Mondy	15	WNW	2	Here is a larg island and the river near a mile wide, sort of a lake [*at Holcombe Flowage*].

[18] On Carver's map, the river he designates as the Vermilion is farther north, and flows into the Chippewa River from the northeast; it may be the present Flambeau River or Deer Tail Creek.

[19] Probably covered in the creation of Lake Wissota by the dam at Chippewa Falls, Wis.

Weeks Days	Months Days	Course	Distance Miles	Remarks &c
		NNE	1	A river [*Jump?*] comes in here from ye NE. About here several islands.
		N	1	
Monday	June 15	NNW	1	
		NNE	1	
		WNW	2	
		W	5	
Tuesdy	16	W	1	To the forks. On[e] half [*Flambeau R.*] of the [*Chippewa*] river comes from ye north.
		NW	6	This is up the western branch [*Chippewa R.*].
		ENE	2	
		SE	1	
		NNE	3	
		W	1	
		NNE	7	Many very short turns.
Wednsdy	17			Stormy weath[er]. Lay by.
Thursdy	18	N	3	At the beginning of this 3 mi. comes in a river [*Thornapple*] from ye NE.
		NNE	12	Some very short turns.
Frydy	19	N	3	Some hard rapids [*at Imalone, Wis.?*]. A very small river [*Nail Creek?*] comes from east.
		NW	2	
		N	4	At the end of this comes in a small rivr [*Brunet?*] from ye east.
		NNE	1	At the end of this mile left the main branch on the east.

Weeks Days	Months Days	Course	Distance Miles	Remarks &c
Saturdy	20	N	2	This is up a small river [*Couderay*] about 30 yards wide, very stony.
Sundy	21			Lay by to dry our baggage [*near Radisson, Wis.*].
Mondy	22	WNW	2	
		NNW	3	
		NW	2	
		WNW	2	
		WSW	2	
		W	4	Very many short turns.
		N	3	About a mile of the last of this 3 is much wider and dead water.
		NE	2	The last of this 2 mi. is dead water and much wd. Is like a lake.
		N	1	The river narrow as usual.
		N	1	This 1 mi. is a lake a mile broad [*Little Lac Court Oreilles*]. At the up[p]er end stands an Indian castle[20] containg a great no. of houses calld Chippawy of the small lakes.
Continued in this castle till June the 29				Against the castle is a narrow channel of water run[n]ing swift about 20 rod. The houses stand on both sides having a bridge of logs between. Above the town is a lake [*Lac Court Oreilles*] ten mile long NW & SE

[20] On this Chippewa "castle," see pp. 127–129, above.

Weeks Days	Months Days	Course	Distance Miles	Remarks &c
				length, and about 5 mile wide in the middle. Something indentd shor.
Monday	29	N	3	This 3 mi. is across the lake above the town or castle.
		N	2	This is up a small river only sufficient for our canoes [*east of North-woods Beach, Wis.*].
		NW	6	This 6 mi. is all the way a lake [*Grindstone*] 3 mile broad.
		NW	1	This is a carryg place by land, no sort of water communican.
		NW	2	This 2 mi. is a lake [*Windigo*] 1 mile broad.
Tuesdy	30	NW	6	This is all the way carryg place [*Namekagon-Lac Court Oreilles Portage*]. Could see no water com[m]unication.
Wednsdy	July 1	NW	5	This 5 mi. is down a branch [*Namekagon R.*] of the River St. Croix five rods wide.
		W	2	
		SW	13	Some hard rapids, some short crooks [*near Spring-brook, Wis.*].
		NW	2	This same branch being part of St. Croix that falls in to the Mississippi between the Lake of Tears and the Falls of St. Anthony of Padau.
		NNW	2	
		SW	1	

Weeks Days	Months Days	Course	Distance Miles	Remarks &c
Wednsdy	July 1	S	1	
		SE	2	
		S	2	
		SW	5	
Thursdy	2	W	4	
		NW	6	
		NNW	14	All the [way] in this river is very full of short crooks which if alowd for will make the way much shorter.
		N	6	
		NW	14	
Frydy	3	W	10	This joins another large branch of Rivr St. Croix about 18 rods wide [*St. Croix R., northern Burnett Co., Wis.*].
		NE	5	This is up the other branch. At the junction is about 24 rods wd.
		N	3	Some hard rapids [*near Clemeng Creek*].
		NE	5	
Saturdy	4	NE	8	
		E	7	The last mi. of this begins Sturgeon Lake [*St. Croix Flowage*] about 60 rods wide.
Sundy	5			Stormy weather.
Mondy	6	E	6	Two of the first miles is in Sturgeon Lake the same width as before.
		ENE	3	This is dead water.
Tuesdy	7	NE	2	At the end of this is a small bay on the east side.

Weeks Days	Months Days	Course	Distance Miles	Remarks &c
		N	2	The river here is very narrow.
		NNW	1	
		NW	1	
		N	3	This 3 mi. is in a lake I calld Lilly Lake [*Upper St. Croix L.*], a mile wd in ye midle but mor narrow at each end.
		NE	2	This 2 mi. is in Lilly Lake. This lake has an island [*Crowhart*] in the middle.
		NNE	2	This 2 mi. is a carryg place [*St. Croix-Brule Portage*] over land being the head of the River St. Croix on the high land. This divids the waters of Misspi from that of Lake Superior.
Wednsdy	8	NE	9	This is down a small brook [*Brule R.*] six feet wide but soon grows larger.
Thursdy	9	ENE	5	
		NE	4	Some high hills on east.
		NNE	3	
		N	7	Joins here a river from ye west [*Nebagamon Creek*]. Here our river is six rods wide.
		NNE	6	
		N	8	
Frydy	10	N	16	To a carryg place [*north of Brule, Wis.*].
		N	14	Here is three short car–

Weeks Days	Months Days	Course	Distance Miles	Remarks &c
				rying places near each other [*at Lenroot and Clubhouse falls?*].
Saturdy	11	N	9	To a short carryg place.
		N	15	Here I came in to Lake Superiour, SW part. A small island near the mouth of the [*Brule*] riv[er].[21] This river all the way is very full of short turns, and when it enters the lake is about 20 rods wide.
Sundy	12	W	22	This is in Lake Superiour on the south part. High shore of red clay.
		NW	3	To the enterance of a large river [*St. Louis*] which has a bay [*Superior*] a little back discribd by a rough draught.[22]
		N	1	To a small castle of Chippeway & this bay mentiond before is large, is enclosd by two narrow capes [*Wisconsin and Minnesota pts.*] a mile and half long where the river falls in the lake from the west.
Mondy	13			Lay by.
Tuesdy	14	NW	2	
		NNW	3	Indented shore along here — this is round the

[21] This island has since disappeared.
[22] This rough draft is not with Carver's journals in the British Museum.

Weeks Days	Months Days	Course	Distance Miles	Remarks &c
				west end of Lake Superiour [at Duluth, Minn.].
		ENE	9	
Wedy	15	NE	6	
		ENE	3	
		NE	2	Passd a small river [Sucker?].
		E	2	
Wednsy	July 15	NNE	2	
		ENE	2	Here is a small island near shore [Knife I., at Knife River, Minn.?].
		N	2	Here passd a small river [Knife?].
		NE	4	
		E	2	At the end of this is Bloody Point calld so by the natives [at Two Harbors, Minn.?].
		NE	1	
		E	1	Here is a small island [Encampment?].
		NE	12	To a great point [Split Rock?].
		NE	2	Very indented shore, many bluff points.
Thursdy	16	NE	18	
		NNE	3	Indented shore all the way, high bluff point.
		NE	22	
		NNE	1	To a small river [Two Island?] and a small island [Bear or Gull I.?] against the mouth [at Taconite Harbor, Minn.?].

Weeks Days	Months Days	Course	Distance Miles	Remarks &c
Frydy	17	NE	10	All the way indentd shore, high bluff point.
		ENE	5	To a small river [*Poplar?*].
Saturdy	18	ENE	7	Very indented shore.
		NNE	3	Begins some high mountains [*Sawtooth Range*] of in land, indented sho[re].
		E10°N	8	
		ENE	34	All the way some small bays & pts. At the end of this a few islands near shore [*Blueberry, Pancake, and Arch I.*].
Sundy	19	ENE	4	To the bay at the Great Carryg Place [*Grand Portage*].
Mondy	20	NW	2	Back of this is a high mountain [*Mt. Rose*].
		NE	1-1/2	This mile and half brings to the landing place and Indian castle.[23]
		ENE	1-1/2	Back of this is a high mountain [*Mt. Josephine*].
		ESE	3	In this small bay is an island in the chops of it [*Grand Portage I.*].

Continued at the Great Carryg Place till the 8th of August

Saturday	Augt. 8	N	1	This is from the east pt. of the carryg place bay [*Hat Pt.*].
		E	1	
		SE	1	Along here is several islands [*Governor, High, and Magnet I.*].

23 On the Indian village, see p. 130, above.

Weeks Days	Months Days	Course	Distance Miles	Remarks &c
		E by N	6	Very indented shore.
		ENE	9	Very indented shore and rocky, several islands with mountains [*Boundary, Marin, Owen I.*].
Sundy	9	ENE	24	Very indented shore. Passd thru narrow bay, a mile deep east, & islands all the way, some with high mountains on ym [*Big Trout Bay?*].
Mondy	10	ENE	19	This is over a bay [*Thunder*] fourteen mile deep — with an island [*Pie*] in the middle six mile long, a mountain on [it].
		ENE	10	All the way some small islands [*Angus, Shangoina I.*].
		E	14	This 14 mi. is over a bay [*Black*] 20 mi. deep lying north, some islands in it [*Grey, Edward, Ariel I.*].
Tuesdy	11	NE	20	The first after passing at the bay go between shore and several islands, a narrow passage [*Magnet Pt.*].
Wednsdy	12	ENE	12	Several narrow bays [*Sturgeon, Shesheeb Bays*] and a no. of islands some very large [*Swede, Gourdeau, Lasher, and Brodeur I.*].
		ENE	5	Very indented shore. A small island.

Weeks Days	Months Days	Course	Distance Miles	Remarks &c
Thursdy	13	N	7	
		NE	6	To a very larg island [*Fluor*] with a mountain on it.
		N	4	
		NE	14	Over a bay [*Nipigon*] ten mile deep, several islands in it. The river [*Nipigon*] comes in here from Nipegon [Lake].
		E	16	Here is an island [*St. Ignace*] 30 mile long & 4 broad in general. Here we pass between this island and the bay mentiond last. This island begins with the last 14 mile.
Frydy	14	ENE	8	Across the east end of the isle to main land [*Crow Pt.*].
		ENE	4	
		ESE	18	Several islands [*Salter, Wilson, Copper I.*]. Here is a high rocky bluff point [*near Schreiber, Ont.*].
Saturdy	Augt. 15	E	15	
		ESE	9	To a great island [*Patterson*] far from land, very indented sh[ore].
		NE	8	
		E	5	Several islands along here [*Lawson, Barclay, and Pic I.*].
		SE	4	

Weeks Days	Months Days	Course	Distance Miles	Remarks &c
		S	5	To a high rocky mounn. Very indented shore [*near Guse Pt.*].
Sundy	16	E	10	To three high rocky islands [*near Marathon, Ont.*].
		S	18	
		E	3	To a large rivr [*Pic?*], has a communication with James Bay.[24]
Mondy	17	S10°E	23	Very indented shore.
		SSE	26	To a rock calld Otter Head. About this is some small islands.
		SE	16	To the enterence of a small river [*Pukaskwa?*], very indentd shore.
Tuesday	18	SE	9	At the end of this is a large isled six mile out in lake [*Michipicoten*].
		ESE	7	
		E	6	
		ENE	8	All this way is very indented shore and high ro[cks].
Wednsdy	19	ENE	14	
		SE	6	Some island [*Clergue*] at the bottom of this bay [*Michipicoten*].
		SW	4	
		S by W	8	

[24] The most common way to reach James Bay from Lake Superior was via the Michipicoten and Missinaibi rivers. However, it would have been possible to ascend the Pic River, portage to the Pagwachuan, and reach James Bay via the Albany River system. See Morse, *Fur Trade Canoe Routes*, 71. On the Pic area's importance in the fur trade, see Grace Lee Nute, "Peninsula, the Pic River Region, and Modern Marathon," in *Inland Seas*, 4: 3–14 (Spring, 1948).

Weeks Days	Months Days	Course	Distance Miles	Remarks &c
		S	8	
		SSW	7	
		SE	3	
		S	3	
		SW	2	
		S	3	
		SE	4	This is through a no. of small islds calld ye Stone Cross [*Cape Gargantua*].
Thursdy	20th	SE	5	Very indented shore.
		ESE	9	Comes in a rr. [*Baldhead*] north of a mounn [*Bald Head*], sevrl islands near shore and three low islands off in ye lake [*Leach, Rowe, and S. Lizard I.*].
Frydy	21	SSE	14	To where a rivr [*Sand*] enters and a long sandy beach and several small rocky islands [*Barrett, Sinclair, Agawa*] near shore and two low islands off further in the lake [*Rowe, S. Lizard I.*].
Saturdy	22	SSW	11	To a sml rivr [*Agawa*].
		SSW	11	Some sml bays and points [*MacGregor, Alona bays, Theano Pt.*].
Sundy	23	S	6	
		SW	7	To some small rocky islands calld Copper Islands, indented [*near Pointe aux Mines?*].[25]

[25] On the extensive copper-mining enterprises from the Montreal River to Coppermine Point in the mid-19th century, see John J. Bigsby, *The Shoe and Canoe: Or Pictures of Travel in the Canadas*, 2: 191–193 (London, 1850).

Weeks Days	Months Days	Course	Distance Miles	Remarks &c
Mondy	24			Lay by.
Tuesday	25	S	6	Across a bay [*Mica?*].
		SSE	4	
		SE	7	
		ENE	3	
		SSE	4	Something indinted shore all the way [*near Pancake Bay*].
		SW	4	
		S	3	
		SE	4	
Wednsdy	Augt. 26	ENE	5	
		SE	11	This is in a bay [*Batchawana*]. Some large islands, 2 out in the lake [*Batchawana, N. Sandy, S. Sandy I.*].
		W	3	
		SW	6	Against this is another island [*Maple*] a little out in ye lake.
		SSW	6	Much indented all along here.
		S	5	
		S	2	
		SE	2	
		E	8	
		SE	5	
		S	4	
		SW	16	
Thursdy	27	S	3	
		SSE	3	Here is a sml island [*Chêne*] nr shore. This begins the Straits of St. Marie's [*St. Mary's R.*].
		SE	9	This is in the straits. This forms somthing of

Weeks Days	Months Days	Course	Distance Miles	Remarks &c
				a bason [*Mosquito Bay*].
		E	3	To Puden Pt. [*Pointe aux Pins*]. Here 'tis near three mile wide, more narrow at pt.
		NE	4	This is 3 mile wide in middle somthing of a bay NW [*Pointe aux Pins Bay*].
		ESE	2	This is down the rapids to St. Marie's, near a mile wide [*Sault Ste. Marie*].
Frydy	28	ESE	2	From St. Marie's down ye rr. [*St. Mary's*]. A rivr [*Old Channel*] comes in from east.
		SSE	6	Thro a great no. of islands some very sml.
		S	10	
		SSE	6	Here is a no. of islands and a large one cald St. Joseph.
		SE	14	This is across a bay [*Munuscong L., west end*] 6 mi. wide in the midle more narrow at each end.
		SSE	6	A cross a bay [*Raber*] 5 mile wide sevl island here.
		SSE	6	This is a bay divided from other by two pts. [*Detour Passage*]. Here begins Lake Huron.
Saturdy	29	NW	3	This is in Lake Huron.
		W	3	

Weeks Days	Months Days	Course	Distance Miles	Remarks &c
		S	3	
		WNW	8	
		WSW	17	Some islands near shore [*Les Cheneaux Islands*].
		WSW	3	
		SSW	12	
		WSW	8	
		S	5	An island.
		SW	3	
	30	S	6	This is over the straits between Lakes Huron & Michiga[n] [*Straits of Mackinac*].

❧ Chapter Three ❧

JOURNAL OF A VOYAGE
1766-67

BY JAMES STANLEY GODDARD

Edited by Carolyn Gilman

THE only known copy of this journal is in the Rare Book Room of McGill University Library, Montreal. It is entitled "Journal of a Voyage under the Command of Captain James Tute, James Stanley Goddard Second, and Secretary to the Detachment; Joseph Reaume, Interpreter, Andrew Stewart Commissary, Augustus Ange, Lorange and Gabriel Loring, Engages." The manuscript is an 18th-century copy, but the date and purpose for which it was made are unknown. The only contemporary reference to Goddard's account found by the editor is in Sir William Johnson's journal of Indian affairs on November 6, 1767. Johnson noted there, "Mr. Goddard a Trader, and Joseph Rheaum a French Interpreter, Arrived here [*Johnson Hall, Johnstown, N.Y.*], & brought me Sundry letters & Accts. of Indn. Expences incurred by Major Rojers orders . . . I . . . desired Mr. Goddard to Send me his Journal, & opinion of the Disposition of the Sevrl. Nats. he had been amongst." The surviving copy may have been made for Sir William Johnson's use. The copyist was evidently a person who had little knowledge of the West, for the errors (for instance, miscopying Prairie du Chien as "Parie de lahun," although it was subsequently spelled more correctly) indicate little recognition of the names and places mentioned in the journal.[1]

[1] Hamilton, ed., *Johnson Papers,* 12: 386. On Joseph Reaume, see p. 125n, above. An Andrew Stuart accompanied Rogers from London, and was employed at Michilimackinac as the latter's servant. Stuart was accused of smuggling rum out

There are no major differences between Goddard's and Carver's accounts. There is, however, one interesting omission from Goddard's journal: he never mentioned the northwest passage. At Rogers' court-martial Goddard stated that his intention in going west was "to bring in the Indians," or persuade them to trade at Michilimackinac rather than New Orleans, and that is the purpose reflected throughout his journal.

THE JOURNAL

Wednesday morning about 6 o'clock the 17th September, 1766, set out in a bark canoe with goods & proper necessaries from Michilimackinac with a light breese from the north east up Lake Mishagan: this lake is so well known, that it would be needles[s] to say anything; only that it's the worst navigation for boats of any lake in the up country.

About thirty leagues [*95 miles*] west and be[aring] south of Michilimackinac, there is a river called Amanistick [*Manistique*], which the Indians winter in, and has a communication by several small carrying places with Lake Superior. About thirty leagues [*70 miles*] W.S.W. of this river is an island called Little Detroit, on which there is a small Indian town, consisting of about twenty five war[r]iors &ca., mostly Ottawas, of which Mamick-guoine is chief.[2]

During the summer season, the Indians of this place live on

of Michilimackinac with Rogers' connivance on August 20, 1767; if it was the same man, he must have parted with Tute's group, which only arrived at Michilimackinac on August 29. On Stuart and for Goddard's comments below, see Armour, ed., *Treason?*, 43, 55; memorial of Benjamin Roberts, August 21, 1767, and declaration of Charles Lavoine, John Chinn, and Alexander Henry, in Flick, ed., *Johnson Papers*, 5:633, 640. Augustin Ange was a Canadian trader who, after working in the Kaskaskia region, moved to Prairie du Chien, where he was one of the first settlers. In 1781 he was one of a deputation who received a grant of land at Prairie du Chien from Governor Patrick Sinclair at Michilimackinac. He married a Sioux woman and is said to have gone to live on the Missouri River. See Kellogg, *British Régime*, 171; Scanlan, *Prairie du Chien*, 70, 71; Brisbois, in *Wisconsin Historical Collections*, 9:285. The editor has been unable to identify the *engagés* L'Orange and Gabriel Loring.

   [2] On Little Detroit, see p. 73, above. The editor has been unable to identify Mamickguoine. Goddard's estimates of Indian population are usually equal to or less than Carver's; for example, see pp. 76, 80, 83, above. Other contemporary estimates can be found in Hicks, ed., Hutchins, *Topographical Description*, 135–137; Gorrell, in *Wisconsin Historical Collections*, 1:32; Jenks, in Bureau of American Ethnology, *Nineteenth Annual Report*, 2:1108.

fish, Indian corn, squashes, &ca., of which they raise large quantities. We having bad weather on the lake caused our arrival at this place so late the Indians were set off for their winter hunting before we arrived; however, we overtook the chief a few leagues from the town, gave him a little rum, and inticed him to come in the spring to Michilimackinac to see his father.[3]

Twelve leagues [35 miles] to the west north west of this island, is a river called Menomenecon [Menominee]: about two miles up this river, on the north shore, is an Indian village of the Menominies, consisting of eighty warriours: Nekick, or the Otter, is chief. This river also has a communication with Lake Superior: many Indians winter in the neighbourhood of this river, being plenty of beaver, martins, bears, &ca.[4]

Eighteen leagues [50 miles] to the W.S.W. of this river is the entrance of the River du Renard [Fox R.]: a mile up this river, on the north shore, is a small picqueted fort, which in the French time was garrisoned with an officer and a few men, who were paid by the person who farmed the post of La Baye: every winter the officer, with the men, went out wintering with the Indians.[5]

About half a mile up this river on the same shore is another town of the Minominies, containing about 40 warriours. In this town live the principal chiefs of this nation; the head of which is called the Horse, or Econeme — Caron, who acts for him, having more sense — Le Ne Coupe, or Ecowene, Paqueton: these are chiefs of the village; the war chiefs are, Chickiconawa, Tabasha, Whychet.[6]

[3] By "his father" Goddard means Rogers. This passage demonstrates the Tute party's role as advance men for Rogers' great council of Indian tribes in the spring of 1767. On the council, see Cuneo, Rogers, 202–205.

[4] On this village, see p. 76n, above. Goddard was mistaken in placing it northwest of Little Detroit; it was really to the southwest. The editor has been unable to identify Nekick.

[5] On Fort La Baye, see p. 75, above. By "farmed" Goddard probably means "farmed out"; the French owners of posts often leased the trading rights to fur merchants. François Arnaud, Marquis de Rigaud, was the owner of La Baye in the last years of the French regime. See contract of Rigaud de Vaudreuil, I. G. Hubert, and Jacque Giasson, September 30, 1757, and grant of La Baye to Rigaud, January 26, 1759, in Wisconsin Historical Collections, 18: 197–199, 207; Kellogg, French Régime, 382.

[6] According to the genealogy given by Walter J. Hoffman, The Menomini Indians, 44–60 (Reprint Ed., New York, 1970), Carron was a French trader who married a Menomini woman and founded a line of chiefs; he died around 1780.

The Menominies are the bravest warriors and best hunters of all the Indians in the upper country, of which, when they are in company with other nations, they don't forget to boast, by telling them they have killed and bound all other nations, at the same time saving theirs; not an Indian on earth can boast of taking a Menominies prisoner, not even a woman.

The 14th October 1761, this post was garrisoned by Captain Belford [*Henry Balfour*], of General [*Thomas*] Gage's infantry. He left Lieutenant James Gorrell of the Royal Americans, a serjeant, corporal and fifteen soldiers, who continued unmolested 'till all the posts were cut off in 1763, and then the chiefs, with some young warriors, escorted the garrison, with their arms, traders with their goods, &ca. down to Michilimackinac; and by their care and influence opened the road through the Ottawas, and Chippawas for the English that came from La Baye, as well as all other English prisoners in that country, and persuaded the Ottawas to carry them to Montreal.[7]

The current of this [*Fox*] river is very strong, having several rapids, and one carrying place [*Grand Kakaling*] of about one mile long.[8]

Fourteen leagues [*40 miles*] from the fort is a small lake [*Winnebago*]; 7 leagues [*10 miles*] from east to west, and about two leagues [*29 miles*] from north to south. In the entrance of this lake is an Indian town of the Whynipicons [*Winnebago*], or Puiants, in which are near 80 warriors; the chiefs of the village are two, called Labra and Caramane [*Caromanie*]: the war chiefs, Wacon-

---

Goddard knew him as early as 1763; see Gorrell, in *Wisconsin Historical Collections*, 1:38. The "Old Chief" Tshekatshakemau (also spelled Cha-kau-cho-ka-ma) may be Goddard's Chickiconawa. Either Econeme or Ecowene may have been Hoffman's Akwinemi, son of the "Old Chief." One of these two may also be "Ogemawnee" or "Okimasay," both cited by the British for loyalty; for this and other information, see Grignon, certificates of William Johnson to Ogemawnee, August 1, 1764, and Robert Rogers to Okimasay, July 3, 1767, all in *Wisconsin Historical Collections*, 3:217, 226, 265–268, 283–285; 18:268, 286; Father Anthony M. Gachet, "Five Years in America," in *Wisconsin Magazine of History*, 18:347–350, 356–358 (March, 1935).

[7] This is an eyewitness account, for Goddard arrived at Fort La Baye with the garrison on October 12, 1761, and left in 1763. On Goddard and Balfour, see Gorrell and Thwaites, in *Wisconsin Historical Collections*, 1:26; 18:233n. Gage's Light Infantry was the 80th Regiment of Foot. For another account of the evacuation, see p. 75, above.

[8] On the Fox River rapids, see p. 152n, above.

haw and Huckemawpelo. This nation are brave and intriped, but very indifferent hunters.[9]

Five leagues [*15 miles*] to the west and be[aring] north of this town the same River du Renard falls into this lake: in this river are several small lakes; the first [*Butte des Morts*] takes its name from the river, the next is called Lake Apoquoy [*Puckaway*]. On the south side of this lake is another small village of the Whynipicons. In this are thirty warriours; the chiefs of the village are named Chungepaw and Whynschuk: war chiefs Huckemawcemon and Whynixchiga [*Winneshiek?*].[10]

Fifteen leagues up this river is another small lake called Lake le Boeuf [*Buffalo L.*], six leagues [*13 miles*] from east to west, and one league [*1 mile*] from north to south. On the south shore are two Indian houses who raise Indian corn. From this lake to the carrying place [*Portage, Wis.*] is fifteen leagues [*16 miles*]: this river is very serpentine, and makes every point of the compass several times cross the country to Fort La Baye, being but 36 hours march.

The above carrying place is near three miles over; half of which is a swamp, the other half high champion [*champaign*] land: when over this carrying place we fall into a fine river called Ouisconsang [*Wisconsin*], which takes its source from a lake called the Fallovine Lake, distance 40 leagues bearing north. As this river's course is north and south; a strong current, and is one hundred leagues [*430 miles*] long; about one mile across: the river is full of islands and sand banks, which makes the channel crooked and difficult to sail in.[11]

[9] Goddard's dimensions for Lake Winnebago would be more correct if his north-south and east-west measurements were reversed. On the town at Doty Island and Caromanie, see pp. 78n, 79n, above. Waconhaw or Waukon Decorah was the name of a line of chiefs prominent into the 19th century; for a summary of information about them, see Hexom, *Indian History*, n.p.; Hodge, ed., McKenney and Hall, *Indian Tribes*, 2: 298–302, 308–315. The editor has been unable to identify Labra and Huckemawpelo.

[10] Again Goddard confuses north and south here. The entrance of the Fox River into Lake Winnebago is southwest of the Doty Island village. "Apoquoy" is a version of the Chippewa *apakwei*, the leaves of the cattail plant. "Puckaway" is a corruption of this. See Blair, ed., *Indian Tribes*, 2: 227n. According to Hexom, *Indian History*, n.p., Winneshiek was originally a Fox name, properly spelled "Winnishiga." On this and other Winnebago chiefs, see Lawson, in *Wisconsin Archeologist*, 6: 136–159.

[11] The source of the Wisconsin River is Lac Vieux Desert in present Vilas County, Wis. What Goddard calls Fallovine (folle avoine or wild rice) Lake may be one of the many Rice lakes in northern Wisconsin enumerated by Jenks, in

Two leagues distant from the carrying-place, on the west side, is a small river called River de Baraboux [*Baraboo*], so called from a Frenchman of that name, wintering in it many years ago: the Indians frequently go up this river to their winter hunting, in which they make a tolerable hunt, having plenty of deer, bears, raccoons, beaver &ca.[12]

Twelve leagues down Ouisconsang on the west shore is a large Indian town of Sackies [*Sauk*], in which are three hundred warriours. The principal chiefs of the town are Peshepau & Cagigameg: the war chiefs are Sigets, Otokgick & Washehone. This nation are warlike and good hunters, have a quantity of horses which they use to hunt buffeloes on in the summer season. This town is situated on the banks of Ousisconsang [*Wisconsin*]: behind the town is a very extensive plain [*Sauk Prairie*], on which the Indians raise large quantities of Indian corn, squashes, mellons & tobacco; they raise sufficient to supply themselves and sell vast quantities to the traders. They have a perpetual war with the Illinois Indians, which I have heard the war-chief declare should endure as long as the sun, moon and stars.[13]

A French officer endeavouring to make a peace betwixt these two nations, the war chief answered, father, how can you expect we can be at peace, for was it possible our bones should meet after death, they would fight together 'till they would be broke to pieces; how then father can you expect I should be at peace while I am living, and have any flesh on my bones.[14]

Bureau of American Ethnology, *Nineteenth Annual Report,* 2:1124. Scattering Rice Lake, on the border of Vilas and Forest counties, is drained by the Wisconsin River.

[12] H. E. Cole, *Baraboo And Other Place Names In Sauk County, Wisconsin,* 7–17 (Baraboo, Wis., 1912), lists many variations of Baraboo, Baribeau, or Baribault, a French trader. See also Brisbois, in *Wisconsin Historical Collections,* 9:301.

[13] On this town and the war with the Illinois, see pp. 83, 84, above. "Peshepau" resembles the name of the Sauk chief Pashipaho, who was prominent in the early 19th century, and who may have been a descendant of this chief. See Hodge, *Handbook,* 2:205. The editor has been unable to identify the chiefs mentioned, although several of the names survived into the 19th century; see, for example, an 1839 list of Sauk and Fox chiefs in A. R. Fulton, *The Red Men of Iowa,* 278–280 (Des Moines, Ia., 1882). The Fox Indians were the main aggressors against the Illinois, with the Sauk acting as their frequent allies.

[14] On French efforts to make peace and their reports of Sauk-Fox answers, see Kellogg, *French Régime,* 304–306; letter of Constant Marchand de Lignery to Pierre Dugué de Boisbriant, August 23, 1724, in *Wisconsin Historical Collections,* 16:444–446.

Twenty five leagues [*43 miles*] down the river, on the same side, is the town of Otagamies, or Renards [*Fox*], containing about 300 warriors: chiefs of the town are Macketochick and Chekequey: the war chiefs, La Port, or Kipahone & Wasala; this nation raise a good deal of corn, &ca.: have much the same language and manners of the Sackies.[15]

Eighteen leagues [*40 miles*] below this town Ousconsang falls into Missisippi, or the Superior River: the season was so far advanced that the Indians were all on their hunting ground before we past their towns, so that we had no opportunity of speaking with them. We concluded to winter on a river, called River du Dard [*Turkey*], on the west side the Missisippi 12 leagues [*23 miles*] below Ousconsang.[16]

This river comes from the westward, is very rapid, many Indians winter in it, as well as traders; we got our house built; just as it was finisht Mr. [*William*] Bruce came down and persuaded Captain [*James*] Tute to go and winter in a river, called Jone [*Yellow*]: accordingly Captain Tute left me some goods; sent off the canoe with the other goods the 29th November to the River Jone, and on the 30th he and Mr. Bruce set out on foot for the above river, leaving Mr. Reaume, Stewart and L'Orange with me.[17]

Nothing material happened 'till about the 1st January, when Mr. Pratt and Cagigamang, chief of the Sackies, came to see me,

[15] This is probably the town near Muscoda, Wis., mentioned above, p. 84. The chiefs have not been identified. La Port or Kipahone is the man mentioned below (p. 187) as the founder of the Fox settlement at Prairie du Chien. Many sources claim that Prairie du Chien was founded by a chief named Dog or Dog's Head, from which the name of the town was derived. G[iacomo] C. Beltrami, *A Pilgrimage in Europe and America, Leading to the Discovery of the Sources of the Mississippi and Bloody River,* 2:170 (London, 1828) gives his name as "Kigigad, or dog." Joseph M. Street to William Clark, October 14, 1830, gives it as "Shon-Kar-Paw"; see National Archives Microcopy 234, Roll 696, U.S. Office of Indian Affairs, Letters Received (Prairie du Chien Agency, 1824–33), microfilm in Minnesota Historical Society. However, the French "La Port" probably means "door," not "dog." The Fox and Sauk were so closely related as to suggest they were originally branches of the same tribe, according to Hodge, *Handbook,* 1:472.

[16] "Superior River" is an unusual name for the Mississippi, perhaps a translation into French of "Great River." See Upham, *Minnesota Geographic Names,* 4–6. By wintering on the Iowa side of the river, Goddard and Tute were among many British traders illegally in Spanish territory.

[17] According to Rogers' instructions, p. 193, below, Bruce should have been wintering with Carver.

by whom I heard the said Cagigamang had received presents with a belt of wampum from Monsr. [*Louis de*] St. Ange [*de Bellerive*], French commanding officer of the Illinois, in order to get the neighbouring Indians to leave their towns, and establish themselves on the west side of the Missisppi. I used every method in my power to persuade them to the contrary, and likewise to go to Michilimackinac the spring following.[18]

During the winter I made him several visits and at the last with much difficulty got his promise to take his young men to Michilimackinac: we had a very fine winter; saw a great many Indians; amongst the rest the chief of the Renards: I made use of the same arguments to him to go to Michilimackinac with his young men: I got his promise much easier than the other, he being an old acquaintance of mine.

The 16th of April we left winter quarters for La Parie de Lahun [*Prairie du Chien*] an Indian town on the east side of the Missisppi, two leagues above where Ousconsang falls into the Missisippi: the chief of this town is La Port or Kapahane. This town was established in 1763 by the abovenamed chief, since which there are 12 large huts of Autagamies [*Fox*] and Sackies [*Sauk*], in which may be one hundred warriors; the chief's name is [*blank in ms.*]

When we arrived at the place, the Indians were not returned from hunting: Captain Tute ask't me if I would fetch some liquor from La Bay; as I thought it would strengthen our endeavours to get the Indians to Michilimackinac, I accordingly set off the 21st April with a small canoe and five men: I got to Fort La Bay in 11 days; bought one keg of common brandy, being all that was to be got, and two kegs of wine; made the Menomenices that wintered about La Bay a present of two gallons of brandy, and desired them to go see their father at Michilimackinac, which they promised.

On my return I met the different nations of Indians who had

---

[18] The Pratte family was prominent in the fur trade of St. Louis. This could have been Jean Baptiste Sebastian Pratte (1739–1826), a French trader who was living at Ste. Genevieve in present Missouri by at least 1771. See "The Reminiscences of General Bernard Pratte, Jr.," in *Missouri Historical Society Bulletin*, 6: 60n, 61n (October, 1949). St. Ange, who had been French commandant at Post Vincennes since 1736, was at St. Louis in 1767, where he commanded with the consent of the Spanish. See Reuben G. Thwaites, ed., "The French Regime in Wisconsin," in *Wisconsin Historical Collections*, 16: 443n.

held council with Capt. James Tute, and had orders for liquor on me; I contented them as well as possible; bought some Indian corn and grease with half the brandy for our voyage: as the Menominies had no order on me for liquor, I had a keg of wine for my own use. I gave it them, and begg'd them to go see their father at Michilimackinac.[19]

I was 23 days on this voyage; at my return found Capt. Jona. Carver had joined the detachment, and that Captain Tute had engaged Charles Gaultier as interpreter, he being the interpreter at La Bay the year the posts was cut off, and was instrumental to the saving that fort. It gave me great pleasure to find a person so capable had joined the detachment: Capt. Tute had also engaged five Indians and two Frenchmen to go as far as the great carrying-place [Grand Portage] in Lake Superior; from this place I wrote to Major Rogers, and inclosed him the different speeches of the Indians.[20]

This town is the place where all the different Indians meet every spring and fall, as well as the traders. A fine situation for a fort, being the center of trade in this country, both from Canada and the Illinois; and if a fort was established on this spot, it would greatly augment trade, and keep the Indians in our interest: there is plenty of venison, wild fowl, fish, corn &ca. &ca.: so that I take it a garrison might be kept at little expence.[21]

The 21st May set out on our voyage in two small canoes up the Missisippi: this river is large, an easy current and full of islands, aboun[d]ing with animals, fish and fowl at the proper seasons; many small rivers on each side where the Indians go to winter in. The fourth night after our departure, we were alarmed about midnight with a party of Indians coming upon us well armed, and I verily believe had we not been superior in number, they would have plundered us, if not kill'd us.[22]

[19] For the amount of rum and other gifts given to the Indians here, see p. 204, below. On the official reaction, see p. 18, above.

[20] Goddard would have arrived back at Prairie du Chien on May 13; Carver had joined the party on May 6. On Gautier, see p. 125n, above. Though he served as Lieut. James Gorrell's interpreter at La Baye, Gautier was dismissed before the posts were cut off. See Kellogg, British Régime, 13, 18. On Grand Portage, see p. 17n, above. Goddard's letters to Rogers have not been found.

[21] Peter Pond, in Gates, ed., Five Fur Traders, 44–46, also described Prairie du Chien as a meeting ground of Indians and traders. No fort was established there until the American Fort Shelby, founded in 1814. See Scanlan, Prairie du Chien, 117.

[22] For this episode, see above, p. 125.

The eighth day we arrived at the Chippawa River; held a council what road to take as our pilot [*Acopewine*] was a Chippawa, and the other road must have past us thro' the S[i]oux country, who have a perpetual war together: we concluded it the safest way to proceed up this river; accordingly the next morning we set off.

This is a fine river on the north side of the Missisippi 70 leagues [*120 miles*] from the La Prairie du Chine in the entrance of Lake Papan [*Pepin*], runs near north and south, the current very strong, serpentines very much, as it's an enemies country; there is plenty of animals, such as stag, deer, bears & buffeloes, of which we killed every day one sort or other.[23]

Thirty leagues of this river is a strong regular current, and fine land, and about thirty leagues is rocky and rapid with several carrying places; the navigation is so difficult that very few traders attempt it: it has a communication by several carrying places with La Pointe in Lake Superior; however, we took a small branch of a river [*Couderay*] to the southward, in order to visit an Indian village situated on Lake Ottawa [*Lac Court Oreilles*], so called from one of the Ottawas being buried there.[24]

The Indians of this town are looked upon by traders to be the worst Indians in the country, and it's my opinion they really are so. This town consists of 60 warriours; the chiefs of the town are Andickweas[?], Megose and Ochick; the war chief Acopewine, who was our pilot: they live in continual fear, being so near the S[i]oux nation. They raise within these few years sufficient corn &ca. for themselves: we s[t]aid six days at this town; made them a considerable present, and got some of their young people to help us over two carrying places [*Lac Court Oreilles-Namekagon Portage*].[25]

This country is well watered by several small lakes; it's little

[23] See p. 127, above, on Chippewa-Dakota warfare along the Chippewa River; this may be the meaning of "enemies country." This phrase may also be a copyist's error. Lake Pepin received its name as early as 1703, according to Upham, *Minnesota Geographic Names*, 10.

[24] The route to La Pointe on Madeline Island was via the west fork of the Chippewa River, portages being made through Clam Lake to the Bad River, which empties into Lake Superior near present Odanah in Ashland County, Wis. See James D. Doty, "Northern Wisconsin in 1820," in *Wisconsin Historical Collections*, 7:203. On the name "Ottawa Lake," see p. 128, above.

[25] "Years" may be a copyist's error. According to Carver, pp. 127–129, 166, above, they stayed at Lac Court Oreilles from the evening of June 22 to the morning of June 29. The chiefs have not been identified.

known, we being the first white people that ever passed this road. The last carrying place is near two leagues across, and falls into a small river called Mickaxgan [*Namekagon*]: where we joined this river it is 50 leagues, course S.W. & N.E. It is a very pleasent country, and plenty of deer in it; when we left this we fell into a branch of St. Croix, our course N.W. & be[aring] west: this river is very shallow with a small current: we mounted this river about fifty leagues [*30 miles*] and fell into a small lake, called [*Upper*] Lake St. Croix about five leagues [*4 miles*] long, and one league [*½ mile*] across. At the end of this lake we made a carrying place of 2 miles [*St. Croix-Brule Portage*], which brought us to the head of a river called Nacisaquoit [*Brule*]; we were obliged to stay and make dams to stop the river, in order to get water enough to pass our canoe. This river is narrow and rapid; we had two small carrying places [*Lenroot and Clubhouse falls?*], is forty leagues [*30 miles*] long, and falls into Lake Superior.[26]

About seven leagues [*25 miles*] to the S.E. of the bottom of the lake to which we proceeded the next day, expected to find a great many Indians; when we got there, we only found one hutt, the rest of this village were a hunting: they have no established houses, but move them occasionally, the[y] consist of near 100 warriours; the head of the house we found there, was brother to our pilot: we made him a small present, and invited him and the people of his town to see the commandant of Michilimackinac. Our provisions were very low, neither could we purchase any at this place: we set out along the north shore of the lake for the great carrying place [*Grand Portage*]; this shore is mountanious, well watered, having many small rivers. The sixth day got to the great carrying place; it's about 70 leagues [*150 miles*] from the bottom of the lake, to our great joy, as we had not one mouthfull of provisions left.[27]

[26] On the claim that Tute's party was the first group of whites to visit Lac Court Oreilles, see p. 129n, above. The name Namekagon is Chippewa, from *name* (sturgeon), *kagan* (place). See Chrysostom Verwyst, "Geographical Names in Wisconsin, Minnesota, and Michigan, Having a Chippewa Origin," in *Wisconsin Historical Collections*, 12:394. Goddard's directions are again inaccurate; the party was traveling northeast on the St. Croix. "Nacisaquoit" is probably a version of "Nemitsakouat," the Chippewa name for the Brule River. See Warren, *History of the Ojibway*, 410.

[27] On the Fond du Lac village, see p. 129, above. At Rogers' court-martial, Goddard testified of this part of the journey that they "had very near been Starved." Armour, ed., *Treason?*, 55.

We found 14 or 15 huts of Christinos [*Cree*] and some of the Chippawas; they told us had they had provisions for their voyage they would have gone to see their father at Michilimackinac.

We got now and then a few fish and a little fallovine, or wild rice; we sent a canoe off to meet the French canoes from Michilimackinac, which returned the sixth day with a small replenish of provisions; the next day six canoes came in, we assembled the Christinos and Chippawas, gave a stand of colours to the chief of the carrying-place, invited him to go see his father, as well as the Christinos, which they promised the next spring.[28]

We had a meeting, consulted, and found we had not necessaries to proceed, & we agreed to return to Michilimackinac. Captain Tute set off with Mr. Carver and Mr. Autherenton [*Phinehas Atherton*] two days after myself; Monsr. Reaume & Gaultier embarked in two canoes which Monsr. Boyiz [*Charles Boyer?*] sent to Mr. Grovesbeek [*Stephen Groesbeck*]; we met several French traders along the lake.[29]

The north shore of this lake is very rocky; notwithstanding you meet frequently small bays, so that you march without much fear: the sea in this lake is more regular than in any of the other lakes I've been in. On the 29th August 1767, we arrived safe at Michilimackinac.

(Signed) JAMES STANLEY GODDARD,
Secretary to the Detachment

[28] On the Grand Portage Indians and this council, see pp. 130, 131, above.

[29] On Atherton, see p. 18, above. Boyer was a trader who had been at Rainy Lake since 1744. In 1767 he was in partnership with Forrest Oakes, but by 1781 he was with William Bruce and James Tute on the Assiniboine River. His last years he spent in charge of Rainy Lake, where he was described as an old but excellent trader in 1793–95. See Morton, in Royal Society of Canada, *Proceedings and Transactions*, third series, v. 31, sec. 2, pp. 92–95. He is probably the "Mr. Boyce" Rogers refers to in his letter to Tute, p. 197, below. Groesbeck was one of the traders Rogers was heavily in debt to. He was under suspicion for sending a man out to persuade the Indians to support Rogers' supposed treason. It is likely this man was Boyer; Rogers said in his letter below that "Boyce" was going to Rainy Lake, and Groesbeck outfitted the only canoes which went to Rainy Lake in 1767. See Robert Rogers, statements of debt to Stephen Groesbeck, September 20, 1766, February 2 and May 25, 1767, and letter to Sir William Johnson, September 23, 1766, in Flick and Hamilton, eds., *Johnson Papers*, 5: 380, 488, 553; 12: 194; Roberts to Johnson, August 20, 1767, in *Michigan Pioneer and Historical Collections*, 10: 225; Lart, ed., in *Canadian Historical Review*, 3: 353.

❧ Appendix One ❧

SELECTED DOCUMENTS

1. Jonathan Carver's Commission from "Robert Rogers Esqr. Agent to the Western Indians and Governor Commandant of His Majesty's Garrison of Michillmakinac and it's Dependances," dated at Michilimackinac, August 12, 1766.[1]

To Captain Johnothan Carver Esqr:

Whereas it will be to the honour and dignity of the nation as well as for the good of His Majesty's service to have some good suravies of the interior parts of North America espeeseely to the west and north west from this garrison,

I do by vartiue of the authority given me apoint you for that purpose at eight shillings starling p[er] day until discharged. And you are heareby directed to set out from this post emmediently and proceed along the north side of Lake Missigan [*Michigan*] to the [*Green*] bay, and from thence to the Falls of St. Antinoies [*Anthony*] on the Missipee, taking an exact plans of the country by the way marking down all Indian towns with their numbers, as also to take survaies of the diffrant posts, lakes, and rivers as also the mountains.

And at the Falles of St. Antoines and about that as far as you can explore this winter, and make your reports to me early in the spring. Should you receive orders from me to march further to the westward with any other detachment that I may send this fall or winter you are to do it and send back your journals by Mr. Browe [*Bruce?*] or some other safe hand. But should you not receive any you are to return by the Ilim way [*Illinois*] River, and from thence to Saint Joseph [*at Niles, Michigan*], and from thence

[1] Original in P.R.O., Treasury Solicitor, 11, Class 1069, vol. 4957. Copy in Minnesota Historical Society.

along the east side of Lake Misigan to this place taking all the way exact plans of the country and for so doing this shall be your sufficient warrant.

2. Robert Rogers' Instructions to James Tute, dated at Michilimackinac, September 12, 1766.[2]

By the Honourable Robert Rogers Major & Governor of the Lakes Huron, Missigan & Superior and the Suronding Country to the Heads of the Several Bays and Rivers that Discharge their Waters into the Said Lakes Subordent Agent and Superintendent to Sr. William Johnson for the Western Indians Captn. Commandant of Michilimackinac and its Dependences &c. &c.

Instructions to Captn. James Tute Esqr. commanding a party for the discovery of the North West Passage from the Atlantick into the Passifick Occian, if any such passage there be or for the discovery of the great Reriver Ourigan[3] that fall into the Passifick Occian about the latitude fifty.

You are to set out imediatly with this detatchment and with them proceed to La Bay from thence to the Falls of St. Antonies and further up the said [*Mississippi*] river to a conveniant place to winter amongest the Sioux, carring with you the necessary artickls now delivred to your care for boons to gain the friendship of they Indians and to retain and desmiss them from time to time as you approch on your way and pass the cuntry they are best acquanted with. You are when you arrive at the Falls of St. Antonies to endavour to find out where Mr. [*William*] Bruce winters and from him take Captn. Johnathan Carver under your command who is to be draftsman for the detachment. He with Mr. James Stanley Goddard and the interperter [*Joseph Reaume*] is to make up a consull which you may on every occasion that appears necessary order that they may with you consult the expedeancy of the voyage by which with these instructions you are to guard [*guide*] your selves.[4] Mr. Goddard has an appointment as your secetatary for Indian affairs. He is to be second in command, Mr. Carver third, Mr. Reaume has my appointment

[2] Original in Collection Baby, Université de Montréal; copy in Rogers Papers, Minnesota Historical Society.
[3] On Rogers' use of Ourigan, here and below, see p. 13n, above.
[4] On Reaume, see p. 125, above.

for your interperter and fourth in command. You will from where you winter early in the spring endeavor to get some good guides from the Souix and proceed with your party to the north west and make what discoverys you can during the summer and at the close of which you will fall in with your party to winter at Fort La Parrie [*des Prairies*]⁵ at which place you shall have sent you a further suploy of goods next fall that you may take of them what is necessary to carry on the expedition, and from Fort La Parrie you will travel west bering to the north west and do your endeavor to fall in with the great River Ourgan which rises in several diffrent branches between the latitudes of fifty six and forty eight and runs westward for near three hundred legu[e]s, when it is at no great distance from each other joyned by one from the south and a little up the stream by one from the north. About these forkes you will find an inhabited cuntry and great riches. The gold is up that river that comes in from the north at about three days' journey from their great town, near the mouth of it at the south west side of a large mountain.⁶ But there is not any iron ore that is known to be workt among them. From this town the inhabitints carry their gold neare two thousand miles to traffick with the Japancies and it's said they have some kind of beasts of burden.

From where the above rivers joyn this great River Ouregan it becomes much larger and about four hundred leagues as the river runs from this twon above mentioned it discharges itself into an arm or bay of the sea at near the latitude of fifty four and bends southerdly and emtys into the Pacefick Occian about forty eight nine or fifty where it's narrow, but to the northwest where you joyn this bay of the sea at the entrence of the River Ourigan the bay is wide and supposed to have a comunication with the Hudson Bay about the latitude of fifty nine near Dobsies Point.⁷ From the above discription you will do your utmost endeavor to find out and discover the said cuntry and take all possable means

---

⁵ On Fort des Prairies, see p. 16n, above.

⁶ Charlevoix also told of a race in the Canadian Northwest mining and using gold; see Kellogg, ed., *Charlevoix Journal*, 1 : 265.

⁷ Cape Dobbs, on the south point of the mouth of Wager Bay, is now in the District of Keewatin, Northwest Territories. It was named for Arthur Dobbs, to whose tireless promotion of northwest passage schemes Rogers may have owed some of his inspiration. A fanciful account of the West somewhat similar to Rogers' may be found in Dobbs, *An Account Of the Countries adjoining to Hudson's Bay, In the North-west Part of America*, 18–25 (London, 1744).

to obtain a draft of it as well as by the way reporting from time to time to me all your proceedings, at every oppertunity sending such scetches or plans as your draftsman has taken, and you are further disired to make all the interest you possibly can with the diffrent nations that others may pass after your return to open a trade a cross the continent to those people equaly advantatious to them selves as to us. On your way should you have occasion you may draw bills on me at any time for the purchase of goods and merchandize of traders that you may meet or for the payment of Indians that you may employ for carring on the expedition, shoud your goods that you have with you and those I will send you next fall to Fort La Parrie not be sufficient, and such drafts at a small sight shall meet with due honor.

And when you have any thing to send back as no doubt they Indians will give you presents take care to convey them to me by some carefull person that will honorably deliver them here.

And over and above eight shillings sterling pr. day you are entiled if you discover a northwest passage from the Atlantick to the Pacifick Occian twenty thousand pounds sterling to be payed to the detachment which is equaly to be divided amongest them by the honorable Lords of His Majesty's Treasury of England and for the other discovery of the River Ourigan you will be considerd by the government and paid according to the value of the discovry that you may make to be likewise devided amongest the detatchment.[8]

You must take great care not to be deceaved by the Rivers Missisure [*Missouri*] or by that falls into Hudson's Bay [*Nelson, Churchill rivers*] or by other rivers that emty into the Gulf of Californee: as every attempt of this kind is attended with som defulilty. When ever that appears to you call to mind your courrage and resolution and not lett that faill you in the attempt. Consider the honor it will be to you and the detatchment with you besides the great advantages that must arrive to the undertakers of it. Behave in it like a man that is devoted to his king and brave out every difficulty and you may be sure of susess.

You are to take great care not to leave the least suspicion

[8] The sum of £ 20,000 was offered at the instigation of Arthur Dobbs by the British government to encourage northwest passage searches then being made in Hudson Bay. It would only have applied to a sea route, not an overland or river route. See pp. 7, 13, above; Crouse, *Western Ocean,* 434.

among the many differnt nations of Indians that your design is
any other than to open a tread with them. Beware of their
women not to take them without consent of their chiefs. Pay
them punticaly for what you have of them which is the sure way
to have sucess.

And when you have made all the discovery you can you must
return to this place in the way and manner you think most
conveniant and easy for your self and party either by Hudson's
Bay or back the way you go out a cross the cuntry observing
proper places for posts goeing and coming, but I strongly rec-
omend to you not to touch at any of our Hudson Bay posts as
th[e]y may detain you and make advantages of your journey to
themselves.[9] But shoud you find out a North West Passage as I
do not doubt but you will or a short carring place cross over to
Fort La Parrie where you may be assured to meet relif.

I heartly wish you success and that God may preserve you and
the detachment through this undertaking, and that you may
meet the reward of deserving officer at your return over and
above the mon[e]y offered for the discovery, to effect which my
good offices shall not be wanting to every individual. You are
strictly commanded to make your report to me at your return
where ever I may be or in case of my death to the Honorable
Charles Townsend [10] or in case of both our deaths to the Honorable Lords of Trade and Plantations and for so doing this shall be
your sufficient warrent and instructions.

*3. Robert Rogers' Commission to James Stanley Goddard, dated at
Michilimackinac, September 12, 1766.* [11]

By the Honourable Robert Rogers Major & Governor of the
Lakes Huron, Missigan, & Superior and the Suronding Cuntry
to the Heads of the Several Bays & Rivers that Discharge their
Waters into the Said Lakes, Surbordent Agent and Superinten-
dent to Sr. William Johnson for the Western Indians, Captn.
Commandant of Michilimakinac and its Dependencies &c. &c.

[9] The Hudson's Bay Company was accused of concealing information and
obstructing exploration for a northwest passage, in order to maintain its trading
monopoly. See Dobbs, *Account,* 18, 48; Crouse, *Western Ocean,* 423–425.

[10] On Townshend, see p. 13, above.

[11] Original in P.R.O., Treasury Solicitor, 11, Class 1069, vol. 4957:242. Copy
in Minnesota Historical Society.

To James Stanley Goddard Esqr.:

I do by virtue of the power and authority to me given appoint you secretary to a detachment under the command of Captain James Tute (as also one of the consill to the said detachment) ordered for the discovery of the River Ourigan and the North West Passage at eight shilling sterling p day, and over and above an equal share of the reward offered by the government for that discovery. And you are hereby order'd to do, act, and perform the office of secretary for the detachment to the utmost of your power by keeping exact journals [12] and entering every useful remark that you think can attend to future knowledge of the country which you pass through as also to take down the talks of they Indians, their numbers &c.

And for so doing this shall be your sufficient warrant and authority to demand your payment at your return.

Reced the 29th Septr. 1767 of Major Rogers — a sett of bills of exchange value one hundred and forty [pounds] sixteen shillings sterg when paid will be in full for subsistance due to me for the within warrent. The bills are drawn by Major Robert Rogers in my favour on Mr. Benjn Hammet mercht in London Street, London. James Stanley Goddard.

4. Robert Rogers to James Tute, dated at Michilimackinac, June 10, 1767. [13]

Dear Sir,

I had the pleasure to receive your letter dated sometime last winter and am oblidged to you for the intelligence. I have sent Mr. Boyce [*Charles Boyer?*] to be stationed at the lakes Laplu [*Rainy*] & De Bocue [*Lake of the Woods?*] to keep that passag open from Lake Wennepeck to Lake Superiouer. Mr. Francois [*Le Blanc*] is to follow him with ten canoes. He sets out the begining of next month. Those last canoes is to go to Fort La Pierre and Lake Wennepeck so that you and your party will have plenty of suploys, and Mr. Boyce as allso Mr. Otherington [*Phinehas Atherton*] is to give you any immediate asistance that

[12] See Chapter 3, above.
[13] Original in P.R.O., Treasury Solicitor, 11, Class 1069, vol. 4957:246. Copy in Minnesota Historical Society.

you stand in need of before Francois' arrival.[14] By Francois you shall have all the news of every kind. At present every thing is quiet hear. I am sir with esteem,

Your most obedient humble servant
ROBT. ROGERS

5. Robert Rogers to "Captn. Tuke," dated at Michilimackinac, July 15, 1767.[15]

SIR,

I observe what you say in regard to a person you want to have appointed an officer. That intirely depends on you, and what appointment you make for that gentelman will always be valued accordingly. I am sir,

Your humble servant
ROBT. ROGERS

You never should put on the great man, but pass as a trader only, otherways your expences will run two high.

6. Robert Rogers to "Captn. Tute," dated at Michilimackinac, July 20, 1767.[16]

SIR,

I received your several letters from the Misspy and take this opportunity to answer them. It is very bad to me that you did not send me in the peltrys that you promised me last spring and am astonished at your heavy drafts on me but that convince me on the other hand that you must have now goods enough with you to compleat your expedition and expect that Franco [*François Le Blanc*] will make good returns or am otherwise ruined by your extragance.

I shall send up some bo[a]ts the next spring very early, and desire that you will push on your jorny with all speed and be more prudent than you have hitherto been.[17]

---

[14] On Atherton, Le Blanc, and Boyer, see pp. 18, 132n, 191n, above.

[15] Original in P.R.O., Treasury Solicitor, 11, Class 1069, vol. 4957: 247. Copy in Minnesota Historical Society.

[16] Original in P.R.O., Treasury Solicitor, 11, Class 1069, vol. 4957: 247. Copy in Minnesota Historical Society.

[17] On Le Blanc, see p. 132n, above.

Mr. [*Benjamin*] Roberts the commissary for Indians affairs ariv'd here about a month since but that doth not effect me in my command and I expect the rangers in lieu. I intend to go to the great carrying place next spring myself to meet the canoes that are coming down. I recommend it to you to be prudent and will all that is concerned with you, bid that you'll not pretend any command over such traders as is gon your way with the commissary's licens and my pass. Mr. [*Alexander*] Baxter the gentleman that I wrote you is a going to England on my account emediately & heare I shall remain till your expedision is over to supourt you on your return. I hope to come with some rangers to the great carring place. & am sir, [18]

Your humble servt
ROBERT ROGERS

7. Jonathan Carver to his wife Abigail, in Montague, dated at Michilimackinac, September 24, 1767. [19]

MY DEAR,

I arrived at this place the 30th of last month, [20] from the westward; last winter I spent among the Naudoussee of the plains, a roving nation of Indians, near the river St. Piere [*Minnesota*], one of the western branches of the Mississipi, near fourteen hundred miles west of Michillimackinac. This nation live in bands, and continually march like the roving Arabians in Asia. They live in tents of leather and are very powerful. I have learned and procured a specimen of their dialect, and to the utmost of my power, have made minute remarks on their customs and manners, and likewise of many other nations that I have passed through; which I dare say, you and my acquaintance will think well worth hearing, and which I hope (by the continuation of the same divine Providence that has hitherto in this my journeying, in a most remarkable manner guarded over me in all my ways) personally to communicate. It would require a volume to relate all the hardships and dangers I have suffered since I left you, by stormy tempests on these lakes and rivers, by hunger and cold, in danger of savage beasts, and men more savage than they; for a

[18] On Roberts and Baxter, see pp. 18, 19n, above.
[19] *Boston Chronicle,* February 22, 1768.
[20] Carver gave this date as August 29 on p. 133, above.

long time no one to speak with in my native language, having only two men with me, the one a French man, the other an Indian [*Jacko*] of the Iroquois, which I had hired to work in the canoe. I never received any considerable insult during my voyage, except on the 4th of November last, a little below Lake Pepin on the Mississipi. About sun down, having stopt in order to encamp, we made fast our canoe, and built a hut to sleep in, dressed some victuals and supped. In the evening, my people being fatigued, lay down to sleep: I sat a while and wrote some time by fire light, after which I stept out of my hut. It being star light only, I saw a number of Indians about eight rods off, creeping on the banks of the river. I thought at first they had been some wild beasts, but soon found them to be Indians. I ran into my hut, awakened my two men, took my pistol in one hand, and sword in the other, being followed by my two men well armed. I told them as 'twas dark, not to fire till we could touch them with the muzzle of our pieces. I rushed down upon them, just as they were about to cut off our communication from the canoe, where was our baggage, and some goods for presents to the Indians; but on seeing our resolution they soon retreated. I pursued within ten feet of a large party. I could not tell what sort of weapons of war they had, but believe they had bows and arrows. I don't impute this resolution of mine to any thing more than the entire impossibility I saw of any retreat. The rest of the night I took my turn about with the men in watching. The next morning proceeded up the Mississipi as usual, though importuned by my people to return, for fear of another onset from these barbarians, who often infest those parts as robbers, at some seasons of the year.[21]

My travels last year, by computing my journal, amount to two thousand seven hundred miles, and this year, from the place where I wintered, round the west, north, and east parts of Lake Superior, to Michillimakinac, are two thousand one hundred miles; the total of my travels since I left New-England, is, four thousand eight hundred miles, by a moderate computation. Part of the plans and journals, with some letters concerning the situation of the country, I sent back with some Indians, which plans and letters Governour Rogers has sent sometime ago by Mr. [*Alexander*] Baxter, a gentleman belonging to London, to be laid

---

[21] On p. 90, above, Carver indicated that this episode occurred on November 1.

before the Lords of Trade. My travels this summer I am now preparing for the same purpose, which is the reason of my not coming home this fall.[22]

I have seen the places where the Spaniards came and carried away silver and gold formerly, till the Indians drove them away, undoubtedly there is a great plenty of gold in many places of the Mississipi and westward.[23] I trust I have made many valuable discoveries for the good of my king and country.

I cannot conclude without mentioning something of the superstition of the Naudoussees where I spent the last winter which agrees with the account that the Father [Louis] Hennipin, a French Recollect or a fryar of that order, (who some years ago traveled among some part of the Naudoussees, tho' not so far west as I have been) has given of that people concerning books. I had with me some books necessary for my employment, which they supposed to be spirits, for as I by looking on the page when I first opened the book, could tell them how many leaves there were in the book to that place, they then would count over the leaves and found I told true; supposing the book was a spirit, and had told me the number, which otherways they judged impossible for me to know, they would immediately lay their hands on their mouths, and cry out in their language, *wokonchee, wokonchee,* which signifies, he is a god, he is a god; and often when I desired to be rid of my guests in my hut, I would open the book and read aloud, they would soon begin to go away, saying to one another, he talks with the gods. Many other remarks of the like kind I have made of that people.[24]

They believe there is a superior spirit, or God, who is infinitely good, and that there is a bad spirit, or devil. When they are in trouble, they pray to the devil, because, say they, that God being good, will not hurt them, but the evil spirit that hurts them, can only avert their misery. I have seen them pray to the sun and moon and all the elements, and often hold a pipe for the sun and moon and the waters, to smoak.[25]

On my return to this place, I received the thanks of the gov-

[22] On Baxter and Carver's first reports, see p. 19, above.
[23] On Spanish and French mines, see pp. 81n, 86, above.
[24] See Thwaites, ed., Hennepin, *New Discovery*, 1:260. *Wokonchee* corresponds to the Dakota *wakan* (spirit), *ći* (objective pronoun you). See Appendix 2, J36, T29, 34.
[25] On Dakota religious beliefs and smoking customs, see pp. 111, 112, above.

ernor commandant, who has promised he will take special care to acquaint the government at home of my services.

I have had my health ever since I left home, blessed be God, I hope you and all our children are well. I have not heard from you since I came away. Give my most affectionate love to my children. I long to see you all. I expect to be at home next July. I have two hundred pounds sterling due to me from the crown, which I shall have in the spring. Give my compliments to all friends and acquaintances.   I am,

My dear, your's forever,
JONATHAN CARVER

8. Jonathan Carver's sworn statement that he accompanied Tute, dated at Michilimackinac, May 26, 1768.[26]

These may certifie that I the subscriber being by appointment a draughtsman for a party commanded by Capt. James Tute that I joynd him about the first of May 1767 at Lapraire Lechien [*Prairie du Chien*] on the Mississipi that he was obliged at that place to give very large presents to the several nations assembled there in order to prevail with them not to go to Spanish Louissiania but to remain in the English interest, after which the party under his direction proceeded to the north passd through several Indian vil[l]ages, that I was knowing to his giving large presents to the several bands we passd, which appears to me he could no ways avoid in the situation we at that time was under, and that I verily beleave that Cap. Tute used the utmost discretion on that account that was in his power, and by what I have seen in his accounts that they are very just as to the publick and perticilar expences of the voyage.[27]   Attest JON. CARVER

Capt. Carver acknauledges this to be his hand writting in presence of us — Geo. McBeath, Gregor MacGreger[28]

[26] Original in Collection Baby, Université de Montréal. Copy in Carver Papers, Minnesota Historical Society.

[27] On p. 121, above, Carver states he joined Tute on May 6, 1767. The purpose of this certificate seems to have been to defend Tute against criticism about the immoderate expense and possible treasonous intent of the expedition. See pp. 17, 18, above. It was written shortly before Rogers was taken east for his treason trial. See Cuneo, *Rogers,* 230.

[28] George McBeath was a prominent Mackinac trader and Gregor McGregor was an early British merchant at Detroit; see Reuben G. Thwaites, ed., "Fur-Trade on the Upper Lakes 1778–1815," in *Wisconsin Historical Collections,* 19: 236n, 278n (1910).

9. Jonathan Carver's "Proposal to the Public," September 12, 1768.[29]

Jonathan Carver,

Formerly a Captain in the provincial troops of the Maſſachuſetts-Bay, during the late war in America, and ſince employed as a ſurveyor and draughtſman in exploring the interior and upper parts of the continent, adjoining to, and beyond lake Superior, and to the weſtward of the great river Miſſiſſippi, offers the following

PROPOSALS to the PUBLIC, To publiſh, as ſoon as a proper number of ſubſcribers encourage him in the deſign, An EXACT JOURNAL of his

TRAVELS

In the Years 1766, and 1767, In which time he travelled upwards of 2700 miles, among the remote nations of Indians, many of whom had never before ſeen a white perſon.

This JOURNAL will alſo contain Deſcriptions of the Indian nations. Of their manners and cuſtoms—Of the ſoil and produce of the country—Of the great lakes Huron, Michagan, and Superior,&c. &c. &c.—Of the Miſſiſſippi and other great rivers that run in that part of the continent; and in particular, a full account of the Naudoweſſe Indians, the moſt numerous nation of Indians in North-America, who live in tents of leather, and can raiſe 6000 fighting men, and among whom the author wintered in 1766.

DRAUGHTS and PLANS of theſe countries will be annexed, together with curious figures of the Indian tents, arms, and of the Buffaloe Snake which they worſhip.

Each Subſcriber to pay TWO SPANISH DOLLARS for every copy of the propoſed work; and as ſoon as a ſufficient number have ſubſcribed, to indemnify the expence of the printing and engraving, the publication will immediately enſue. SUBSCRIPTIONS are taken in by Capt. CARVER at MONTAGUE, and by J. MEIN, at the LONDON BOOK-STORE North-ſide of King-ſtreet BOSTON.

10. Jonathan Carver's estimate of goods given to the Indians, undated, possibly 1768.[30]

An estimate of the amount of goods given as presents by several different interpreters and other persons sent by Major

---

[29] *Boston Chronicle*, September 12, 1768. On Carver's military service, see p. 4, above. John Mein, below, was a Boston bookseller and editor of the *Chronicle*. Due to his loyalist sentiments he was forced to leave America for London in November of 1769. See Lorenzo Sabine, *The American Loyalists, or Biographical Sketches of Adherents to the British Crown in the War of the Revolution*, 463 (Boston, 1847).

[30] Original in P.R.O., Treasury, Class 1, vol. 478: 367. Copy in Carver Papers. On this estimate, see p. 124n, above.

Rogers from Michilimackinac to bring in the chiefs of the nations hereafter mentioned, who live on the eastern banks of the Mississipi between the Falls of St. Anthony and the River Illinois, viz., the Ottigaumies [*Fox*] and Sawkies [*Sauk*], the Winobagoes [*Winnebago*] and one or two bands of the Naudowessie [*Dakota*] to the English interest who were at that time strongly importuned by the French and Spaniards from Louissiania to settle on the west side of the Mississippi which removal from the English side to the Spaniards were prevented by the following presents & these Indians are now firmly fixed in the English interest.

To whom delivered	Pieces of strouds at £14	Blankets at 18s	Coats at 16s	Shirts at 12s	Bed gowns at 16	Mds. [?] of wampum at 60	Galls. of rum @ 20	Pounds of verm[illio]n at 20	New York Currency
To the Ottigamies	10	50	20	80	20	8	9	6	£304. 0.0
Do. the Sakies	7	32	20	68	30	10	7	5	249.12.0
Do. the Winebaygoes	8	40	15	80	10	10	14	8	268. 0.0
Do. the Naudowessie River Bands	5	20	10	40	10	5	0	10	153. 0.0
									£974.12.0

I the subscriber do certify that in the year 1767 as I was returning from my travells beyond the Mississipi I join'd a party at a place on the Mississipi called Lapraira Le Chien [*Prairie du Chien*] that Major Rogers had sent to bring in the chiefs of several nations about the Mississipi. That I was present in several counsels which Mr. Tute, Mr. Goddard, and Mr. Reaum held with those Indians where were many presents given them which according to the best of my judgment might amount near to the sum of £500 sterling given by the aforementioned persons to prevent them from going to the French and Spaniards at Louissiania. That by these presents I do verily believe they were induced to continue in the English interest and of consequence an advantage to the public.

JONATHAN CARVER

11. "To the Right Honourable the Lords Commissioners of His Majesty's Treasury The Humble Petition of Jonathan Carver late a Commander of a Company of Provincial Troops of Massachusetts Bay in New England," undated, possibly January, 1770, London. [31]

Most Humbly Sheweth. That in April 1769 your petitioner preferred his humble petition to his majesty in council praying his majesty to take his case into consideration and afford him some recompence for his service and expence in exploring the interior and unfrequented parts of America which petition on the 3d of May last was referred to the Lords Committee of Council who were pleased on the 21 of June last to referr the same to the Lords Commissioners for Trade and Plantations to enquire into the several facts stated in the said petition whereupon the said Lords Commissioners reported that they had been attended by your petr. in person. That your petitioner had undertook and performed a journey of great extent through the interior and unfrequented parts of the continent of America traveling to the westward of Michillemackinac as far as the heads of the great river Missisipi directing his course from thence westward almost to the South Sea and in return exploring the whole circuit of the great Lake Superior. That in this service he was engaged for a considerable course of time with great hazard and fatigue incuring thereby an expence which on account of his pay at the rate of 8s. p day (which he was also promised by Major Rogers then commanding at Michillimackina) together with other incidental charges amounted in the whole to the sum of £735.11.3 the particulars of which is hereto annexed in a schedule No. 1.

That upon the whole of your petitioner's case it clearly appear'd to the said Lord Commissioners that your petitioner having engaged in this expedition under a commission from Major Rogers which that officer was by no means authoriz'd to grant, he cannot now by virtue of such an appointment make any regular demand for indemnification for his labour and expences nevertheless as the hardships and difficulties which your petitionr asserted to have undergone had the testimony of General [*Thomas*] Gage for their truth and as your petitoner did appear as well from the above certificate of General Gage as like wise by a letter from Brigadier Ruggels [*Timothy Ruggles*] to Governor [*Francis*] Bernard[32] to have acquitted himself in his majesty's service with reputation and fidelity the said Lords Commissioners thought it a case of composition [*compassion*] and as such submitted it to the Lords Committee of Council to act thereupon either for your petitioner's releif or otherwise as should be thought meet. The lords on the 20th November 1769 did agree humbly to recommend your petitioner to his majesty for his royal bounty upon condition that your petitioner did deliver up to the Lords Commissioners for Trade and Plantation all maps charts plans discoveries and observations made by him during the course of his expedition which he hath accordingly done.

That his majesty on the 29th day of November 1769 taking the said report into consideration was pleased by and with the advice of his privy council to approve thereof and was pleased to declare his gracious intention to bestow his royal bounty upon your petioner and orderd the right honoble the Lords Commrs. of this honoble board to give such direction therein as to them should seem proper.

That your petr. humbly apprehending his majesty will at least be graciously pleased of his royal bounty to defray all his reasonable and necessary expence your petitioner hath been at during the course of his said expedition and also his costs and expence since his return in drawing and correcting the several maps charts plans and observations and journals made by him during the course of his said expedition as also to allow your petitioner a compensation for time whilst in the said service according to his rank and merit, all which your petitioner is rather encouraged to expect as he is well assur'd from his observation on his said expedition great advantages may arise to the publick and that

---

[32] On Bernard, the governor of Massachusetts Bay Colony, and Ruggles, a brigadier general in the French and Indian War and loyalist in the Revolution, see *Dictionary of American Biography*, 2:221 (1929); 16:221 (1935). The certificates of character from Gage and Ruggles to Carver are printed by Lee, in *Proceedings*, 1912, p. 113.

great encouragement hath ever been given by all states to them who in like manner explored the unknown parts of the world, your petioner therefore begs leave to lay before this honourable board an accot. of his expence and required compensation in Shedule No. 2 amounting to the sum of £570.4 which with the sum of £735.11.3 in the schedule hereto annexed amounts to the sum of £1305.15.3.

Your petitioner therefore most humbly prays that your lordships will please to order the said sum of £1305.15.3 to be paid to your petioner as his majesties royal bounty or make such other order as your lordships shall think fit.

And your petitioner will pray &c.

JONATHAN CARVER

Schedule No. 1

	£	s	d
To goods purchased of several traders after I left Michillimackinac untill my return again to that place which goods were given to the difft. nations of Indians on or near the Mississippi River & to the west of that toward the South Sea where I passed to procure their interest in trade and their friendship to the Brittish government	180	12	4
To the hire of an interpreter 105 days @ 4s. 6 p day	23	12	6
To the hire of two men for the voyage	30	6	5
To the hire of a servant 13 months at 2s. p day	39	12	
To expences in purchasing canoes of the Indians in my march	9	10	
To 3 large belts of wampam at £3 each	9		
To 3 ream of paper @ 30s. p ream	4	10	
To a quadrant of Hadley's [33]	4	15	
To 6 compasses at 12s. each	3	12	
To quills for writing pens		18	
To a trunk for the preservation of my papers		12	

[33] On the quadrant, see p. 68n, above.

To 3 blanketts for to secure my papers at 14s. each	2	2	
To the hire of carriage for my baggage from Albany to Michillimackinac in 1766	7	3	
To exps. in returning from Michilimackinac to New England in 1768	27	14	0
To my wages from the 1st May 1766 to ye last of Decr. 1768 it being 976 days inclusive @ eight shillings p day	391	12	
Total	£735	11	3

Sched[u]le No. 2

To provisions for self & 2 men from 1st May 1766 to 1st Decr. 1767 omitted in the 1st accot. being 606 days at 4 p day necessaries being exceed dear in ye country	121	4
To expence of board cloaths washing & lodging from 1st Janry 1769 to 1st Janry 1770 while drawing & correcting the plans & journals of my travels being 365 days at 8s. p day	146	
To my pay from 1st Janry 1769 to 1st Janry 1770 whilst drawing & correcting the plans & journals of my travels @ 8s. p diem	146	
To my passage & necessary stores from America to Londo[n]	21	
Do. from London to America	21	
Pd Mr. Kitchener [Thomas Kitchin] ingraver for a copper plate delivered with my plans & journals to ye Board of Trade [34]	12	12
To expce in London from 1st Janry 1770 to 1st May 1770 the time expected to sail for America 120 dys at 10s. p day	60	

[34] On Kitchin and the engraving, see p. 34, above.

To pay from 1st Janry 1770 to 1st July 1770
the time expected to arrive in America
181 days at 8s. p day

	72	8
£ 570	4	
The former accot. exhibited	735	11	3
Total	£ 1305	15	3

❧ Appendix Two ❧

CARVER'S
DAKOTA DICTIONARY

Edited by Raymond J. DeMallie

THE "NAUDOWESSIE VOCABULARY" published in Carver's *Travels* (pp. 433–440) is the earliest Dakota lexicon to appear in print. It differs somewhat from the manuscript "Dictionary of the Naudowessee Language" in Carver's hand in Version I of the journals. The manuscript version, for example, contains 145 entries; the printed vocabulary contains 106 entries, 36 of which do not appear in the manuscript.

The two vocabularies are compared in the lists that follow. The first list presents entries from the manuscript dictionary in the journals; these entries (which have been arranged in alphabetical order) are preceded by a number and the letter "J" to indicate journals. An asterisk indicates that the word is also in the vocabulary published in *Travels*. The second alphabetically arranged list contains those words which appeared in *Travels* only. These entries are numbered and preceded by a "T." As printed in *Travels,* all the entries were capitalized (a device not used here), but accents were given in only two cases — T23 and T33. All significant variations between the manuscript dictionary and the printed versions have been collated.[1]

---

[1] Carver's spellings of some Dakota words in the text of the manuscript journals differ from those given in these vocabulary lists. For example, *Waukon Teebee* appears on p. 91 of the text while *wàhkon* and *tèebe* are given in the dictionary entries; *shandnuapaw* is given as the spelling for the word meaning pipe on p. 111, while the dictionary gives *shanuapàw* (J70). Although these and other examples offer inconsistent spellings of Dakota words, the variation is not meaningful phonetically. Carver is notably inconsistent in the spelling of English words, and he is similarly inconsistent in his spelling of Dakota terms.

Columns 1 and 2 list Carver's English and Naudowessee forms. Column 3 gives the Dakota word which seems closest to the form given by Carver, except for the numerals in entries J113–141, where the usual Dakota method of counting is presented. Column 4 gives English glosses. The material in the last two columns is taken from Stephen R. Riggs, *A Dakota-English Dictionary*, edited by J. Owen Dorsey (*Contributions to North American Ethnology*, Vol. 7 — Washington, D.C., 1890).[2]

On the basis of these comparisons, Carver seems to have acquired a fair speaking knowledge of a good number of Dakota words and phrases, though his English glosses were sometimes not quite right (see J5, 8, 13, 33, 40, T3), and sometimes entirely wrong (J12, 25, 32, 82, 90, 99). Carver apparently learned little Dakota grammar. He rarely noticed that adjectives generally follow nouns, though he gave correct forms in some cases where he undoubtedly learned the phrases as single units — "white blanket," "red blanket" (J11, 112). He confessed in *Travels* (p. 416) that he was not able to "reduce" the languages of the Chippewa and Naudowessee "to the rules of grammar." Many of his "compounds" in the manuscript version put Dakota words into English grammatical constructions. Some probably would have been readily understood by the Dakota (T32, 33), but others would have been confusing or unintelligible unless accompanied by meaningful gestures (J108, 109, 111, T31, 34–36).

In *Travels* (p. 440), Carver offered the following brief text of a song to show, he said, how the Naudowessee "unite their words" (the glosses are taken from his vocabularies):

1. *Meoh accoowah eshtaw paatah negushtawgaw shejah menah.*
    I   go   see   light   kill   bad   water.

---

[2] For further references on the Dakota language, see J. Owen Dorsey, ed., Stephen R. Riggs, *Dakota Grammar, Texts, and Ethnography* (*Contributions to North American Ethnology*, vol. 9 — Washington, D.C., 1893); Franz Boas and Ella Deloria, *Dakota Grammar* (*Memoirs of the National Academy of Sciences*, vol. 23, no. 2 — 1941); Eugene A. Buechel, *A Grammar of Lakota, the Language of the Teton Sioux Indians* (St. Louis, 1939); Paul Manhart, ed., Eugene A. Buechel, *A Dictionary of the Teton Dakota Sioux Language* (Pine Ridge, S. Dak., 1970); Williamson, *English-Dakota Dictionary*; James C. Pilling, *Bibliography of the Siouan Languages* (Bureau of American Ethnology, *Bulletin*, no. 5 — Washington, D.C., 1887); J. Owen Dorsey, "On the Comparative Phonology of Four Siouan Languages," Smithsonian Institution, *Annual Report for 1883*, part 2, 919–929 (Washington, D.C., 1885); Stephen R. Riggs, ed., *Grammar and Dictionary of the Dakota Language* (*Smithsonian Contributions to Knowledge*, vol. 4 — Washington, D.C., 1852).

2. *Tongo Wakon meoh woshta, paatah accoowah.*   3. *Hopiniyahie*
   Great Spirit I   good, light give me.   Oh
oweeh accooyee meoh, woshta patah otoh tohinjoh meoh teebee.
moon give   me,   good light many deer   my   tent.

The free translation provided by Carver reads as follows: 1. "I will arise before the sun, and ascend yonder hill, to see the new light chase away the vapours, and disperse the clouds." 2. "Great Spirit give me success." 3. "And when the sun is gone, lend me, oh moon, light sufficient to guide me with safety back to my tent loaden with deer!"

Although this text clearly demonstrates Carver's lack of knowledge of Dakota grammar, it is valuable as an example of the type of "pidgin" Dakota probably used by Carver and many early traders. Each of the three sentences is grammatically correct in English, with the best possible substitutions of Dakota words as Carver knew them. Syntax depends mainly on contiguity. It is doubtful that the Naudowessee would have understood more than a few disconnected phrases such as "Great Spirit," "I am good," "many deer," and "my tent." It might be noted that a Frenchman, applying the method Carver used here, would have had a better chance of being understood, since he would have emerged with the correct Dakota syntactic relation between nouns and adjectives and would have been accustomed to nasalized vowels.

We can assume that Carver himself could not have carried on much successful intercourse in the Dakota language, largely due to almost total ignorance of verbal forms. Although he claimed only to speak Dakota "after an imperfect manner," the evidence presented by the vocabulary and especially by the text in *Travels* suggests that Carver could not possibly have composed the long speech in Dakota which he claimed to have delivered to the assembled Naudowessee (pp. 118–120, above) and probably could not have understood much beyond disconnected phrases of spoken Dakota.

Without any doubt, however, that which Carver did report concerning the language of the Naudowessee is genuinely Dakota, of the Eastern or Santee dialect. He is the first to give a vocabulary of this language, and his journals and *Travels* therefore provide the beginnings of the extensive literature on the Dakota language. It is interesting to find that there are very few words which Carver reported that can be considered archaic. The Dakota language seems to have changed little from Carver's time to the present.

Carver apparently made no attempt to use a systematic method for writing the sounds of the Dakota language. For example, for "a" he wrote: a, aa, aah, au, aw, o, oh, oa, oah, e, ee, u, etc. His orthography is equally variable throughout. In some cases his rendering of a word is so far from phonetic that it may be questioned whether the term would have been understood by a Dakota speaker, or whether we have correctly identified the word he was attempting to write (J18, 65, 75, T20). In some cases it was not possible to make a reasonable guess at which word Carver intended (T2, T5, T8).

In the lists that follow, the orthography used by Riggs is basically phonetic, though it fails to distinguish between aspirated and unaspirated consonants. Vowels are pronounced roughly as follows:

a	as in father	o	as in go
e	as in they	u	as in food
i	as in me		

Special symbols:

ć	ch
ǧ	back velar fricative, voiced
ħ	back velar fricative, unvoiced
ŋ	makes the preceding vowel nasal
ś	sh
ź	as in pleasure; like French *j*

subscript dot indicates that the consonant is glottalized or followed by a glottal stop

In the lists that follow N.G. signifies phrases which are nongrammatical in Dakota; notes are keyed by number of entry.

	Carver		Riggs	
	1	2	3	4
J1.	arm	ishpàw	iśpá	lower part of the forearm
J2.	ass	netàh	nité	rump
J3.	ax	auspàh; *ashpaw	oŋspé	ax
J4.	bad; *evil	shèjah	śíća	bad, ugly, wicked
J5.	beads	tawhinnoh	totódaŋ	blue or green beads
J6.	bear; *a bear	wakunshèjah; *wakonshejah	waȟáŋksića	black bear
J7.	beaver	chawboh; *chawbah	ćápa	beaver
J8.	belt	weokèah	wiyókihedaŋ	wampum
J9.	big; *great	tòngo; *tongo	táŋka	large, great
J10.	bird	wàhkeah	wakíye	birds
J11.	blanket	shenòeketo	śiná; śináȟota	blanket; common white blanket
J12.	boy child; *child, a male	wahchèekseh; *wechoakseh	mićíŋkśi	my son[3]
J13.	brother	sungàwgo	suŋkáku	his or her younger brother
J14.	buffeloe [sic]; *buffalo	tawtòngo; *tawtongo	tatáŋka	buffalo bull
J15.	canoe	waahtoàh; *waahtoh	wata	canoe
J16.	cold	shenèe or mechùata; *mechuetah	sni; maćúwita	cold; I am cold
J17.	comb	nepaiogochàw	ipákća	comb
J18.	corn	kishcàh	wamnáheza[4]	maize
J19.	deer	*tohinjoh	táȟiŋća	deer
J20.	die	nepoo	nipó	dead[5]
J21.	dish	wakeshèjah	wakśíća	dish
J22.	dog	shewngoòsh;[6] *shungush	śúŋka	dog

[3] The Naudowessee terms for "boy child" and "girl child" are transposed in *Travels*. The substitution of initial "w" for "m" is puzzling. See J33.

[4] Carver perhaps thought "wamna" to be a separate word.

[5] According to Riggs, *nipó* is probably from Ojibway, but was frequently used by the Dakota when speaking with white people who did not understand their language. Carver's printed Ojibway vocabulary, *Travels*, 420–433, gives Neepoo, "dead." See also T1, below.

[6] The suffix -oosh is apparently Ojibway. See Carver's Ojibway vocabulary, Sagaunosh, "English," Wawpoos, "Hare," etc., in *Travels*, 420–433.

	Carver		Riggs	
	I	2	3	4

J23.	door	weopah	tiyópa	door
J24.	ear; *ears	nookàh	nóǧe	ear
J25.	eat	wachonechaw	waćónića	dried or wild meat. See T2.
J26.	*eyes	*eshtike⁷	iśtá	eyes
J27.	*father; *king or chief	otàh	até	my father. See J38.
J28.	fire	*paahtàh	péta	fire
J29.	fish	onguòh	hokúwa	to fish
J30.	flint	wahhèe	waŋhí	flint
J31.	foot	chehhah	sihá	foot
J32.	girl	hawpawnàw⁸	hápaŋ	name given to the second child in a family, if a girl. See T30.
J33.	girl child; *child, a female	weechockssèe; *whacheekseh⁹	mićúŋkśi	my daughter
J34.	give me; *give	accòoyeh	ku	to give¹⁰
J35.	go	accooyouwiàh	kúwa; iyáya; iyáyeya	to follow after, chase, hunt; to have gone; to send. See J108.
J36.	*God or a spirit; *the Great Spirit	wàhkon; *wakon	wakáŋ; wakáŋtaŋka	a spirit, something consecrated; God ("great spirit")
J37.	good	washtà; *woshtah	waśté	good
J38.	great or much	otòh	óta	much, many
J39.	gun	muzawàhkon; *muzah wakon	mázawakaŋ	gun ("spirit metal")
J40.	hair	nausàu	nasú	upper part of the head; brain
J41.	hand	nappèe	napé	hand
J42.	hat	wappàh	wapáha	hat
J43.	hazelnut	òmo	úma	hazelnuts
J44.	head	paah	pa	head
J45.	hear	noawkeshòn; *nookishon	nakíȟoŋ	to hear one's own

---

⁷ The final -ke is probably *kiŋ*, the definite article: *iśta kiŋ*, "the eyes."

⁸ The final -nàw is probably *-na*, diminutive suffix.

⁹ See J12. Carver may have had in mind the term *wićíŋćadaŋ*, "little girl." There is no parallel term for "little boy." The term *ćíŋća* means "child."

¹⁰ Carver made no attempt at systematic verbal conjugations. See J35, 108, 109, T31.

	Carver		Riggs	
	1	2	3	4

J46.	horse	shuatòngo; *shuetongo	śuktáŋka	horse ("big dog")
J47.	house	tèebe; *teebee	típi	tent, house
J48.	I;*or me	meah; *meoh	míye	I, me
J49.	*iron	*muzah	máza	metal
J50.	kill	negushtawgàw; *negushtaugaw	See J20, note 5	
J51.	kittle [sic]	shàhhah	ćéǧa	kettle
J52.	knife	esaùgh	isáŋ	knife
J53.	little	jeèstin; *jestin	ćístiŋna	little
J54.	long	tòngo; *tongoom[11]	See J9	
J55.	me	meah	See J48	
J56.	milk	oatsaẁbee; *etsawboh	asáŋpi	milk
J57.	Mississip[p]i	Wattahpàwtongo	watpá taŋka[12]	("big river")
J58.	Montreal	Moòneock	[not given]	
J59.	moon	weeh; *oweeh	wi; haŋyétuwi	sun; moon ("night sun")[13]
J60.	more	noòkoh	nakúŋ	and, also
J61.	*mouth	*eeh	i	mouth
J62.	never or not at all	wohneèjoh	waníća	none, without any
J63.	no	heyàh; *heyah	hiyá	no
J64.	nose	passòo	pasú	nose
J65.	old man	waẁkoinjoh[14]	wićáȟća	old man
J66.	old wooman [sic]	wawkhùngo	wakáŋka	old woman
J67.	otter	ptah	ptaŋ	otter
J68.	paddle	wawmenàwhe-chàw	wamnáheća	oar, paddle
J69.	p---k	chah	će	penis
J70.	pipe	shanuapàw; *shanuapaw	ćaŋdúhupa	pipe

[11] The suffix -oom may be Ojibway. It is not Dakota.

[12] According to Riggs, the Mississippi was called *ȟaȟáwakpa,* "river of the falls." *Watpá* and *wakpá* are apparently interchangeable.

[13] In Dakota, the moon is called "night sun." Carver confused the terms, and took the word for sun, *wi,* to mean moon. For sun, he consistently used the word for fire (see J90).

[14] Carver is apparently using a form for old man, *"wakáŋća,"* parallel to the term for old woman, *wakáŋka.* This form is not recorded by Riggs.

	Carver		Riggs	
	1	2	3	4
J71.	pistol	muzawakon jestin	mázawakaŋ ćístiŋna	("little gun") [15]
J72.	pouch	pthah [16]	See J67	
J73.	powder	shawhandee	ćaȟdí	gunpowder
J74.	rain	megràusuc	maǧáźu	rain. See T16.
J75.	rattlesnake; *snake	omelìshcaw; *omlishcaw	wamdúśka	snakes
J76.	rice	psheen	psiŋ	rice; wild rice
J77.	ring	muzamchùpah; *muzamchupah	mázanapćupe	finger ring
J78.	rum; *spirituous [sic] liquors	menewàwkon; *meneh wakon	míniwakaŋ	whisky ("spirit water")
J79.	St. Pierre [Minnesota River]	Wattahpaw-mènesoter	watpá mínisota	("whitish water river")
J80.	salt; *salt water	menisquèah; *menis queah	miniskúya	salt
J81.	shoes	hawpàw	háŋpa	moccasins
J82.	sister	towinjòh	tawíću	his wife [17]
J83.	sleep	esteemàh; *eshteemo	iśtíŋma	to sleep
J84.	snow	owàh; *sinnee	wa; See J16	snow
J85.	speak [18]	tyishpàwgochaw	?	
J86.	spoon	toogehàh	tukíha	spoon
J87.	stink	shechòmonee	śićámna	bad smelling
J88.	stockings	ooscàh	huŋská	leggings
J89.	sugar	chawhompèe	ćaŋháŋpi	sugar (tree sap)
J90.	sun	paatàh; *paahtah	See J28	
J91.	tobacco	shawhandèe	ćaŋdí	tobacco
J92.	tomehawk [sic]	spaychopès	oŋspéćaŋduhupa	a pipe-hatchet
J93.	turkle [turtle]	caoh	kéya	large tortoise
J94.	vermilion	wahsissaw	waśéśa	vermilion
J95.	wampam [sic]	weokèah	See J8	
J96.	*water	mèneh; *meneh	míni	water
J97.	what	tàwgo; *tawgo	táku	what

[15] The usual Dakota word for pistol is mázakaŋptećedaŋ, "short gun." The form recorded by Carver may be archaic.
[16] Referring to a pouch made from a whole otter skin.
[17] Carver reversed the meanings of the terms for wife and sister. See J99.
[18] The terms for speaking (see T22) are puzzling. The verb to speak is éya. The form given here by Carver may be ekíćiya.

	Carver		Riggs	
	1	2	3	4

J98.	where	toogetà	tókiya	where
J99.	wife	taẇkshedego	taŋkśítku	his younger sister. See J82.
J100.	wood	chuah	See T25	
J101.	you	neah; *chee	níye	you. See T29.
J102.	young men	weochèster	wićáśta	man
J103.	a great water or lake	meneh tongo; *tongo meneh	míni táŋka	"big water" [19]
J104.	a silver broach [sic]	muzascah	mázaska	silver ("white† metal")
J105.	a silver medel [sic]	shunehah	?	
J106.	a wrist clap [sic]; *broach	muzahhoohoo; *muzahootoo	mázahuhu	bracelets, armbands
J107.	an iron spear	wahhookechah	wahúkeza	spear
J108.	come here	coowahre; *accooyouiyare	kúwa	come here. See J35.
J109.	go there	accooyouwiyah	See J35, 108	
J110.	I thank you friend; *friend	kitchewah; *kitchiwah	kićúwa	friend
J111.	on the other side	aucotsompaw	akó; sáŋpa	beyond, on the other side of; more, over, beyond
J112.	red strouds	shewnooscah	śináśa	red blanket

The Naudowessee manner of counting

J113.	1	*wonchaw	waŋźí
J114.	2	*noompaw	nóŋpa
J115.	3	yawmones; *yawmonee	yámni
J116.	4	tobah; *toboh	tópa
J117.	5	sawbotah; *sawbuttee	záptaŋ
J118.	6	shockopee; *shawco [20]	śákpe
J119.	7	shocko; *shawcopee	śakówiŋ
J120.	8	shawindohin; *shahindohin	śahdóǧaŋ
J121.	9	nebochungenung; *nebochunganong	napćíŋwaŋka
J122.	10	wegochungenung; *wegochunganong	wikćémna

†NB Iron and silver is the same only the[y] call one white ye other gray.

[19] The Dakota word for lake is *mde*.
[20] The terms for 6 and 7 are incorrectly transposed in *Travels*.

	Carver			Riggs
1		2	3	4

J123.	11	wegochungenung wonchaw; *wegochunganong wonchaw	akéwaŋźidaŋ
J124.	12	wegochungenung noompaw²¹	akénoŋpa
J125.	13	wegochungenung yawmonee	akéyamni
J126.	14	wegochungenung-tobah	akétopa
J127.	15	wegochungenung-sawbotah	akézaptaŋ
J128.	16	wegochungenung-shockopee	akéśakpe
J129.	17	wegochengonung-shocko	akéśakowiŋ
J130.	18	wegochungonung-shawindohn	akéśahdoǧaŋ
J131.	19	wegochungenung- nebochungenung	úŋmanapćiŋwaŋka
J132.	20	noompah-wegochunegenung; *wegochunganong noompaw	wikćémna noŋpa
J133.	30	yamonee-wegochungonung; *wegochunganong yawmonee	wikćémna yamni
J134.	40	toboh-wegochengonung; *wegochunganong toboh	wikćémna topa
J135.	50	sawbotah-wegochungonung; *wegochunganong sawbuttee	wikćémna zaptaŋ
J136.	60	shockopee-wegochungenung; *wegochunganong shawco	wikćémna śakpe
J137.	70	shocko-wegochungonung; *wegochunganong shawcopee	wikćémna śakowiŋ
J138.	80	shawhindohin wegochungenung; *wegochunganong shahindohin	wikćémna śahdoǧaŋ
J139.	90	nebochengonung wegochungonung; *wegochunganong nebochunganong	wikćémna napćiŋwaŋka
J140.	100	opongh; *opohng	opáwiŋǧe
J141.	1000	wegochungonung opongh; *wegochunganong opohng	kektópawiŋǧe

Cardinal points of the compass

J142.	north or north wind	wazaahtah	wazíyata	north

²¹ The forms given here for 12–19 are translated as 20, 30 . . . 90 in *Travels*.
Carver's Dakota numeral system is clearly idiosyncratic, although it is based on
the Dakota words for 1 to 10 and 100. It is not idiomatic Dakota, but
supplemented with signs it probably would have been understood well enough
for purposes of trade.

	Carver		Riggs	
	1	2	3	4

J143.	east DO [ditto]	weoheah paatah [22]	wiyóhiyaŋpata	east
J144.	south DO	enticah	itókağa	south
J145.	west DO	weoh paahtoh	wiyóħpeyata	west
T1.	dead	negush	See J20	
T2.	eat	echawmenaw [23]	?	
T3.	falls of water	owah menah	owámniyomni	eddy, whirlpool
T4.	Frenchman	Neehteegush [24]	?	
T5.	gold	muzaham [25]	?	
T6.	heaven	woshta tebee	N.G. waśté típi	("good house") [26]
T7.	home, or domestic	shuah	śaŋ	vagina [27]
T8.	love	ehwahmeah [28]	?	
T9.	medal	muzah otah [29]	máza óta	"much metal"
T10.	mine	mewah	mitáwa	mine
T11.	more	otenaw	See J38	
T12.	much	otah	See J38	
T13.	near	jeestinaw	See J53	
T14.	oh!	hopiniyahie! [30]	iníhaŋya	to frighten, scare, amaze, or astonish
T15.	pipe of peace	shanuapaw wakon	ćaŋdúhupa wakáŋ	consecrated pipe
T16.	rain	oway meneh	See T3, J74	

[22] Carver's renderings of the words for east and west appear to be based on the incorrect assumptions that *paatah* signified sun, and that the terms for east and west terminated in the word for sun.

[23] Riggs lists the cognate Dakota form *ićámna*, "to blow, bluster, storm, drive." The verb "to eat" is *yúta*.

[24] This is apparently an Ojibway term. Carver's printed Ojibway vocabulary gives Nechtegoosh, "French." The Dakota word is *waśíćuŋ*.

[25] Carver gives the same term for silver (T19). The Dakota words given by Riggs are *mázaska*, "silver (white metal)," and *mázaskazi*, "gold (yellow silver)." It would be tempting to think that the form given by Carver is an archaic one, but he clearly states above (after J111) that silver is called "white metal," and gives the latter form for "silver broach" (J104). "Muzaham" seems to be an error on Carver's part.

[26] The Dakota later used the word *maħpíya*, "clouds, sky," to mean "heaven."

[27] Perhaps a joke on Carver's part (or on the part of the Dakota from whom he learned the word), or a now-obsolete double entendre.

[28] This form may derive from *ihákta*, "to love," and *míye*, "me."

[29] This construction is apparently Carver's own, medals being the "metal" (*maza*) given to chiefs. Riggs gives the Dakota word for medal as *mázaska-wanapiŋ*, "silver necklace."

[30] Initial ho- may be *ho*, "yes, yea."

	Carver		Riggs	
	1	2	3	4

T17.	round	chupah[31]	?	
T18.	see, to	eshtaw	See J26	
T19.	silver	muzaham	See T5	
T20.	smoke	shaweah	śóta[32]	smoke
T21.	surprising	hopiniayare	See T14	
T22.	talk	owehchin	See J85	
T23.	there	daché	déći	here, in this place
T24.	tobacco	shawsassaw	ćaŋśáśa	bark which the Dakota mix with their tobacco for smoking. See J91.
T25.	tree	ochaw	ćaŋ	tree, wood
T26.	wicked	heyahachta[33]	?	
T27.	woman	winnokejah	winóȟiŋća	woman
T28.	wonderful	hopiniyare	See T14, 21	
T29.	you	chee	ći	a double pronoun infixed in verbs, meaning "I, thee" (nominative, objective)
T30.	young	hawpawnaw	See J32	

Compounds:

T31.	go away	accoowah	See J35, 108	
T32.	no good	heyah washtah	N.G.[34]	
T33.	who is there?	tawgo daché	N.G.[35]	
T34.	you are a spirit	wakon chee	N.G.[36]	
T35.	you are good	washtah chee	N.G.	
T36.	you are my good friend	washtah kitchiwah chee	N.G.	

[31] Carver seems to have thought that the word for finger ring (J77), *mázana-púpe,* meant "round metal," whereas it actually means "finger metal" (from *napćúpe,* "finger"). This seems to be the source of Carver's word for round.

[32] The discrepancy between the two words is puzzling. Perhaps Carver intended some other form.

[33] This appears to be a misprint for *heya wachta.* See T32.

[34] The grammatical expression is *wašté śni,* "not good."

[35] Apparently *táku,* "what" and *déći,* "here." Carver has the significance wrong, and has put them together nongrammatically.

[36] T34–36 are nongrammatical compositions based on Carver's misunderstanding of the pronoun *ći* (see T30). "You are good," for example, is *niwášte.*

❧ Appendix Three ❧

A BIBLIOGRAPHY OF JONATHAN CARVER'S *TRAVELS*

VARIOUS LISTINGS of the editions and issues of Carver's *Travels* exist, the most notable being that of John Thomas Lee in the *Proceedings of the State Historical Society of Wisconsin,* 1909 (Madison, 1910, pp. 143–183). The National Union Catalog also lists editions located in the United States. In both of these sources, however, confusion exists between the editions and issues which have all or most of the complete text, based on the London editions, and those which originated with the abridgment made for juvenile readers by Joachim Heinrich Campe. The following descriptive bibliography is divided into two parts. The first includes those editions and issues appearing prior to the advent of photographic reprints, in which the text is complete, or nearly so. The second lists editions of the Campe abridgment.

COMPLETE TEXTS

I.   1778. Travels through the interior parts of North-America, in the years 1766, 1767, and 1768. London: Printed for the Author; and sold by J. Walter, at Charing-cross, and S. Crowder, in Pater-noster Row. MDCCLXXVIII.

[20], i–xvi, 17–543, [1] pp.; 2 maps, 4 illus. Directions for placing the plates and errata [544]. No directions are given for placing the maps.

Maps: 1. A new map of North America, from the latest discoveries, 1778. Engrav'd for Carvers Travels.

2. A plan of Captain Carvers travels in the interior parts of North America in 1766 and 1767.

Illustrations:

1. The Falls of St. Anthony in the River Mississippi, near 2400 miles from its entrance into the Gulf of Mexico. M. A. Rooker Sculpt. At p. 70.
2. A man and woman of the Ottigaumies. At p. 228.
3. A man & woman of the Naudowessie. At p. 230.
4. [Indian implements: a pipe of peace; a war club, or *casse tête;* a Naudowessie dagger.] At p. 296.

II. 1779. Travels through the interior parts of North America, in the years 1766, 1767, and 1768. London: Printed for the Author, by William Richardson in the Strand; and sold by J. Dodsley, in Pallmall; J. Robson, in New Bond-street; J. Walter, at Charing-cross; J. Bew, in Pater-noster Row; and Mess. Richardson and Urquhart, at the Royal Exchange. MDCCLXXIX.

[24], i–xvi, 17–543, [1] pp.; 2 maps, 4, [1] illus.

Maps: Same as I.

Illustrations: 1, 2, 3, and 4, same as I.

[5] The tobacco plant. This illustration is not listed in the Directions for placing the maps and plates, but contains inscriptions "Drawn and engraved for Carvers Travels as the act directs by F. Sansom No. 16 Maiden Lane Cheapside"; "Published Novr. 1st 1779"; and "Page 522." It is not identical to either of the engravings published in Carver's *A treatise on the culture of the tobacco plant,* London, 1779.

In this second London edition "care has been taken to rectify those errors which have unavoidably proceeded from the hurry of the press." The errata have been corrected, and there are minor changes in the text.

III. 1779. Travels through the interior parts of North-America, in the years 1766, 1767, and 1768. Dublin: Printed for S. Price, R. Cross, W. Watson, W. and H. Whitestone, J. Potts, J. Williams, W. Colles, W. Wilson, R. Moncrieffe, C. Jenkin, G. Burnet, T. Walker, W. Gilbert, L. L. Flin, J. Exshaw, L. White, J. Beatty, and B. Watson. MDCCLXXIX.

[20], i–xiv, 15–508; 1 map, 2 illus.

Map: A new map of North America. (Not based on maps in previous editions).

Illustrations:

1. The Falls of St. Anthony in the River Mississippi near 2400 miles from its entrance into the Gulf of Mexico. At p. 50.
2. [Indian implements: a pipe of peace; a war club or cassa tate; a Naudowessie formerly made of stone [*sic*]. At p. 279.

The text is based on edition I.

IV. 1780. Travels through the interior parts of North America, in the years 1766, 1767, and 1768. The third edition. London: Printed for the Author by William Richardson in the Strand; and sold by J. Dodsley, in Pallmall; J. Robertson, in New Bond-street; J. Walter, at Charing-cross; J. Bew, in Paternoster Row; and Mess. Richardson and Urquhart, at the Royal Exchange, MDCCLXXX.

A reissue of the sheets of the 1779 London edition.

Maps: Same as II.

Illustrations: Same as II; frontispiece, Captn. Jonathan Carver.

V. 1780. Johann Carvers Reisen durch die innern Gegenden von Nord-Amerika in den Jahren 1766, 1767 und 1768, mit einer Landkarte. Aus dem Englischen. Hamburg, Bey Carl Ernst Bohn, 1780. Colophon: Hamburg, gedruckt bey Carl Wilhelm Meyn.

XXIV, 456 pp.; 1 map.

Map: Karte von Hauptman Carvers Reise in den innern Theilen von Nord Amerika. Tingeling sculp: Hamburg. Based on Map 2 in edition I. Inscriptions and legends translated.

The "Vorbericht" states: "Die Uebersetzung ist nicht von mir, allein ich kann für ihre Richtigkeit einstehen." Signed, C. D. Ebeling, Aufseher der Handlungsakademie in Hamburg.

The translator-editor added some brief notes to the text, chiefly in the natural history sections. The same sheets, but with new title page worded exactly the same, were published as Volume I of *Neue Sammlung von Reisebeschreibungen,* edited by Christoph Daniel Ebeling in 10 volumes, 1780–90. The "Vorbericht des Uebersetzers" to volume II of this series by J. P. Ebeling [Johann Theodor Philipp Christian Ebeling] contains comments indicating that he was the translator.

VI. 1781. Travels through the interior parts of North America, in the years 1766, 1767, and 1768 . . . Illustrated with copper plates, coloured. The third edition. London, Printed for C. Dilly, in the Poultry; H. Payne, in Pallmall; and J. Phillips, in George-Yard, Lombard-Street. MDCCLXXXI.

Frontispiece; [4], 1–22, [23–46], i–xvi, 17–543, [544–564] pp.; 2 maps, 4 illus.

Maps: Same as edition II, but colored in outline.

Illustrations: 1, 2, 3 & 4, same as edition II, all but no. 1 colored. No. [5] may be included in this edition.

This is the edition published at the suggestion of John Coakley Lettsom for the benefit of Carver's heirs. The text is a reissue of the sheets from the 1779 London edition, with introductory material and index added, and the maps and three of the illustrations colored.

VII. 1784. Three years travels, through the interior parts of North-America, for more than five thousand miles . . . and an appendix, describing the uncultivated parts of America that are the most proper for forming settlements. Philadelphia: Printed and sold by Joseph Crukshank in Market-Street, and Robert Bell, in Third-Street. MDCCLXXXIV.

xxi, [22]–217 pp. Based on the 1781 issue of the 1779 sheets, but without the "Advertisement," "Some account of Captain J. Carver," and the index included in that issue.

VIII. 1784. Voyage dans les parties intérieures de l'Amérique septentrionale, pendant les années 1766, 1767 & 1768 . . . Ouvrage traduit sur la troisieme édition angloise, par M. de C. . . . avec des remarques & quelques additions du traducteur. Paris, Chez Pissot, Libraire, quai des Augustins. MDCCLXXXIV. Avec approbation & privilége du Roi.

24, xxviii, 451 pp.; 1 map. The approbation is dated 11 Mars 1783.

Map: Carte des voyages du Cape. Carver, dans la partie intérieure de l'Amérique septentrionale, en 1766. et 1767. Benard direxit.

Based on Map 2, edition I; inscriptions and legends translated.

The translator was Jean Étienne Montucla, 1725–1799, a mathematician who wrote several histories of mathematics, and was Censeur royal for scientific works. On page 10 he states, "On a cru pouvoir & devoir y ajouter plusieurs notes, tantôt nécessaires pour modifier des assertions de l'Auteur." In addition to notes added at the foot of the page, he, in some instances, inserts information of his own into the text.

The "Quatrieme partie," second supplément, contains Montucla's observations on western travels from Le Page du Pratz, *Histoire de la Louisiane,* Paris, 1758; Baron Lahontan, *Nouveaux voyages,* The Hague, 1703; and Arthur Dobbs, *An account of the countries adjoining to Hudson's Bay,* London, 1744.

IX. 1784. Voyage dans les parties intérieures de l'Amérique septentrionale, pendant les années 1766, 1767, & 1768 . . . Ouvrage traduit sur la troisieme édition angloise, par M. de C. . . . avec des remarques & quelques additions du traducteur. Yverdon, 1784.

xxxvi, 436 pp. The approbation is dated 10 Août 1784.

This is the Montucla translation, but it omits his statement on the quality of Carver's observations noted in VIII. Fifteen of the translator's notes are also omitted, six of them in the Introduction.

X. 1789. Three years travels through the interior parts of North-America, for more than five thousand miles . . . and an appendix, describing the uncultivated parts of America that are the most proper

for forming settlements. Philadelphia, Joseph Crukshank, in Market-
Street, between Second and Third-Streets, MDCCLXXXIX.

xvi, [i]–vii, [9]–282 pp. A reprint of the Philadelphia, 1784, edition.

XI.   1792.   Three years travels through the interior parts of North-
America, for more than five thousand miles . . . and an appendix,
describing the uncultivated parts of America that are the most proper
for forming settlements. Philadelphia: Printed by Joseph Crukshank,
No. 87, High-Street, 1792.

Collation identical to Philadelphia, 1789, edition, a page-for-page reprint.

XII.   1794.   Three years travels throughout the interior parts of
North-America, for more than five thousand miles, . . . and an appendix, describing the uncultivated parts of America, that are the most
proper for forming settlements. Printed at Portsmouth, New Hampshire, by Charles Peirce, for David West, No. 36, Marlborough-Street,
Boston. M, DCC, XCIV.

Collation identical to Philadelphia, 1789, edition, a page-for-page reprint.

XIII.   1796.   Three years travels through the interior parts of
North-America, for more than five thousand miles . . . and an appendix, describing the uncultivated parts of America that are the most
proper for forming settlements. Philadelphia: Published by Key &
Simpson; –1796.

xx, [i]–ix, 11–360, [1]–20, [1]–8 pp.

The text is the same as the Philadelphia, 1789, edition. Added were:
List of subscribers to Carver's *Travels* [1]–20; List of subscribers to
Carver's *Travels,* residing in New York [1]–8.

XIV.   1796.   Reize door de binnenlanden van Noord-Amerika. Naar
den derden druk uit het Engelsch vertaald door J. D. Pasteur. Te
Leyden, Bij A. en J. Honkoop, 1796.

Vol. I: [4], [i]–xxvi, 248 pp.; 1 map; 5 illus.

Vol. II: [4], 280, [18] pp.; 1 illus.

Map: Kaart van Capitein Carvers Reize in de binnenlanden van
Noord-Amerika in 1766 en 1767. C. van Baarsel sculpt. At Vol.
I, p. 15.

Illustrations:

1. Waterval van St. Anthony in de Rivier Mississippi omtrent
2400 Engelsche mijlen van daar zij in de Golf van Mexico
valt. H. Roosing sculpt. Rotterdam 1794. At Vol. I, p. 66.

2. Amerikaan van de natie der Ottigaumies. At Vol. I, p. 218.

3. Amerikaan van de natie der Naudowessies. At Vol. I, p. 220.

4. Amerikannsche vrouw van de natie der Ottigaumies. At Vol. I, p. 225.

5. Amerikaansche vrouw van de natie der Naudowessies. At Vol. I, p. 225.

6. Naudowessische ponjaard, vreede pijp, oorlogs knods. At Vol. II, p. 99.

Illustrations 2, 3, 4, and 5 are separate portrayals of figures paired in the English edition.

The text is based on the 1781 issue of the 1779 edition. Occasional notes are added by the translator, Jean David Pasteur, 1753–1804, author and translator of many works on natural history and travel.

XV.   1797. Three years travels throughout the interior parts of North-America, for more then five thousand miles . . . and an appendix, describing the uncultivated parts of America, that are the most proper for forming settlements. Printed by John Russell, for David West, No. 56, Cornhill, Boston, 1797.

xvi, [5]–312 pp. The text is the same as the Philadelphia, 1789, edition.

XVI.   1798. Three years travels through the interior parts of North-America, for more than five thousand miles . . . and an appendix, describing the uncultivated parts of America that are the most proper for forming settlements. Edinburgh: Published by James Key. –1798.

xx, 21–380, [1]–4 pp. Based on the London, 1779, edition. Some copies include a List of subscribers to Carver's *Travels* at Glasgow [1]–4.

XVII.   1802. Three years travels throughout the interior parts of North America, for more than five thousand miles . . . and an appendix, describing the uncultivated parts of America, that are the most proper for forming settlements. Fourth American, from the last London edition. Charlestown: Printed by Samuel Etheridge, for West and Greenleaf, No. 56, Cornhill, Boston, 1802.

[i]–xvi, [5]–312 pp. Collation identical to Boston, 1797, edition. Dedication signed John Carver.

This is not the fourth, but the sixth American edition, and it is not based on the last [1779–81] London edition, but is a close reprint of the Boston, 1797, edition.

XVIII.   1805. Three years travels through the interior parts of North America for more than five thousand miles . . . and an appendix, describing the uncultivated parts of America that are most proper for forming settlements. Glasgow: Printed by E. Miller for A. & J. Leslie, Booksellers, Gallowgate, 1805.

A reissue of the Edinburgh, 1798, edition, except for the "List of subscribers," which is omitted.

XIX. 1807. Three years travels through the interior parts of North-America, for more than five thousand miles . . . and an appendix, describing the uncultivated parts of America that are the most proper for forming settlements. Edinburgh: Published by James Key. –1807.

A reissue of the Edinburgh, 1798, edition, except for the "List of subscribers," which is omitted.

XX. 1808. Three years travels through the interior parts of North America, for more than five thousand miles . . . and an appendix, describing the uncultivated parts of America that are the most proper for forming settlements. Edinburgh: Published by J. Key, 1808.

A reissue of the Edinburgh, 1798, edition, except for the "List of subscribers," which is omitted.

XXI. 1813. Three years' travels throughout the interior parts of North America, for more than five thousand miles . . . and an appendix, describing the uncultivated parts of America, that are the most suitable for formirg [sic] settlements. Walpole, N. H., Published by Isaiah Thomas & Co., 1813.

xvi, 17–237, 236–280 pp. [Page numbers 236 and 237 are repeated.] This edition does not include the Dakota and Chippewa vocabularies.

XXII. 1838. Carver's travels in Wisconsin. From the third London edition. New-York: Printed by Harper & Brothers, No. 82 Cliff Street, 1838.

Frontispiece, [i]–v, verso blank; [vii–xiii], xiv–xv, verso blank; [xvii]–xxiv, [xxv]–xxxii, [33]–376 pp.; 2 maps, 5 illus.

Maps: Copies of those in 1778 and 1779 London editions, but with slight reduction in longitudinal dimension.

Illustrations: Copies of plates in 1779 London edition, placed as follows: 1 at p. 60, 2 at p. 152, 3 at p. 153, 4 at p. 188, [5] at p. 300. All are slightly reduced in size. Frontispiece: Captn Jonathan Carver.

The advertisement at [iii]–v is an anonymous statement of Carver's merits as an observer in what was at the time of publication Wisconsin Territory. The addenda at pp. 345–362 is a statement in support of the validity of the Carver grant, including a history of its conveyance through various heirs and claimants to the Mississippi Land Company.

ABRIDGMENTS

Joachim Heinrich Campe's abridgment of Carver's *Travels* was made for juvenile readers. It incorporates most of the narrative of Carver's journal, and includes some of the material from the sections on the Indians and the natural history of North America. The abridgment was part of a collection of travel narratives. The numerous editions and the rarity of complete sets of the collection make this bibliography a tentative one, but the following editions of Carver's *Travels* and its position in the collection have been identified.

A1. *Das Interessanteste aus Johann Carvers Reisen durch die innern Gegenden von Nordamerika,* comprising Vol. IV, Part II in *Sammlung interessanter und durchgängig zweckmässig abgefasster Reisebeschreibungen für die Jugend.* Reutlingen, J. Grözinger, 1786–93. 12 vols.

This collection was issued in subsequent editions as follows:

    A2. [Reutlingen, Johannes Grözinger] 1786–96. 12 vols.

    A3. Reutlingen, J. Grözinger, 1787–1800. 12 vols.

    A4. Reutlingen, Johannes Grözinger, 1800–1808. 12 vols.

    A5. [Hamburg] 1786–96. 12 vols.

    A6. Wolfenbüttel, In der Schulbuchhandlung, 1786–[96?].

    A7. Braunschweig, 1789. [12 vols.?]

B1. *Das Anziehendste und Merkwürdigste aus Johann Carvers Reisen durch die innern Gegenden von Nordamerika* became the title of Vol. XX, Part IV in the series which was newly titled *Sammtliche Kinder- und Jugendschriften von Joachim Heinrich Campe* in the following editions:

    B2. Braunschweig, In der Schulbuchhandlung, 1807. [37 vols.?]

    B3. Braunschweig, In der Schulbuchhandlung, 1829. 37 vols.

    B4. Braunschweig, In der Schulbuchhandlung, 1830–32. 37 vols.

    B5. Braunschweig, Verlag der Schulbuchhandlung, 1831–32. 37 vols.

    B6. Braunschweig, Verlag der Schulbuchhandlung, 1831–36. 34 vols. Siebente verbesserte Ausgabe.

    B7. Braunschweig, Verlag der Schulbuchhandlung, Friedrich Vieweg und Sohn, 1847. Achte verbesserte Ausgabe. [12 vols?]

Carver's *Travels* also comprise all of Part IV in:

C1. *Joachim Heinrich Campes Sammlung interessanter Reisebeschreibungen für die Jugend.* Wien, [B. P. Bauer] 1807–08.

C2. *Sammlung merkwürdiger Reisebeschreibungen für die Jugend.* Stuttgart, A. F. Macklot, 1823. 13 vols.

D1. A Dutch translation from the German, *Reisbeschrijvingen voor de jeugd.* Zwolle, J. de Vri, 1786–1804, was published in five volumes, and included Carver's *Travels.* The series was continued as *Nieuwe reisbeschrijvingen.* Amsterdam, De weduwe J. Dóll, 1805.

E1. Campe's abridgment was published in French as *Choix des détails le plus intéressans que contiennent les voyages de Jean Carver dans l'intérieur de l'Amerique septentrionale,* being Vol. IV, Part II of *Recueil de voyages intéressans pour l'instruction et l'amusement de la jeunesse.* Frankfurt sur le Main, J. P. Streng, 1787–93. 7 vols.

E2. A second French translation was made by Jean-Baptiste-Joseph Breton de la Martiniere. It was titled *Voyage dans l'intérieur de l'Amerique septentrionale,* and was issued as Vols. 5 and 6 of the series titled *Bibliothèque géographique et instructive des jeunes gens, ou recueil de voyages intéressans pour l'instruction et l'amusement de la jeunesse.* Paris, J. E. Gabriel Dufour; et à Amsterdam chez le même, 1802–3.

This translation by Breton de la Martiniere does not differ materially from the earlier Frankfurt edition in its presentation of Carver's *Travels.* Its distinguishing feature is a long introduction titled "Notice historique et geographique sur l'Amérique septentrionale, servant d'instruction pour le voyage de Carver." It also includes a folding map, "Amerique septentrionale d'après les dernières observations par Hérisson." It was reissued in the following editions:

E3. *Bibliothèque géographique et instructive des jeunes gens, ou recueil de voyages intéressans dans toutes les parties du monde.* Nouvelle édition. Paris, 1802–7.

E4. Paris, J. E. Gabriel Dufour, 1804. 12 vols.

E5. Paris, G. Dufour, 1816. 72 vols.

E6. Paris, J. E. Gabriel Dufour, 1816. 12 vols.

F1. The Breton de la Martiniere translation was used by D. Krutmejer in the preparation of a Swedish edition, *Jonathan Carvers resa i Norra Amerika,* comprising Part V and the first 134 pages of Part VI of *Geografiskt bibliotek för ungdom, eller samling af interessanta resebeskrifningar,* Stockholm, C. F. Marquard, 1804–16. 16 vols. The Carver volumes were published in 1805.

In 1845 the first of a series of editions of the Breton de la Martiniere translations was issued separately from the other travel narratives previously associated with it in the Campe collection. These editions are not based on an English edition as claimed by Wilberforce Eames (Lee, in

Proceedings, 1909, p. 178n). Generally referred to as the Tours editions, they are as follows:

G1. *Aventures de Carver chez les sauvages de l'Amérique septentrionale.* Tours, A. Mame et Cie, 1845. (Half-title: *Bibliothèque des écoles Chrétiennes approuvée par Mgr. l'Évêque de Nevers.*)

G2. Deuxieme édition, 1846.

G3. Troisième édition, 1849.

G4. Quatrième édition, 1850.

G5. Cinquième édition, 1852.

G6. Sixième édition, 1858.

G7. Septième édition, 1861.

G8. Huitième édition, A. Mame et fils, 1865.

G9. Neuvième édition, A. Mame et fils, 1870. (Half-title: *Bibliotheque de la jeunesse Chrétienne approuvée par Mgr. l'Archêveque de Tours.* 3e série in-12).

H1. The latest edition of the Campe abridgment was a Greek edition published in 1881. It was translated from the French of Breton de la Martiniere, presumably from one of the Tours editions, by N. G. Nicolaidou. The title page reads as follows: ΙΣΤΟΡΙΚΑΙ ΜΕΛΕΤΑΙ, Η ΣΥΜΒΑΝΤΑ ΤΟΥ ΑΓΓΛΟΥ ΚΑΡΒΕΡ ΠΑΡΑ ΤΟΙΣ ΑΓΡΙΟΙΣ ΤΗΣ ΒΟΡΕΙΟΥ ΑΜΕΡΙΚΗΣ. ΕΝ ΓΑΛΑΖΙΩ, ΕΚ ΤΟΥ ΝΕΟΥ ΤΥΠΟΓΡΑΦΕΙΟΥ "ΔΑΚΙΑ," 1881.

INDEX